DREAM OF
ITALY®:
Travel. Transform. Thrive.™

A COMPANION to the
PUBLIC TELEVISION SPECIAL

Kathy McCabe

Dream of Italy Productions, LLC

Printed in the United States of America

ISBN 978-0-9792309-3-6

Design by Karen Sheets de Gracia

Dream of Italy Productions, LLC
P.O. Box 2025
Denver, CO 80201

For my parents,
who always believed
in my dreams

KATHLEEN NARGI McCABE
1938-2018

STEPHEN J. McCABE
1938-2019

Contents

Foreword

FRANCES MAYES

Trust Kathy. Kathy knows best. She created the *Dream of Italy* television series, magazine, and book club—and now this book—out of her limitless passion and extensive knowledge of the most fascinating country on Earth. Kathy is never a voice from on high, directing you to see this and that. She's a full-on participant wherever she goes.

My introduction to her enthusiasm happened when she came to *Bramasole*, my house in Tuscany, to interview me for her TV show. We didn't sit down in the garden and talk for very long. Soon we were out the door, talking to locals and tourists in town, picking olives, cooking with the chef at the sybaritic *Il Falconiere*, lunching on the *loggia* above the *piazza* while chatting with the waitstaff about truffles. We strung my garden with lights, iced a case of *Prosecco* and threw a party.

When we were invited to participate in a procession prior to a medieval archery tournament, we got to try on gowns from the town's festival costume supply and select the most romantic and regal. Kathy in blue brocade, me in coral, we paraded along *Via Nazionale* in medieval pomp with a glory of drumrolls and blaring trumpets.

By now I've seen her paddling a *gondola,* soaring in a crane to the upper reaches of the *Duomo* façade in Florence, rolling out pasta, tasting wine in the moonlit *piazza* and milking a donkey in the pursuit of fresh milk in *Abruzzo*. The triple focus of this book—*Travel, Transform, Thrive*—comes naturally from the seeker mentality that guides all of Kathy's journeys.

Practical information packs the pages. Where to go, stay, eat, what to see and do. Turn the pages and you'll soon see you're in the good hands of an insider who gives you the chance to step beyond the obvious into a sense of discovery. Isn't that what we long for when we travel? Not only to check off the sites, taste the well-known dishes of the region, stay in approved hotels, but also to find out why the local women are gathering around one truck on market day (edible hyacinth bulbs, anyone?); what the aqua door leads to in the *albergo diffuso* (hotel rooms scattered about a town) listing; who the guy is who holds the key to the chapel where the double-sided *Signorelli* hangs; and how to get that lesson in windsurfing on Lake Como.

These insider travel experiences prove to be keys to the book's philosophy. *Transform. Thrive.* Welcoming spontaneity into the day shakes loose the parameters that almost inevitably settle around us. And, surprise! One spontaneous adventure promotes another. This leads to a fine feeling of thriving. I'd guess for Kathy, that pair of goals for travel manifests most strongly in the art of meeting people. In all of her PBS programs and in this book, *people* are at the heart of her travels. How does she meet so many locals? She never met a stranger, true, but she often talks to dogs. And of course, she then meets the dog's owner. What a simple lesson.

Most Italian towns have a tourist office with tons of information, but through the woman having *cappuccino* next to you in the *piazza*, you find out about a donkey race, cello concert, feast of wild boar in the park, cinema under the stars, whatever is on offer. As Kathy knows, this provides a chance to enter the life of a place and to begin to see why people are the way they are in that particular locale. Find the *genius loci*. That's really traveling.

Oddly enough, this kind of travel often provokes a mysterious sense of home. How many people have I met who arrive in Italy and after a week remark that they *need* to live there, or they feel that they once must have lived there in another life, or they just admire the humanity and ease they find in daily life and see that life makes a new kind of sense?

It certainly happened to me. I found my place to flourish and write. Kathy ventured to the town of her ancestors and was welcomed like a returning heroine, an event that changed her life. In these pages, she takes on this phenomenon of Italian travel, exploring that comforting sense of home as well as the practicalities of buying property, moving to Italy and what sustains you once you've made the leap.

The three Ts: *Travel. Transform. Thrive.* They're seamlessly woven in this book, Kathy's irresistible invitation to Italy. *Buon viaggio.*

Introduction

KATHY McCABE

There is one thing I know for sure: Italy changes lives.

It casts a spell on us and just won't let go. How one place could hold so much magic is almost impossible to comprehend.

"I think it's that soft power that Italy radiates around the world that attracts people here. How does all this stuff come from here? How did the Renaissance come from here? How did these artists come from here? And this music and this wine, this food? There's a reason. I'm not sure I can pinpoint what the reason is, but this is it," the musician Sting shares at the open of the TV special, *Dream of Italy: Travel, Transform and Thrive*, to which this book is a companion.

The premise of the special and this book is that travel to Italy can be a catalyst for personal transformation and provide a road map to thrive, the Italian way. Learning more about the Italian lifestyle can help us to adopt the healthy Italian lifestyle at home, travel to Italy in a more meaningful way or even decide to move there!

In the special and this book, I explore the 11 essential elements of the Italian lifestyle—the land, food, family, art & culture, beauty, pace of life, passion, movement, community, celebrations and sense of home—through the experiences of full- and part-time expats Sting & Trudie Styler, Francis Ford Coppola, *Under the Tuscan Sun* author Frances Mayes, best-selling financial author David Bach, retiree Sally Carrocino and career changer/interior designer Arlene Antoinette Gibbs. They have all been touched deeply by these unique attributes of Italy, which have in turn inspired them to change their lives.

My own life was transformed by just one trip to Italy—my first—26 years ago when my mother and I set off on a quest deep into southern Italy to discover the town my great-grandfather had left more than a century before. The town of *Castelvetere sul Calore* held a mythical place in the family lore as a source of mystery and miracles. My grandfather tried to visit the town in the 1960s when my grandparents were on a cruise that stopped in Naples.

He asked the taxi driver at the port to take him to *Castelvetere* but was taken instead to *Castelvetere in Val Fortore*, the wrong town. The roads in this area of *Campania* were still in bad shape post-war and my grandfather wasn't sure they could make it to the right town and then back to the ship in time and he left Italy without having fulfilled his dream.

In 1995, when my mother and I returned on his behalf, my grandfather was 93 and living in a nursing home in New Jersey. That one day we spent in *Castelvetere* was truly the greatest of my life. Through what can only be divine intervention, we showed up in the town knowing no one and were taken under the wing of distant cousins. We learned that the *Nargi* family only hailed from this town and were originally Norman invaders. Some of the people we met and even some of the etchings on the gravestones looked so much like my mother's family. We saw the churches, cemetery, town hall and even the street where our family lived. My mother said, "This is like *Brigadoon*," referencing the play where the town comes alive only once every 100 years.

Less than two days after leaving the town, we received a message from my father as we arrived at our hotel in Rome that my grandfather was dying. My father back home headed to the nursing home and we called to try to talk to my grandfather. We were too late; he had passed away, never knowing directly that we had found the town. I was extremely close to my grandfather and I always believe he "gave me" *Castlevetere sul Calore* and Italy to stem the brunt of his loss.

Fulfilling my grandfather's *dream of Italy* led me to my own. In 2002, I founded the membership website and travel magazine *Dream of Italy*, now having published 180 issues and counting. In 2015, *Dream of Italy* became a public television travel series with two seasons and the *Dream of Italy: Tuscan Sun Special* preceding this special—and all still airing on PBS, PBS.org, YouTube and Amazon Prime. The premise of all things *Dream of Italy*—there's a podcast too—is authenticity and hands-on experiences with the locals.

I have realized through the thousands of emails I have received from viewers that *Dream of Italy* is about so much more than a trip or a destination; it is about living richer lives and being inspired to fulfill our own very personal dreams. That's how I came up with the concept of *Dream of Italy: Travel, Transform and Thrive* in 2019. Who would have thought then that when the special actually began to air, we would have just endured a worldwide pandemic that made us all think deeply about how we live and what our future holds? If we don't live our dreams now, then when? And Italy is a dream that must be fulfilled—at least once.

After all, as the lovely actor/producer Trudie Styler shares at the end of the special, "I would encourage everyone that I know, if they can get to Italy before they die, then you've come to Paradise a tad early."

I hope if you haven't been that this book will inspire you to travel to Italy and, if you have already visited once, that it will help you to see Italy and indeed the possibilities for your life with new eyes.

How to Use This Book

The premise of the TV special and this book is that one trip can change your life, leading you to make Italy a part of your life in ways big and small. This book isn't meant to be a traditional travel guide about where to go, what to see, where to eat. For that kind of detailed, insider travel advice, I recommend you join *Dream of Italy* as a member and access more than 180 back issues of my award-winning travel magazine at **www.dreamofitaly.com/magazine**

Instead, I include a chapter on *how to* travel, no matter where in Italy you are going. These are lessons I have learned in some 60 trips to *il bel paese* over 26 years. Keep them in mind no matter where you go and what you do. They are the keys to unlocking secret doors all over Italy.

This book follows the outline of the TV special exploring the essentials of Italian life including the land, food, family, art & culture, beauty, pace of life, passion, movement, community, celebrations and sense of home. Each of these short chapters ends with actionable "Thrive Tips" to live like an Italian at home and "Travel Tips" to experience this particular Italian essential on the ground in Italy.

If you share some of my Italian heritage, I then explain how to explore your ancestry so that you might be able to return to your roots like I did and even use *jure sanguinis*, the right of blood, to claim Italian citizenship, which can give you a European Union passport and an easy way to move to Italy.

I believe deeply that Italy is one of the world's greatest catalysts for transformation. But how is it that we change and transform our lives, spiritually and practically? I talk to a handful of wonderful experts about actionable steps to make any dream come true.

Sprinkled throughout the book you will find Q+A interviews with the TV guests and others who have brought their own *dream of Italy* to life in unique and interesting ways. Read them carefully; they share some great advice.

Finally, so many of us dream of living in Italy full- or part-time. A good chunk of this book is devoted to how to make that incredible dream come true, whether it is taking your family on a radical sabbatical like David and Alatia Bach or deciding, as Sally Carrocino did, to age "out of place" in retirement in Italy.

I talk to the experts on everything from how to choose where to live in Italy to what the options are for visas to the nitty gritty of making your dream of renovating a house in Italy come true. This isn't meant to be a full guide to moving to Italy but rather an outline to get you thinking, planning and dreaming.

We live in a world where there are so many demands on our time, especially when it comes to consuming media and information. Your support has made my *dream of Italy* come true. I hope I can help make yours a reality too.

For more about the TV special and how to watch it, including an extended digital version with 30 minutes of additional content, visit **www.dreamofitaly.com/ttt** For updates on this book, please visit **www.dreamofitaly.com/tttbook**

I welcome your feedback at **info@dreamofitaly.com** Please drop me a note if you would like to be added to our list for future *Dream of Italy: Travel, Transform and Thrive Virtual Workshops* on topics such as moving to Italy, renovating a house and claiming citizenship.

Kathy with Trudie Styler and Sting

The Land

The land gives life and inspiration here in Italy. Italians are strongly connected to the earth, which bestows both beauty and bounty.

Italians eat and drink well because the land and coastline provide the fertile sources to harvest the building blocks for the healthy Mediterranean diet. The rich soil produces grapes for wine, olives for oil that is also known as "green gold" and fresh fruits and vegetables of all shapes and sizes. The soil and sea provide sustenance for animals and fish.

Sting and his wife, actor/producer Trudie Styler, were drawn to live part-time at *Tenuta Il Palagio,* south of Florence, where they witness the power of the land firsthand and produce their own wine, olive oil, vegetables, honey and eggs.

There's something more to the land here, a calm and beautiful energy, and I ask Sting why?

"Everything is related: the wine, the way it's grown. It all helps the environment. There are more insects here, more birds here. They treat [the land] kindly. Nature pays you back a hundredfold," Sting says.

While wine has been produced on this property since the 1500s, Sting and Trudie led a replanting of the vines in 2000. When they moved in, the vineyards had been neglected for years, but thanks to their efforts, the grapes now go into a variety of award-winning red, white and rosé wines that are exported worldwide, including a red named *Roxanne* for Sting's famous song.

"I would call ourselves stewards in that we're here to look after [the land], to protect it and, if we can, to make it better than it was when we found it. So far, we've managed to do that," Sting says.

"We wanted to treat the land in an organic way and not put chemicals on it. It's amazing what happens to nature when you allow it to just be nature. It actually revitalizes itself; it heals itself and you see stuff growing out of the ground. I mean, I'm a city boy, just to see something that you plant bear fruit is still a miracle to me," he adds.

Trudie and Sting appreciate the opportunity to share their bounty with their neighbors.

"We have a farm shop that serves the local community," Trudie notes. "They're very grateful for organic vegetables, and our eggs are really good organic eggs, as well as all the wine."

And what is it about that inextricable bond between wine, the land and Italians? I ask local *Tony Sasa,* who works for *Il Palagio.*

"It's essential to the food. That means for Italians, beside that it's part of the culture and the history, is something that, it's a part of our life. When I taste the wines from *Palagio,* talking about *Sister Moon, Casino delle Vie, When We Dance* or *Roxanne,* they're reflecting really beside the soul, but even the personality of Trudie Styler and Sting, who are artists, musicians, but they are smooth, we can say like water. They are like wind. This is what our wines are; they're transmitting your personality and they're giving you the music and the words," Tony says.

Author Frances Mayes also made her part-time home in Italy because of the land.

"I felt like I wanted to put down roots here because I saw how amazingly close to the land the Tuscans still are," Frances says. Her purchase and renovation of the villa *Bramasole* in *Cortona* was made famous in the book and movie *Under the Tuscan Sun.*

"*Bramasole*" means "to yearn for the sun" and the sun of course is an essential element in the alchemy of nature.

Not only do Frances and her husband Ed enjoy the colors, beauty and scents of the land in the exquisite flower-filled garden at the front of their villa, but they also enjoy its nourishment, particularly from the olive trees.

Fall is the time when Italians feel a particularly strong connection to *la terra*.

"Everyone will soon be out hunting mushrooms and truffles and each season has its own foraging things," Frances says.

"You enter into this ancient agricultural cycle that's been going on forever, and it really makes you feel close to the land. It's quite something to participate in an olive harvest," she adds.

I ask Ed when they know it is time to harvest. "Exactly whenever they tell you that they are getting a little darker, they're ready to be picked off the tree. All of our olives are handpicked by poets," he laughs.

Ed tells me that the FDA recommends Americans consume two tablespoons of olive oil per day to improve health and lower the chance of heart disease. It is easy to see that Italians and those who live like Italians likely consume even more. There's a reason Italians call olive oil "green gold." I tend to think my friends who produce and consume olive oil also look younger than everyone else!

As Frances alludes to, the land also gives Italians a strong sense of place and connection through time. Italy as a unified country is a relatively young concept, only becoming a nation-state in 1861.

Italians can trace their families back hundreds of years or even more than a thousand years to a specific *borgo*, town or city, and feel incredibly tied to the swaths of soil they hail from, even if they now live in other parts of Italy or have emigrated.

It was that little speck on the map that brought Francis Ford Coppola back to his roots, his grandfather's birthplace of *Bernalda*.

"Everything originated from the fact that we came from a part of Italy known as *Basilicata*, previously known as *Lucania*, in the town of *Bernalda bella*," he tells me.

Perhaps it is because so much of Italy has a rich rural past that Italians appreciate nature and make time to enjoy it. Italy has 24 national parks that in total cover 5% of the nation's land. Urban Italians make good use of city parks like *Villa Borghese* in Rome (which is one of the biggest parks in Europe) and venture into the countryside for regular nature refills. Even the day after Easter, *Pasquetta,* is set aside for a picnic or jaunt into nature.

Italians are onto something when it comes to their love of nature. Spending as little as two hours a week in nature improves health and feelings of well-being, according to a study in the journal *Nature.* Among the benefits of spending time in nature are lower blood pressure, higher self-esteem, lessened anxiety and lower stress.

Those who live close to the land have even better outcomes. *The Journal of Environmental Health Perspectives* found that those who live around greener areas of vegetation actually live longer than those who live in cities.

There are so many opportunities for travelers to experience the magic of the varying Italian landscapes. Plan time on a farm, in the mountains, on a lake, in a national park, at some hot springs. Staying at an *agriturismo* is a must for those who wish to experience how Italians and the land interact. This is a working farm that welcomes guests. The owners often host farm-to-table cooking classes as well as a plethora of outdoor activities, like participating in an olive or grape harvest, on or near the property.

THRIVE TIPS

- Put spending time in nature on your calendar; even two hours a week can make a difference in your emotional well-being.
- Walk on the grass with your bare feet, a practice known as "earthing" or "grounding."
- Plant your own small garden in your backyard or even on your apartment balcony.
- Join a hiking group to explore the areas around where you live.
- Help clean up local parks and waterways.
- Visit a local farm to appreciate what the earth gives us and buy their products.

- Photograph or paint landscapes to preserve and enjoy the beauty of the land.

TRAVEL TIPS

- Plan a farm stay in one of the many *agriturismi,* where you will see how the land provides us such bounty and how everything is connected.
- Add nature to your itinerary. For those who love mountains, check out the Dolomites. Sicily's beaches are perfect for coastal fans. There's something for everyone.
- Take a hike! Hiking is a perfect way to explore Italy. Explore the *Cinque Terre* by foot, take a trek on a volcano on the island of *Stromboli* in Sicily, hike and take in the views on *Il Sentiero degli Dei* (the Path of the Gods) on the Amalfi Coast.
- Visit one of Italy's 24 national parks.
- Snorkel or scuba dive in one of the four seas surrounding Italy: the Adriatic, Mediterranean, Ionian and Tyrrhenian.
- Explore a *grotta;* natural caves are a fascinating sight and Italy is full of them from north to south.
- Choose eco-friendly destinations like *Bandiera Blu* (blue flag) beaches, which have quality criteria related to the cleanliness of the beaches and water and the services offered, and *Bandiera Arancione* (orange flag) towns that have been recognized by the Italian Touring Club for their quality.
- Visit a vineyard and sip a glass of wine while walking through the vines or stop at an olive mill to see how olive oil is extracted. To taste wine or olive oil when visiting Tuscany, visit the Farm Shop at *Il Palagio.* Sting and Trudie have added a *pizzeria* and wine bar for a full experience.
- Spend the night in the Italian wilderness while glamping, which is a more luxurious form of camping and a vacation you will never forget.

How to Grow an
Italian Garden at Home

Growing your own fresh, organic produce is also an easy way to incorporate the Mediterranean diet into your lifestyle. In your own garden, you can grow varieties that aren't readily available in American supermarkets, including heirlooms that have been passed down through generations. My friends mother-and-son duo Lynn Byczynski and Will Nagengast of Seeds From Italy (**www.growitalian.com**) import heirloom seeds to bring the best of the Italian garden to the U.S. They share some of their best strategies for creating an Italian-inspired garden at home.

1. Grow three kinds of tomatoes and use them in as many ways as possible. Grow a paste tomato such as *San Marzano Redorta* for sauces, a huge slicer such as *Franchi* Red Pear for sandwiches and a salad tomato such as *Principe Borghese* for snacking and roasting.

2. Grow basil the way it's grown in Italy: Direct seed it (i.e., plant the seeds right in the ground) at close spacing, and pull up plants as you need them when about 4 to 6 inches tall. Succession plant it (i.e., plant seeds every week or so) all summer so you always

have fresh, tender leaves at the peak of flavor. This strategy is perfect for growing basil in a pot on your patio.

3. Try *cima di rapa*. This quintessential Italian vegetable is a close relative of broccoli, popular for both its leaves and its small flower stalks. It's super easy to grow—just direct seed it in the garden and harvest anytime before it flowers.

4. Grow chicory in cool weather. This is a huge category of plants— everything from dandelions to *radicchio* to baby salad greens. The flavor is best when the plants mature in fall or early spring.

5. Show off with a *zucchetta* serpent of Sicily! The huge leaves and vigorous vines of this amazing plant will cover a fence or *pergola* quickly. The fruits can be picked young and cooked like zucchini or left to mature into huge gourds for fall decorating. It goes by several names in Italy, including *pergola* vine, *cucuzza* and *gagootza*. If squash bugs and cucumber beetles are a problem for your other squash, try *zucchetta* instead, as it seems to be immune.

6. Grow many kinds of squash. Every region has its favorites and you'll have fun comparing a few every summer. Plus, they'll give you plenty of zucchini blossoms for frying.

7. Ditto for beans—every region has a favorite so try different types to see what works and tastes best in your climate. *Rampicante* means climbing or pole beans, which require a strong trellis but produce all season from the same plants. *Nano* means bush beans, which should be planted several times for a long harvest.

8. Many Italian recipes call for pumpkin, which is not the jack-o-lantern type we associate with the word "pumpkin." In Italy, pumpkin means *zucca*, or winter squash. Heirloom varieties tend to be very large, sprawling plants with gigantic fruits. A few plants will produce enough squash for eating now, freezing and storing.

9. Plant arugula where it won't become a nuisance. This piquant Italian green is a robust grower, ready to eat in about 30 days from direct seeding, and if you let it go to seed you will see it again and again and again. Free food!

10. Don't forget to grow flowers among the veggies to attract the pollinators many of your plants require to set fruit. Sunflowers are our top choice, but you also can't go wrong with zinnias, calendula, poppies or geraniums for an Italian garden.

Kathy and Frances Mayes

Interview with

FRANCES MAYES

Writing the Tuscan Dream

Though an incredibly prolific writer and poet, Frances Mayes is perhaps best known for her worldwide best-selling memoir *Under the Tuscan Sun*, about buying and renovating the villa *Bramasole* in *Cortona* with her husband, Ed. It also became a hit movie. Both gave us—the reading and viewing public—permission to dream our *dream of Italy* and dream big! Her most recent books include *See You in the Piazza* and *Always Italy*, both non-fiction travel books, as well as the novel *Women in Sunlight*, about four retirement-age women who move to Tuscany. Frances and Ed split their time between *Cortona* and North Carolina.

Kathy McCabe: How has *your dream of Italy* evolved over these years?

Frances Mayes: It has become reality more than dream. It was dream at first because I rented a property here in this area kind of by chance and fell in love with it. I started coming here every summer and then finally bought a house. Now I've lived here longer than anywhere else I've ever lived. But you know, some days in early June it's so paradisical you can't help but think you're in a dream.

KM: I'm amazed at how people come back to Italy again and again. Why do you think that is?

FM: They find something here that they need, that they want. You just feel relaxed. I think in a small town like *Cortona*, there's this intense sense of community. You're sitting in the *piazza* and you start talking to someone, and people in the stores are friendly. It's a special ambiance that I don't think is reproducible anywhere else that I've ever been.

KM: Does it remind you of the American South, where you grew up?

FM: It reminds me of the South. Tuscany has a lot to do with hospitality; it has the hot climate and the big sky. Also, Tuscans are very friendly, but after a certain point they're very private. And that's so true in the South.

KM: How did you transition from vacationing to living here?

FM: The first time I ever rented a house here, I put down my little basil plants and saw them grow. I thought I might want to put down roots here too. It was one of those quick decisions. I thought, "I want this to be a part of my life in some way or the other." Italy is 5,000 years deep. It's beautiful. There's all this art, this great food. My husband Ed loved Italy as well. We started just vacationing here and deciding how we were going to do this. We were both university professors, so we had the summers off.

KM: Is it hard to split your time between the U.S. and Italy?

FM: It's not difficult. I love where I live in North Carolina and I love Italy. It's like having two really nice husbands. It's an easy transition, and the joy of it is that you see one place from the perspective of the other and vice versa. You get a little bit more perspective than if you were just living in one place. I love knowing two cultures.

KM: If someone wants to move to Italy, how should they start the process?

FM: Spend a lot of time here before you do anything drastic. The best thing of course is learning the language as much as you can. A little bit of Italian goes a long way.

KM: What have you done that's helped the most to learn Italian?

FM: Restoring the house was kind of a breakthrough because we were working along with everyone else. We picked up a lot of local dialect and of course took courses. My husband went to the *Università per Stranieri di Perugia*. We went to *Istituto Dante Alighieri* in Florence and in *Siena*. Studying along the way is helpful, and then the best thing is picking it up in the *piazza*.

KM: You've shared before that you have to do something when you're here.

FM: Yes. You can't just be a tourist forever. You have to live here and that is the great joy. If you take to country pleasures, it's a country place. *Cortona* is not an exciting city, but as in all the very small towns and villages in Italy, each one has an amazing cultural life. There are photography workshops in *Cortona*, there are concerts, there are lectures. It's like a midsize American city, at least.

KM: Do you recommend people look for a smaller town?

FM: It just depends on what you like. Some people want to be right in the middle of Florence or Rome or *Milano* or *Torino*. Some people want to be in a city, a lot of buzz, a lot of excitement. But I like the country pleasures. I love my garden. I love walking on the Roman roads.

KM: What's it like having friends visit you in Italy?

FM: It's a happy place to have your friends come to visit. It gives a new dimension to your friendship. We love cooking here, so we have at least one dinner party a week and we go out a lot because everybody else likes to cook too. It's very sociable.

KM: How easy is it to make Italian friends?

FM: *See You in the Piazza*? That's it! Yesterday I was there and there was a young woman with her baby and we all ended up holding the baby. You meet people in the shops everywhere you go. There's a nice mix between the foreigners and the local people, and I really enjoy that. We have a book club with people from four different nationalities. There's a whole lot of social life. There's a lot of cooking and entertaining, a lot of beautiful table settings and visiting harmonica players and fun things. A social life is intense. I think meeting people is not the problem. It's more like, how do I get anything done? Because there's so much to do.

KM: What inspired your recent novel *Women in Sunlight*?

FM: I was sitting in the *piazza* in the morning and having my *cappuccino*, which I do often, and I saw a woman reading or taking notes in her notebook, and I knew why she was there. I knew that she was not here just to absorb the sights, but she had a quest. That's why I came here too, on a quest, and I thought I would like to give a voice to these women.

KM: What is it about women and Italy? What do women come here to find?

FM: I've thought about that a lot and I think I've come to the conclusion that it's not so much that it'll change them once they're here. It's more that they are ready to change. Italy is such a lovely catalyst because of being able to feel at home here and to feel encouraged in whatever you want to do. It just opens that possibility. When the student's ready, the teacher appears, in the form of Italy. Every day is a new act in life.

I had this kind of quest, but I stayed because of the warmth of the people and the friends we've made here, and just how close-knit the community is. The people here are so generous. When I get back, I haven't been here a morning before someone says, "Can I bring you some eggs?" or "I've got some beautiful grapes. Would you like some?" The giving here just nourishes you.

KM: You've traveled all over Italy, especially for your travel book *Always Italy*. What have you learned?

FM: Italy is endless. Even a couple of lifetimes would not be enough. Even in *Cortona*, I often see something that I haven't seen before. There's a whole underground layer of *Cortona* that nobody knows about. Under my bank there are Etruscan walls, and when they restore buildings downtown, they find Etruscan walls and remnants that are always coming to light. It's always new. It's always old.

KM: Of course people read about the restoration of *Bramasole*. Would you do it all again?

FM: We keep doing it. Oh, houses are never finished with you. You might be finished with them, but they're not finished with you. The restoration was really fun. I loved it, and we've done a lot of big projects since then. We've restored a second house, although we've always kept *Bramasole*. It's a way into the community. You learn about all the people who are working for you and their families. One of those secret benefits to moving here is that with your team, you really learn a lot about the community. It's just a magnificent sense to be restoring something to the patrimony.

KM: Does it end up costing twice as much?

FM: Oh, of course. But the satisfaction is enormous because the workers here are skilled, beautiful craftsmen, and they really know what they're doing, particularly the stonemasons. They can just cut and shape that stone like it's butter and you can't believe the skill they have, the artistry they bring to their work and their enjoyment of it. Not only are you fixing this place back up again, but you're doing something beautiful to it. It's the satisfaction of working with these amazing people.

KM: Do you think buying *Bramasole* was particularly adventurous?

FM: It was at the time in 1990. I didn't know anyone who'd ever bought a foreign property, but now it's pretty common.

KM: Do you feel like a trendsetter?

FM: I was a pioneer. I don't particularly think about it, but I've seen so many people come to *Cortona*, and most of them live very happily here. They make a real life here. They find something interesting to do and they stick with it. I think a lot of people in the U.S. in their 50s and 60s have the mindset of, "What are you going to do? You're going to live to be 100, so you might as well do something interesting and fun and new." I think it's important to surprise your own life so that you don't fall into doing what you know how to do.

Your life may be very pleasant, but you know what the day is going to be. If you pull up stakes and move to someplace where you don't know what's happening every day, it does something very invigorating to your life. Every morning when I wake up, I think, "What can I do today that I didn't do yesterday?" I'm someone who gets really bored with routine, so I have to shake it up.

———

For more information, visit **www.francesemayes.com**

Kathy and Sally Carrocino at *Mercato Sant'Ambrogio*

Food

Is any nationality more passionate about what they eat than the Italians? Food is the primary topic of conversation in Italy—always. Italians critique the flavors they just enjoyed, anticipate the meal they are going to enjoy next and reminisce about that dish they ate on vacation 10 years ago. Really. And who made it better? *Mamma* or the chef at the restaurant? Well, *mamma* of course.

Food here is beyond fresh and best enjoyed *insieme*—together.

"You can have a watermelon that was in the garden 20 minutes before you eat it. Now that level of freshness is a rare thing in modern life. So I appreciate it," Sting says.

"The tomatoes are the same; they come straight to the table, they taste different. It's an incredible privilege. I'm also immensely grateful. We eat well and we feel well. I also like to share it. We never have less than 30 people at any meal. We're Italian!" Sting exclaims.

Ah the tomatoes! I too can wax poetic about how the tomatoes just burst with flavor in Italy. That's what expat retiree Sally Carrocino and I discuss when we visit the local *Sant'Ambrogio* market in Florence in the special.

She tells me Italians buy produce "every day, because you only buy what you can eat that day. You don't buy for a week." Sally points out that refrigerators in Italian homes are small, so they can only hold so much.

One tip for shopping for produce: Don't touch! *Non si può toccare.*

Shopping at local markets and individual producers also comes back to the sense of community that food inspires in Italy. "You're going to see people if you go out every day to buy your vegetables," I say to Sally. "Yes, and I think that's one of the reasons that Italy has the oldest society here, because they are out. They're not cooped up in their house watching TV. They're meeting people," Sally observes.

Access to fresh, affordable food is one of the primary reasons why the country of Italy often tops the Bloomberg Global Health Index as the healthiest country in the world. The Mediterranean diet, which Italians follow, calls for moderate amounts of wine and moderate to high consumption of fish, legumes, olive oil, fruits and vegetables. Studies show those who follow this diet have a lower risk of obesity, diabetes, cancer and cardiovascular disease.

Best-selling author Dan Buettner has researched and written about "Blue Zones," five areas around the world where people live the longest and healthiest. One of these is on the island of Sardinia, which has the largest concentration of male centenarians in the world. One reason: diet. In his book, *The Blue Zones Solution*, Buettner advises eating a mostly plant-based diet, with 3- to 4-ounce servings of meat only five times a month; eating the smallest meal of the day in the evening; and drinking a moderate amount of alcohol.

Italian recipes are simple to show off the quality of the ingredients. Interior designer Arlene Antoinette Gibbs, who lives in Rome, has discovered the joys of the local snack *pizza bianca.* "It's only olive oil and salt on bread," she says. "That's why it's all about the ingredients, because if you don't have a lot of ingredients, they have to be perfect."

Alatia Bach, who moved to Florence with her husband David and their sons, says, "You don't have to be a good cook to live here because it's about the ingredients, like four ingredients for every meal."

David adds, "I'm not a cook, but here I'm like a chef. The food is such high quality that I can whip something up in five minutes."

"I came to Italy loving Italian food," he explains, "but as anyone who lives here will tell you, once you've had a pizza in Italy, you're ruined for pizza for life. It's the truth about all Italian food. When people tell you that the food tastes better here, it's not just because of the environment. The food truly, deeply tastes better. The fruit, the vegetables, the color, the flavor. Now we realize it's because they don't have all the chemicals."

Another bonus about food in Italy: You can eat well on a budget.

"I'm constantly shocked at how much less I pay for food," Sally says, compared to prices when she lived in California.

Italians and those who live like Italians—like Sting and Trudie—grow their own vegetable gardens, providing a hyper-local source of food. It is called *km zero* here, meaning zero kilometers. Sting and Trudie share their produce with locals (and visitors) who visit the *Il Palagio* Farm Shop. They've just added a wine bar and *pizzeria* too.

Much of the cuisine of Italy is *cucina povera*, the poor kitchen, dating back to peasant times when food was scarce. Nothing is wasted. Every part of the pig is used. Even days-old bread makes for an important ingredient, as it did in *ribollita*, the Tuscan bread soup I made in the Florence episode of *Dream of Italy*.

Italians nearly always sit down to eat a full meal for lunch and dinner. (Breakfast can be a coffee and *cornetto* standing up at the local bar.) They enjoy multiple courses during a meal: *Primo* is first and often a pasta, *secondo* is often meat or seafood and *dolce* is dessert. Portion sizes are smaller and Italians take the time to eat, savoring all the flavors.

Italians take food seriously even when they are traveling. Enter the *Autogrill,* which, in true Italian fashion, is an over-the-top version of a rest stop that you can find on the main A1 highway and other major roads. You can sit down for an entire meal at an *Autogrill*—steak made to order, fresh *mozzarella, arancini* (fried rice balls), side salads, wine, pastries and more. It is truly an Italian experience so be sure to stop at one if you are driving through Italy.

Food is like a passport to the history and culture of the 20 regions of Italy that only in recent times came together to be known as *Italia*. There are commonalities, of course, like pasta, but you would be surprised at the differences in recipes and ingredients even a few miles apart.

Since rediscovering his ancestral hometown of *Bernalda*, Francis Ford Coppola has delighted in discovering local dishes. "I must be honest that there was the attraction of eating all these exotic foods that you couldn't get anywhere else," he says. His favorite is *lampascioni*, something resembling fried hyacinth bulbs. "They only really have it in *Puglia* and *Basilicata*," he says. Another specialty in *Bernalda,* and an example of *cucina povera*, is *capuzzelle*, a sheep's or lamb's head cooked with all the innards intact. Coppola says, "As a kid I tried to sample the brains, because I thought if I ate the brains, I would be smart."

No matter where you travel in Italy, try to find out what the local specialties are—*ragù* in *Bologna, cacio e pepe* in Rome, *orecchiette* and *burrata* in *Puglia*—and partake in those. At least one cooking class is a must when traveling—usually it includes a market visit and a lesson by a local chef and the enjoyment of the meal together. You can take your skills home and live and eat like an Italian in your everyday life.

Try to enjoy a meal with locals. If you don't know any Italians in the places you're visiting, sign up for a meal with **Cesarine.com** (formerly known as *Home Food*) where you can dine in a local home, with vetted hosts around the country, and not only taste local specialties but also get to know a family in their home.

THRIVE TIPS

- Follow the Mediterranean diet. (See page 20.)
- Eat in-season, organic and non-GMO. You will taste the difference.
- Seek out local farmer's markets.
- Focus on the quality of your ingredients.
- Start a small garden to grow your own fresh fruits and vegetables.

■ Don't eat anything out of a wrapper or a box!

■ Use type oo flour from Italy. It is more finely ground and has less gluten.

■ Spend money on a good Italian olive oil and use it, don't save it. Store it in a dark cool place.

■ Don't eat between meals.

■ Don't drink without eating—that's how the Italians do it.

■ Take digestion seriously and have a *digestivo* after dinner.

TRAVEL TIPS

■ Research the local delicacies in the towns and regions you will be visiting.

■ Take a cooking class. If you can, take one in each of the different areas you are visiting as cuisine varies so widely. Look for a class that is hands-on and includes a market visit with the chef.

■ Visit a food factory such as a *prosciuttificio* where *prosciutto crudo* (dry-cured ham) is prepared and aged, or a *caseificio*, a dairy farm that makes products like cheese. In the south, visit a buffalo farm to try the freshest *mozzarella di bufala*.

■ Enjoy a half-day urban food tour such as the ones offered by **EatingEurope.com** and **TasteFlorence.com**

■ When planning your days in Italy, do as the Italians do, and enjoy sit-down meals with multiple courses.

■ Tour a vineyard and enjoy a wine tasting. Harvest season in the fall can be a great time to go.

■ Ask locals for restaurant recommendations. Frances Mayes suggests stopping in the local *enoteca* (wine store/bar) as the wine experts always know the best places to go.

■ Plan to attend a food or wine event to explore the richness and traditions that Italy offers. *Vinitaly* is an international wine and spirits exhibition held every year in April, or *Salone del Gusto,* a huge gastronomy event hosted by Slow Food that takes place every two years in Turin, is worth planning a trip around.

- Hosted in honor of everything from artichokes to truffles to potatoes, a *sagra* is a local festival that is often organized around food and can include historical elements such as processions or parades. Look up the local events of the town you are visiting and you might be surprised about the variety of festivals taking place during your stay.

- When stopping for *gelato,* be wary of the colorful and fluffy industrial flavors. Instead, eat *gelato artigianale,* handcrafted *gelato* made of quality ingredients that can be found in the authentic *gelateria.* Want to take a serious course of study to make *gelato* or start a *gelateria*? Go to *Carpigiani Gelato University,* which I visited in the *Bologna* episode of *Dream of Italy.*

- Visit as many local markets—featuring fish, fruit, vegetables, olive oil, honey—as you can and specialty stores like the *salumeria* (cured meat shop), the *pasticceria* (for pastry) and all the rest with "...ria" in the name. The local *bottega* or *gastronomia,* as well as the *Autogrill,* are great places to buy portable fine foods, *prodotti gastronomici.*

How to Follow the
Mediterranean Diet

You've no doubt heard of the Mediterranean diet as a way to eat healthier and live longer. Studies have shown that older Italians who follow this diet live longer and have lower rates of diabetes, cancer, cognitive decline and heart disease.

But what exactly is the Mediterranean diet in Italy? In the *bel paese*, emphasis in the kitchen is not only given to the type of ingredients selected for each meal but also to their freshness and origin. Locally sourced, fresh and authentic products are the secret for delicious and healthy dishes that can be enjoyed in every region of Italy.

In Italy, the *km zero* movement emphasizes local ingredients that have traveled zero kilometers from farm to plate. Most importantly, seasonality is another crucial aspect of Italian cuisine. Every season brings its own bounty of products and colorful and creative recipes that not only reflect the chronological time but also become traditions, much awaited moments and memories that families cherish together. The Mediterranean diet in Italy is poetry, love for the land and respect for nature at its best.

Here are tips for how to incorporate the Mediterranean diet into your own life, no matter where you live:

- Search for simple but authentic ingredients (fruits, vegetables, grains, potatoes, beans, nuts and seeds) and shop at a farmer's market on a near-daily basis.
- Opt for smaller portion sizes with an emphasis on moderate amounts of lean protein, such as fish, chicken or eggs.
- Limit the amount of unhealthy saturated fats such as the ones found in cream, butter and red meat.
- Include olive oil as your primary fat source.
- Choose larger amounts of fresh, seasonal fruit and vegetables, grains, olive oil, beans, nuts, herbs and spices.
- Drink moderate amounts of red wine.
- Consume sugar in moderation.
- Take the time to sit down for each meal and enjoy simple and creative recipes with family and friends.

HOW OFTEN SHOULD YOU EAT EACH OF THESE FOOD GROUPS?

- **Fruit and vegetables:** Give priority to fruit and vegetables during all meals.
- **Carbohydrates:** One portion of pasta or rice can be eaten every day, especially if combined with fresh seasonal vegetables and seasoned with extra virgin olive oil. Pasta can also be combined with legumes, making it a nutritious and delicious meal.
- **Protein:** One portion of milk or yogurt can be eaten every day; fish and eggs two to three times a week; lean meat and cheese twice a week; and legumes twice a week.
- **Fat:** Italy's favorite condiment is extra virgin olive oil, but don't exceed two tablespoons a day. Herbs are an excellent substitute for salt, and they flavor dishes without adding fat or calories.
- **Red wine:** Moderate consumption of red wine at mealtime is allowed and especially recommended by those who emphasize the beneficial effect that certain substances contained in

wine, such as resveratrol (a powerful antioxidant), have on our bodies. Servings can range from one small glass a day to several glasses. As always, consult your doctor.

How to Cook Pasta
Like an Italian

Italians take their pasta seriously: which shapes and sizes to use, which ingredients are superior and how to cook it properly. Of course, it's always best to make fresh, homemade pasta, but if you need something fast, we love *De Cecco* (**www.dececco.com**) for its authenticity and flavor. The second-largest pasta brand in the world makes its pasta with high-quality durum wheat from Italy and the U.S. and with water from its own spring in the beautiful mountains of *Abruzzo*. My Italian friend *Maria Pradissitto* shares some quick tips for cooking pasta the Italian way.

CHOOSING YOUR PASTA

Begin by carefully selecting the right type of pasta for your sauce.

Long pasta

- *Tagliatelle* and *fettuccine* are ideal for rich and full-bodied sauces such as beef or wild boar *ragù*, sausage and *porcini* mushrooms, or four-cheese sauce.
- *Paccheri* (a tube-shaped pasta), *conchiglioni* (large shells) and *lasagnette* are perfect for baking in the oven with cheese and meat sauce.

- *Spaghetti*, *vermicelli*, *bucatini* and *linguine* go well with tomatoes, tuna, sardines, crustaceans and shellfish. Generally, *spaghetti* can be combined with any ingredients, but it is especially suitable in dishes that require the final *mantecatura* (explained below).
- Angel hair can be used in soups or broth.
- *Tagliolini* are fantastic with crab or simply with eggs and *Romano* cheese, more commonly known as *carbonara*.

Short pasta

- *Fusilli* go perfectly with light sauces, fresh tomatoes and vegetables.
- *Farfalle* and *penne* (smooth or ridged) are the most suitable shapes for cold salads.
- *Pipette* (ridged elbows) or *sedanini* (ridged, tube-shaped pasta) are the most versatile: They do well both in soups and with sauces.
- Sardinian *gnocchetti* are good with sauces based on fresh tomatoes and basil or seafood.
- *Orecchiette* are good with *pesto*, eggplants, tomatoes or broccoli rabe.
- *Trofie* (twisted pasta) are perfect with *pesto* or seafood.

Choose pasta made from the finest durum wheat and bronze-drawn texture, which holds the sauce better and keeps its firmness for a longer time.

COOKING YOUR PASTA

- When cooking your pasta, salt must be added to the water a few moments before boiling. Salt can alter the flavor of the food to which it is added. It is important to appropriately dose the salt, keeping in mind the type of sauce selected to achieve balance in the flavors of the final dish. For example, if the sauce contains mussels, it is recommended to use a moderate quantity of salt in the pasta water so that the final dish won't be overly salty.

■ Don't add olive oil to the boiling water; this is not necessary. Instead, bring water to a boil before adding pasta and cook for the recommended amount of time to reach the *al dente* texture, stirring occasionally.

■ Drain your pasta before adding it to the sauce. It is a good idea to reserve some of the cooking water to make a creamy dish, a process known as *mantecatura*, which means "to amalgamate." For this process, it is necessary to drain the pasta when it is still very *al dente* to avoid a drenched consistency.

■ Pour the pasta into the pan with the sauce and finish cooking it by gradually adding ladles of cooking water, which will be absorbed by the pasta. By constantly stirring, part of the cooking water evaporates and more is absorbed by the pasta, which continues to cook, creating a creamy sauce. The starch, a natural thickener contained in the flour, will ensure that the pasta and the sauce create a long-lasting bond that will make your dish unique.

■ Make a simple, fresh sauce from scratch like *marinara*, *pesto* or *carbonara*. Italians almost never use store-bought sauce.

Mediterranean *Spaghetti* with Swordfish

My Italian friend *Maria Pradissitto* says this is one of her favorite simple, classic recipes. She tells me, "This recipe reminds me of Sicily, of its wonderful smell of citrus and mulberry and its warm salty sea breeze on a beautiful summer day. What a perfect representation of the Mediterranean diet in one simple dish: pasta combined with fish, vegetables and olive oil. This recipe is a wonderful and fun way to add your daily share of vegetables or lean protein to your table. I hope you enjoy this dish as much as I do!"

Serves 4

Ingredients

- 16 oz durum wheat *spaghetti*
- 1 cup olives
- 2 Tbsp capers
- 10 oz cherry tomatoes, halved
- 1 lb 1-inch thick swordfish steaks, cut into small cubes
- ¼ cup white wine

- 4 garlic cloves, minced
- 5 leaves fresh basil, minced; or 1 tsp dried basil
- 4 Tbsp extra virgin olive oil, plus some extra virgin olive oil to finish
- Salt and pepper

Directions

1. Fill a large pot with about 6 quarts of water and put it on the stove to boil.

2. Heat 2 Tbsp extra virgin olive oil in a medium skillet over medium heat. When warm, add 2 Tbsp minced garlic and let sit for a few seconds, making sure the garlic doesn't turn brown. Add the tomatoes and season with salt and pepper. Simmer and let cook for about 15 minutes or until the tomatoes are soft, stirring occasionally. After 10 minutes, add the olives, capers and basil.

3. Heat 2 Tbsp extra virgin olive oil in a large skillet. When warm, add 2 Tbsp minced garlic and let sit for a few seconds before adding the swordfish. Sear the fish on all sides. Add the white wine and let evaporate. Add salt and pepper and simmer for about 15 minutes, stirring occasionally. A few minutes before turning off the stove, add the tomato sauce with olives and capers and stir.

4. Add a large pinch of salt to the boiling water for pasta. Add *spaghetti* and stir occasionally until *al dente,* typically 10 minutes. When ready, drain the *spaghetti* in a large colander and reserve half a cup of pasta water.

5. Pour the *spaghetti* into the large skillet and combine with the swordfish and tomato sauce on low heat. Add a little of the reserved pasta water—just enough to make sure the sauce becomes creamy but not overly watery.

6. Divide the pasta among four plates, drizzle with extra virgin olive oil and enjoy. *Buon pranzo!* (Enjoy your lunch!)

Kathy (right) and her mother in *Castelvetere sul Calore*

Family

Family is at the heart of Italian life. Italians have great reverence for their ancestors and the places where they come from. Since Italy is relatively young as a unified country, it isn't surprising that the Italian allegiance to *la mia famiglia* overrides everything else.

"To me, there's nothing more important than my family," says director of *The Godfather* Francis Ford Coppola. "Who we are, where we came from and those who came before define who we are. It's our challenge and our duty to carry this heritage forward and share it with the world. We're Italians; we like to share our food, our wine, our history and our culture."

Many households in Italy are multi-generational with *nonna* and *nonno* (grandma and grandpa) often living with their children and grandchildren, or at least nearby. Those who don't live together still see each other often, especially for a traditional Sunday lunch. Researchers say these strong family ties also help Italians age better and live longer and happier lives.

For many people who visit Italy, it all begins with a search for these family roots. That was the case for Coppola and actor Joe Mantegna—and for me, too—as we all made that first trip to Italy in our 20s to find our ancestral hometowns.

That quest led Coppola to *Bernalda* in southern Italy, the birthplace and home of his grandfather, *Agostino Coppola*, who always referred to it affectionately as *"Bernalda bella."* Ultimately, he opened *Palazzo Margherita*, a boutique hotel, not only to honor his heritage, but also as a place to spend time with family, including his Uncle Kiki and Aunt Almerinda, who are featured in the *Basilicata* episode of *Dream of Italy* and make another appearance in this TV special.

"We knew we were half Italian and half American," Coppola explains. "Everything originated from the fact that we came from a part of Italy known as *Basilicata.*"

Mantegna has a similar family story that began in 1975 shortly after he got married. He and his wife, Arlene Vrhel, were traveling with a theater company in Europe, and he wanted to honor his grandfather's request to visit the family in Italy.

"I'd never been there," he recounts. "I thought, 'Okay, this is a good opportunity to go to my grandparents' hometown and say hello to the family.' I told my wife, 'We'll stop in, and we'll have coffee. We'll spend the day. It'll be great.' "

That one day turned into 12 days. "They basically kidnapped us," he says, "and I'll never forget being at that train station on the day we had to leave, my wife and I both crying our eyes out, knowing we now had a family here in Italy that we would be close to for the rest of our lives. Now that's my Italian family story."

Like Coppola and Mantegna, it was the search for my own Italian roots that also brought me to Italy. My mother and I were the first of our family to return to our ancestral hometown of *Castelvetere sul Calore* in more than 100 years. Italy and our travels here—more than 20 trips in total, all over the Italian boot and also to Sardinia—brought us much closer.

Traveling as a family, like I did with my mother, can bring families closer together and be a bonding experience, particularly for children. That's been the case for author and life coach Sarah Centrella, whose great-grandparents came from Italy, and has visited as a single mother with her three children.

"Travel has been the most important thing I could teach my kids," she says. Sarah enhances the experience by having each child research and plan visits to specific locations. Empowering them to make those decisions ensures they are invested in the trip and helps them build confidence that carries over when they return home.

Traveling together as a family also led to changes in their day-to-day life as she incorporated the "spirit of Italy" by shopping for local foods, making traditional meals or listening to Italian music—focusing on having experiences rather than accumulating things.

Research underscores Sarah's point. Studies have shown that people in societies where money plays a minimal role can have very high levels of happiness. That's because it focuses them on other values, including family and the beauty of nature, explain scientists.

"I wanted to teach my children that having that experience and being touched by Italy in just such a magical way is how you can build your life," she says. "It doesn't have to be just two weeks. It can really be who you are."

While travel can be a great way for families to bond, studies show vacations and living abroad also can increase brain function, academic grades and aspirations for children. Author David Bach and his wife, Alatia, moved from New York City to Florence to experience the Italian lifestyle with their two sons.

"Our *dream of Italy* was to live rich now," he says. "It was not to do it someday when we retire. It was to live rich now, to experience this with our family together. And the fact that we're getting to do that right now, to me that's our *dream of Italy*."

It didn't take long for both parents to see the effects on their family. "We've never spent this much time together nonstop, and it's become a different way of life," says David Bach. "We're all more present in our lives right now than I think we've ever been. We're less distracted. We're more here right now, and I think that's giving all of us a sense of joy."

From her vantage point in *Cortona*, author Frances Mayes also has observed that children growing up in Italy have more freedom.

"It's amazing," she says. "On a summer night, at 11:00 p.m., the kids are running all over town having *gelato*. They're still playing soccer. Children have a lot of freedom here. Our children in America are much more protected, more restricted."

In Italy, family also means business, with 73% of businesses, big and small, being family owned. That's something the Bachs have seen first-hand as they frequent shops in Florence.

"You go to the local businesses here, and they're businesses that have been in families for generations," says Bach. "So, whether it's the laundry store or the hardware store or the florist or the *tabaccheria*, sometimes you have three generations—you have grandma, you have dad and you have the granddaughters all working together, having a great life and servicing the community where everyone is friends."

While Italy may seem very traditional in terms of family structure, Arlene Antoinette Gibbs feels welcomed into a different kind of family as a single woman living in Rome. Research shows friendships are positively associated with life satisfaction, including a recent study on Italians living as couples that found friendship relationships, beyond those within an individual's family, are an important source of support.

"I feel like America is really geared for couples," she says. "If you're not married and you don't have children, people don't know what to do with you. I think it's changing because there are quite a few women who are single and don't have children in America, but I didn't feel that here. It's because the concept of family is different. There are many ways to be a family in Italy."

Italy's emphasis on family may inspire you to take a closer look at your own family ties—improving them, learning more about them or even looking for a sense of family in those who are not related by blood.

Whether your roots are in Italy or elsewhere, the strong ties so many feel to the land where they are from can inspire you to search out your own ancestry and see where you are from with your own eyes. This is a fantastic way to travel.

THRIVE TIPS

- Start a tradition of a weekly, multi-generational meal. Add a virtual component to include the out-of-town members.
- Replicate the Italian Sunday lunch. If you don't have blood family nearby, create a family of friends.
- Interview your relatives and record their responses—even with your phone—to preserve family stories for generations to come.
- Be sure to have older relatives identify people in old family photographs.
- Frame some of those old family photos to keep your ancestors nearby.
- Research your genealogy by building a family tree.
- Explore whether your ancestry might allow you to reclaim citizenship in another country, like Italy, which considers citizenship *jure sanguinis* (by right of blood).
- Try to support family-owned businesses no matter where you live.

TRAVEL TIPS

- Use your ancestry to plan a trip to find your family roots, whether that is in Italy or another country. Even if you can't travel at the moment, this is a great time to plan your itinerary.
- Plan to spend a portion of your stay with your Italian family members. Italians are very hospitable and would likely be delighted to show you around or have you as a guest.
- Italy is the perfect multi-generational family vacation destination. Not only are there activities for all ages, but Italy is also built around a family lifestyle, so you'll find traveling with kids natural and safe.

- Feel free to enjoy a late night out with your family. In Italy, gatherings often include people of all ages, so it's common to see children out late in restaurants or bars with the rest of the family.

- A large part of the Italian family's social life involves eating and celebrating together, so take any opportunity to celebrate—a birthday or anniversary, for instance—while in Italy. Remember to do it with a glass of *Prosecco*.

- Italian design, with its many *piazzas* and walkable areas, encourages families to go out onto the streets. Enjoy being outside and join the locals while shopping, eating and drinking together.

- Wherever you stay, support family-owned businesses and get to know the owners. They will be happy to share their business story with you.

Interview with

FRANCIS FORD COPPOLA

A Grandson Discovers His Roots

Growing up in New York, Hollywood film director Francis Ford Coppola was regaled with tales of a mythical place called *Bernalda*, deep in the south of Italy, the birthplace of his grandfather *Agostino*. Little did he know that later in life, Coppola would become a part-time resident of his ancestral hometown and purchase a *palazzo* (with ties to his grandfather), *Palazzo Margherita*, that he would add to his collection of boutique hotels around the world, now known as The Family Coppola Hideaways. For Coppola, family is inextricably linked to Italy.

Kathy McCabe: Tell me how you first set eyes on the town of *Bernalda*.

Francis Ford Coppola: When I was a little kid, I had six uncles, and they all were imitating my grandfather. He died when I was six. The uncles told all these crazy stories about him, of what he was like when he was young, and his adventures from this mythical place he called *bella Bernalda*. We knew we were half Italian and half American by virtue of living in America. Everything originated from the fact that we came from a part of Italy known as *Basilicata*, previously known as *Lucania*, in the town of *Bernalda bella*.

When I went to Italy for the first time in 1962, I put my car on a ferry while working in Croatia and I just drove to *Bernalda*. I drove up the hill and I saw this little town on the hill, which looked just as I had imagined. With my six words of Italian I said, "I'm Francis Coppola, and I'm the grandson of *Agostino Coppola*, who was born here." No one in my family had ever come back here. My grandfather never had, and none of the uncles had.

I remember being in a little tiny room with the whole family of this elderly lady who was *Agostino*'s first cousin. We spoke as well as I could with the few words I had, and the few words they had. When it was getting late and I realized that I didn't know where I was going to sleep, and I asked, "Is there a hotel?" They said, "No, there is no hotel." There were two newlyweds there. They said, "You can go and stay with this cousin." I followed them in my car and we went to a house, and I remember we went into their little very modest place, but there was all this elaborate wedding furniture gifts, big dressers, and beds, and stuff.

The next thing I know, the bride, the young woman, disappeared, and the husband appears out of the bathroom in pajamas and he indicated the bed and turned the cover down. It said *Signor Franco*. I realized I was going to sleep with him. I got in my side, and he got in his side, then went to sleep. The next morning the wife showed up. I never knew where she slept. I guess in the barn or whatever. She made coffee and then I went on my way. That was a profound form of hospitality.

KM: Did you imagine you would come back to *Bernalda* after that?

FFC: No, I was 22. I didn't have a girlfriend. I was just finishing UCLA film school, so my mind was on a career. I very much wanted to get married because I wanted to have children. *Bernalda* at that point was a footnote.

KM: Did you speak Italian at home?

FFC: We kids were not taught Italian because to be Italian in those days, you were a little bit underclass. I was named after my mother's father, *Francesco Pennino*, but they called me Francis.

KM: Tell me about *Agostino* and his life. Why did he leave Italy?

FFC: In those days, the south, and particularly *Lucania*, was incredibly poor. There's a famous book and movie called *Christ Stopped at Eboli*, which deals with that, because the Italian Fascists were Fascist and pretty tough. If you were out of favor with them, they didn't shoot you, they exiled you to the south, because this was considered a no man's land. *Eboli* is a town on the railroad line further north, and even Christ got out [of the train], because where he was going was so impoverished.

The south was pretty bleak, and had no power politically because the power was in *Piemonte*, which is where the kingdom was. They had no representation. When my grandfather was a little boy, there was very little employment. His mother, *Filomena Coppola*, was an extraordinary woman and an extremely talented dressmaker. She would make the embroidery on the beautiful dresses for the rich ladies.

My grandfather was the only of the boys in his family who made it to the fifth grade. He was sent to school because he was bright. When he finished the fifth grade, he became apprentice to the local genius, whose name was *Ciccio Panio* (*Francesco Panio*), who was a significant figure in the south of Italy at that time with all sorts of infamous exploits of how he solved problems, and ultimately brought electricity to these towns in *Magna Grecia*. (*Ciccio* is *Francesco*. I'm *Ciccio Coppola*.)

My grandfather developed good skills from this apprenticeship and joined the Italian army. Italians in that period either went to Argentina or New York, and he had two brothers who had gone to New York and he went in the Italian army. Italy was a very young nation, and the people of the south had no idea who the people in the north were. They were really different people. The people in the north were French and German and Austrians. Italy was controlled by many different European countries, and the northerners thought the southerners were Africans. The people in the south said, "Who is *Italia*?"

KM: How did you come to buy *Palazzo Margherita*?

FFC: It was really only after *The Godfather* was made, which was pretty early in my life. It was a tough and miserable experience, but it made me very famous in Italy and in *Bernalda*, because no one ever heard of *Bernalda*, no one ever heard of *Basilicata*, no one ever heard of *Matera*. In those days no one ever heard of *Puglia*. All these regions—*Puglia, Basilicata,* even *Calabria*—all now are the very fertile new places of Italy because they are fresh and they haven't been compromised by 1,000 years of tourism.

I was invited by the then-mayor of *Bernalda* to become an honorary citizen. I came with my wife and my children, and the whole town turned out to welcome me and cheer me on. I was especially touched because they had a parade of the schoolchildren in the cute little uniforms. I realized that *Bernalda*, and *Basilicata* and the south of Italy, were enjoying the fact that some of their people who had gone to America, land of opportunity, now spoke for the first time of the achievement.

While filming *The Godfather* in Rome, I met *Michele Russo*, who was an actor and a nice young man from *Bernalda*. I decided to visit *Bernalda* again with all my family because in the summer they have the *Festa di San Bernardino*. In *Bernalda*, they didn't have any money to have television and theater. They had a movie theater, but it closed. So there are a lot of events on the weekends in the streets: a beauty contest, a cooking day or a reggae festival. Nowadays, we live in a time where everyone's watching television. Movies are beautiful, but they're also canned. To have a festival, it's something live.

Some of my newfound cousins said, "The *Palazzo Margherita* is right across from the *festa*. The ladies who live there, they're two sisters, they will let you come in."

Another cousin was now in the real estate business. He said, "Oh, you should buy the *palazzo*." I said, "What do I need a *palazzo* in *Bernalda* for?" I wasn't interested.

Time went by and, on different occasions, I came with my family. I always loved to see this *festa* because it's so colorful. It's so beautiful and so exciting, with strange parades with knights going by and people flagellating themselves. It's like some sort of medieval experience.

Years later, *Michele Russo* said to me, "You know, there's a law in the government of Italy called the 488 Law. If you do something in the south that helps create employment, you can be a candidate for this law. If you win, you will get a subsidy from the government depending on how many people you're going to employ. It could be very substantial." By then, I had some hotels. I thought, if I would get a subsidy from the government to help me redo it, much less buy it, then maybe I could make it a hotel with the other hotels. To make a long story short, I never got the subsidy.

KM: What did you dream of this *palazzo*?

FFC: When you make a hotel, it's like a film. You have a big concept. Our concept was that we weren't going to restore the *palazzo* as if it were brand new. We were going to restore it with a patina of its age, which is 100 years, and serve fabulous food and make the garden, which is an historical site and protected by law.

There are only nine suites. They're beautiful; they're handpainted. The food is incredible. The garden is magical. Then we have this wonderful *Cinecittà* bar, which is a tribute to my old memory of being in Rome at the *Cinecittà* bar, where we used to get an *espresso* with a shot of brandy. We loved having pictures of all the people who worked at *Cinecittà*.

One story I remember from my childhood is that my grandfather was having an affair with the maid, whose name was *Palmetta*. She happened to have a little room that you could get to from the roof. When I came to this *palazzo* when we were planning how to reconstruct it, there was the roof and there was a little room, and then the little stairs going down to one of the rooms. They said, "That was the maid's room." I said, "Wow, maybe that was *Palmetta*'s room." There was a time when I was fantasizing that I was going to call it *Palazzo Palmetta*, which I thought would be the supreme irony because the ladies who lived here were a little snobby. I thought it was pretty funny if I named it after *Palmetta*.

─────

For more information on *Palazzo Margherita,* visit
www.thefamilycoppolahideaways.com

Art and Culture

Italy is synonymous with art and culture, and for good reason. This is the birthplace of the Renaissance and home to the majority of the world's artistic treasures. We feel the cultural impact of Italy every day not only in the art we admire, the books we read and the music we appreciate, but also in the science we advance, the cars we drive and the movies we watch.

For Francis Ford Coppola, it's a lesson he learned from his parents as a child. "My mother used to say when we were kids, I remember very vividly, 'Francis, you're so lucky you're an American, and America is the greatest country in the world.' And my father would say, 'Yes, you're American, but you're also Italian, and the Italians are the greatest culture in the world.'"

With that perspective in mind, many have wondered: What is it about Italy that has produced what has been characterized as a "cultural superpower"?

"I think it's that soft power that Italy radiates around the world that attracts people here," says musician Sting, who has made the country his part-time home. "How does all this stuff come from here? How did the Renaissance come from here? How did these artists come from here? And this music and this wine, this food? There's a reason. I'm not sure I can pinpoint what the reason is, but this is it."

That rich culture is a key reason so many people visit Italy again and again. The nation, which reveres its history, is home to 58 World Heritage Sites, as designated by the United Nations Educational, Scientific and Cultural Organization (UNESCO), the largest number of any country in the world.

"You have the tradition not only of the great composers and of the opera and of the very origins of great classical music, but also the great minds like *Leonardo da Vinci* and *Michelangelo* in art," says Coppola.

Much of Western civilization springs directly from Italian culture, influencing everything from the arts and music to architecture and design to science and technology. The cultural impact of Italians extends worldwide—from the achievements of scientists such as *Galileo Galilei, Enrico Fermi* and *Guglielmo Marconi;* artists such as *Botticelli, Donatello* and *Caravaggio;* and writers such as *Dante Alighieri, Umberto Eco* and *Elena Ferrante.* The names that are famous for a reason go on and on, from automaker *Enzo Ferrari to* educator *Maria Montessori* to filmmaker *Federico Fellini.*

Italy honors its culture in thousands of museums, monuments, churches, theaters, libraries and archaeological sites that testify to a remarkable history with roots in ancient civilizations dating to the Romans and Etruscans.

Research has found that visiting these sites can have positive effects on the brain in unexpected ways. Viewing art—and taking in all kinds of culture—can improve our moods and cognitive functions as well as increase analytical and problem-solving skills. Looking at a piece of art can even have the same effect on the brain as looking at someone you love.

Music also can be a key to living better, the Italian way. Italians are noted musicians and makers of instruments. Music writing began in Italy when *Guido of Arezzo* invented modern staff notation. As a result, Italian words continue to universally indicate whether music should be played *forte* or *piano* or somewhere in between. Italy's musical heritage ranges from Gregorian chants to regional folk songs.

When it comes to classical music, Italy has an innovative history, and opera originated here in the late 16th century. These musical traditions thrived under conductors such as *Arturo Toscanini;* composers such as *Giuseppe Verdi, Antonio Vivaldi* and *Giacomo Puccini;* and performers such as *Enrico Caruso* and *Luciano Pavarotti.*

Opera, steeped with music and drama, seems like it was invented to be the soundtrack for Italian life.

"There was an opera singer at *La Scala,*" Coppola recounts, "and he sang an *aria* and those other people were saying, '*Un'altra volta, un'altra volta.*' And he says, '*Molte grazie,* I'm so moved.' And he sang it again. And when it was over—'*Un'altra volta.*' And he sang it again. Finally, he said, 'Please, everyone, how many times do you want me to sing this?' And they said, 'Until you get it right!'"

While music may indeed "hath charms to soothe a savage breast," according to a poem by William Congreve, researchers at Johns Hopkins University have found that listening to music can reduce anxiety, blood pressure and pain. It also can improve sleep quality, mental alertness, mood and memory.

While listening to music or viewing art have numerous health benefits, taking the next step and actually participating in artistic pursuits also can have positive results at every age.

For author Frances Mayes, the ability to do just that, taking the time to explore an interest in a hands-on way, is one of her favorite things about Italian culture.

"You get the freedom to explore your interests," she explains. "And I think that comes from the fact that there's so much art. Art seems natural. It doesn't seem like something that is taking place in a museum or an art school. Air you breathe is art. And so it feels natural to you to want to connect with that and want to do that yourself."

Research from the George Washington University Medical Center found that people who took part in creative endeavors in their later years had both positive physical and psychological outcomes, including boosting the immune system. A separate study by Canadian researchers concluded that drawing, in particular, can improve memory.

All these findings are good news in a country where art can be found, literally, on every street corner.

Even if it wasn't created by a noteworthy artist, ordinary things in Italy can seem like works of art. For author David Bach, that exposure to a creative culture was a central reason he moved to Florence with his wife and two boys.

"We have a young son who's really into art," Bach says. "He even said this morning, 'Dad, I want to be an artist.' So what better place to be bring him?"

His son, James Bach, elaborates, "There's a statue on the *Ponte Vecchio*, the person's face is actually the same person that made that sculpture. We love to look at the doors and doorknobs. They're carved and they have all this cool artwork on them."

Art and culture, of course, aren't exclusive to Italy. You can find them anywhere you live and tap into them virtually too.

If you are traveling to Italy, remember to look for the bigger picture on your visits. Find a local guide who can help explain the historical context and add meaning to what you're seeing.

Keep in mind that it's impossible to see all the art and culture that Italy has to offer. So pick a few favorites—the *Caravaggio* in Rome or the *Signorelli* in *Cortona*—and treat yourself to a treasure hunt.

And don't be afraid to get your hands dirty. Take a class in painting or ceramics or photography. You may be surprised by what you'll learn from the change in perspective you get by being an artisan for a day.

On one of my visits to Florence, I wanted to gain a better under-standing of the city's famed frescoes, so I took a lesson from an expert. By tracing the shape of the face and transferring the pigment onto the fresh plaster, I got a firsthand view not only of the technique, but also the skill required to make these unique mural paintings. Now when I see a fresco, I have renewed appreciation for what the artist did to create it.

THRIVE TIPS

- Visit a museum. Many museum websites now have virtual tours, so you're not limited in what you can see. Many smaller museums—near where you live and even in Italy—get overlooked so seek out art off the beaten path.
- The same holds true for art galleries. Visit a local gallery and you may find local artists to support.
- Start listening to new kinds of music.
- Embrace opera and learn about the Italian composers who invented this tradition.
- Try your hand at playing a musical instrument. Learning a new skill, especially later in life, helps prevent cognitive decline.
- Learn to make your own art. Again, these new skills help brain function.
- Become a patron of a museum or an artist near where you live. This tradition was prevalent in the Renaissance and it isn't just about Italy.
- Use art and culture to plan a trip to Italy. Center your trip around a special performance or plan an itinerary related to an artist's work. There are also plenty of small group tours centered around making art of all kinds, from jewelry to watercolors to photography.

TRAVEL TIPS

- Follow our friend art historian Paola Vojnovic's tips on page 45.
- Italian cities are open-air museums that can be enjoyed on foot. A day of exploring can lead to the discovery of artisan shops, markets, festivals and theaters that combine traditions, culture and entertainment.

- Discover Italy's many museums. While the famed museums house renowned treasures, don't overlook the smaller museums that can be found in many cities and towns. Entry to some museums is free on Sundays.
- Experience live opera. Plan to see performances at one of the most famous venues in the world including *Arena di Verona, Terme di Caracalla* and *Teatro alla Scala* in Milan.
- Plan to visit the *monumenti nazionali* and *siti archeologici* of the area, local iconic and archaeological sites. Stop by the local tourism office to gather information material and maps that highlight the most important cultural sites.
- Attend one of the many *fiera dell'artigianato,* annual fairs dedicated to handmade crafts. Some of the most popular are *Artigianato e Design Vicenza* and *Mostra dell'Artigianato di Firenze.*
- Enjoy a summer outdoor music festival like *Umbria* Jazz or the *Ravello* Festival.
- Celebrate the *notte bianca,* literally "white night"—but a sleepless night. This event is a cultural initiative that takes place in almost every part of Italy, usually in the spring. During this night, shops and museums are open all night long.
- Visit a literary café with its unique historic charm. There are a multitude of them located in cities like *Trieste,* Florence, Turin, Rome, Naples and *Cosenza.*
- Don't miss the *Dimore Storiche Italiane.* From villas to castles, these are historic homes that are open to the public.

Tips for *Enjoying Italy's Art* to the Fullest

Can it be said that there is almost too much beauty in Italy? Too much art to even begin to get your head around? One of my favorite people in Italy is my friend, Renaissance art historian and private Florence tour guide Paola Vojnovic (**www.paolavojnovic.com**), who is so very brilliant at bringing works of art, and the masters who created them, to life. I asked her advice for how visitors can even begin to manage all the art there is to see in Italy. Here are 10 ways Paola suggests to deeply appreciate Italy's art without being totally overwhelmed.

1. Do your research beforehand on the collections you want to see. A great place to start is **www.smarthistory.org** and do a search by the artist or the city you plan to visit.

2. Give yourself time to linger. Appreciating art takes time and stamina. Make sure you are rested, fed and hydrated.

3. If your time is limited, consider hiring a professional guide. It is an investment well worth the money. You will learn details you

would have never known otherwise. (Members of *Dream of Italy* can access special issues listing Italy's best tour guides. Find out more at **www.dreamofitaly.com/tourguides**)

4. Look into special staff-led museum tours. This service is available with a very reasonable supplement to your ticket and will likely take you into a part of the museum closed to the public. A great example are the tours offered by *Palazzo Vecchio* in Florence (they have tours for kids of all ages) and *Palazzo Ducale* in Venice.

5. Plan to visit the major art museums as soon as they open in the morning, or after 3 p.m., as the museums tend to be less crowded at these times.

6. Do not miss temporary art exhibitions in the local museums— this is often a once-in-a-lifetime opportunity to see major works of art brought together, and in a dialogue with each other that gives much more context to an art period or a specific artist than the permanent museum displays provide.

7. Look for art *in situ.* Italian *piazzas* never disappoint their visitors with sculptures and fountains, created by the best artists of their time. Enter the open doors of any church (usually free or for a small fee). There you will find incredible masterpieces still in the same place their creators intended them to be. If you can, return at different times of the day to see how the works of art change with different light conditions. Be reminded that you are standing on the exact same spot where the artist or the patron stood.

8. Look for art on the street corners. There are incredible tabernacles with images of the Virgin Mary, and different local saints, that have been placed on the intersections of small streets for centuries. The candles lit for them were often the only source of light in the dark medieval cities. These were the spots where one could stop to pray *en passant*, or the only place for prayer in the

times of plagues when locals hesitated to enter the church. Often, when business deals were made, the interested parties would shake hands by the tabernacles, an additional promise that those involved would keep the word given.

9. Visit antique shops to admire extraordinary art by lesser-known masters. Art dealers are usually really interesting characters with great stories to tell!

10. Many incredible works of art are in need of restoration, and giving a small donation can make a big difference. Non-profit organizations such as Friends of Florence, Save Venice and Venetian Heritage all do incredible work, and you can help preserve Italy's remarkable artistic heritage for those who will walk this journey after us.

Arlene Antoinette Gibbs and Kathy filming on the streets of Rome

Beauty

Beauty is so essential to the Italian experience that it almost feels like beauty was invented here. It emanates from everything in Italy, from the landscape to the fashion to the art. *La vita è bella*. Life is beautiful, indeed.

The breathtaking natural allure surrounding *Il Palagio* is like a dream come true for Sting and Trudie Styler and informs their creativity and well-being.

"Well, I'm living in this *dream of Italy*," Sting tells me, gesturing behind me. "If you pan the camera around, you'll see a vista that is dream-like. I mean, it's like the background to a *Da Vinci* painting, without the *Mona Lisa*—there you are—but that background is the same one that the Renaissance artists looked at and were inspired by."

"So as an artist or being a musician," he continues, "I still find this landscape inspiring. I can look at the *Appennini* every night as the sun goes down, and they're changing every second, the shadows are deepening and the colors are so rich and powerful. It's a real inspiration."

"So when I came here, it's like I really died and gone to heaven. All those pictures of heaven, it's like, 'Did I die?'" Trudie tells me as we sit under a *pergola* at their villa. I know what she means and respond, "It's like you couldn't have even dreamt it."

"So when you say the *dream of Italy*, this is the *dream of Italy*. And it's also the reality of Italy," Trudie says.

Author David Bach has witnessed that effect firsthand since moving with his family to Florence.

"One of my favorite things to do here has been walking along the *Arno* with my kids after dinner to watch Jack and James every single day, still taking in the beauty months later," Bach says.

"And there was a moment recently where James looked out, looked at me and goes, 'Dad, it just doesn't get old.' And for my nine-year-old to be taking in the beauty of the *Arno*, having walked past the *Ponte Vecchio* and realize like, this is super special and this is my life, I feel like that's the greatest gift we're giving our children right now."

For the Bach family, beauty has become just part of daily life. "In Florence, everything really feels like a painting," David says. "You literally feel like you're in a painting. We're living in a painting now."

While the colors, tones and textures of the landscape and buildings can feel bold and unmissable, beauty also lives in the details in Italy— ones that others might overlook, but not Italians. No detail is too small, from the sprig of lavender tucked into a carefully folded napkin to an elegant scarf loosely tied around the neck.

When Arlene Antoinette Gibbs tells me, "Straight men here will say 'I really like your shoes,'" I have to laugh and nod in agreement. I've always found Italians and Italian men especially, whether part of a romantic connection or not, super observant. Maybe it all relates back to *la bella figura*.

Fare bella figura literally means to make a good figure or presentation, but it's all about making a good impression, being put together, showing decorum. Arlene says that for Italians, beauty isn't so much an attribute as it is an approach.

"There's more appreciation in general for beauty, and not in a superficial way," Arlene explains. "It's part of the DNA, and it's not just interior design or architecture or physical beauty, like how you wear makeup or how you wear your hair. It's just in a way you approach things in life, and it touches everything."

Italians are some of the most fashionable people on the planet. After all, this is the birthplace of *Prada, Gucci* and *Fendi*, so taking a page from them and dressing as an act of beauty can help anyone feel better. As Arlene and I walk along Rome's charming *Via Monserrato* and pop into her friend's fashion boutique, *L'Archivio di Monserrato*, she notes that Italians own fewer pieces of clothing but make sure they are timeless and of higher quality.

"I personally feel that that's better," she says. "I think it's more sustainable, and also, if you know your sense of style, you don't have to worry about trends so much. I think it's better to have one excellent suit than to have five average suits. That's my philosophy. Everything's on purpose and effortless."

In the home, as an interior designer, Arlene sees Italians create a comfortable mix of decor, often representing multiple generations and blending different styles to create an individual aesthetic. They have a way of taking items passed down in the family, that might not be their taste, and making them work. "Sometimes," she notes, "we are too quick to throw those things away."

In Italy, she explains, "There's the idea of mixing old and new. Most of my Italian friends, when I go into their homes, they're always like, 'Oh that chest came from my *nonna.*' And on top of it will be a piece of modern art. I just love that mix. I think it gives a really great energy to a space."

Italians simply believe in beauty. It's part of everyday life, like the air they breathe, and they give it the respect it deserves. That philosophy isn't surprising in a land rich with rolling hills that have inspired generations of poets and artists that's filled with world-famous art around every corner.

Lisa Cecconi, who owns a boutique wholesale agency *CecconiCo* representing a portfolio of Italian artisans who sell their wares to the American market, knows that when it comes to creating things by hand, beauty is non-negotiable.

"Italian artisans have such a profound sense of pride in their work and are so devoted to their craft, it's almost palpable," she explains. "My theory is that it's partially because when you're raised in a country with such jaw-dropping beauty at every turn, and especially within a family of artisans, it's in your veins! They not only love producing items that will please our clients, but also ones that they themselves are just as taken with. I once had an artist who made a custom piece for a client say that he could hardly bring himself to ship it out of his factory, 'because what I have made is so beautiful.' True love!"

"It comes back to creativity and beauty," Arlene says. "I keep talking about beauty, and I want to be clear, I'm not talking about beauty in a superficial way because to me, it's not superficial at all. There was this famous quote, I can't remember who said it: 'Beauty will save the world.' I feel that, especially now with all this ugliness that surrounds us, there is something very powerful about choosing to look toward the beauty and not the ugliness."

Arlene is onto something that science has been working to confirm. Various studies have shown that visual arts, for instance, can improve stress, memory and empathy, whether the subject is viewing the art or creating it. Looking at art also has been found to cause people to experience joy that is akin to the sensation of falling in love.

Beauty stays with us, even as we age. Several studies have found artistic engagement—both making art and appreciating it—can have beneficial effects not only for patients with Alzheimer's disease, but for their caregivers, too. Patients with Alzheimer's disease have been shown to retain their memories of beauty, recent and past, as well as their aesthetic preferences.

The lasting impact of beauty crosses generations and starts early. Research has shown that children who visit art museums come away with more knowledge about art, stronger critical-thinking skills, increased historical empathy, higher levels of tolerance, and a greater taste for consuming art and culture.

This may be why David Bach says exposing his children to the beauty of Italy is "the greatest gift we're giving our children right now."

But you don't have to move to Florence to enjoy the benefits of art and beauty. No matter where you live, you can infuse your environment with color and design, visit a museum or gallery or simply appreciate the details around you, from the shape and color of the leaves on the trees to the texture of your clothing.

When you travel to Italy, it's not hard to incorporate beauty into your itinerary; you're literally surrounded by it every day. Of course, this is the world capital of art so there is plenty to see in galleries and museums.

But aesthetic enjoyment can also be found in countless other ways, from hiking along an old Roman road to enjoy the local fauna, stopping at a local pottery shop to watch artisans creating their wares or exploring the ruins and observing the silence of a 13th-century abbey.

The key to finding beauty is taking the time to appreciate it. No matter where you are in the world, beauty—and being truly present with all it offers—will simply make you happier.

THRIVE TIPS

- Stop and take in the beauty. Something akin to "stop and smell the flowers." When you see something aesthetically pleasing, take a few moments to stop and enjoy the beauty.
- Make everyday experiences beautiful. For example, even if you are dining alone, set the table with fresh flowers and colorful napkins. It's sure to improve your mood.
- Learn how to create beauty—take an art class, even virtually. Just the act of getting out of your head and using your hands will provide an escape and learning a new skill will help your cognitive function.
- Add a few pieces from local artisans to your home décor. Your business will mean so much to them, and there will be a story behind these items.
- Dress to impress—and not just for a job interview. Even if you're only going to the supermarket, put on a nicer shirt and add a scarf or earrings. It will make you feel better.

- When buying new pieces for your wardrobe, think like the Italians do and think quality—cashmere, leather, silk—not quantity.
- Find new landscapes to admire near your home. Take a walk through an arboretum or visit a state park.
- Take advantage of the cultural attractions in your community. Visit an art gallery and look for local artists to support.

TRAVEL TIPS

- When you're in Italy, beauty is part of every single aspect of life and deeply ingrained in the culture and landscape. Take time to marvel at monumental masterpieces in the city or admire the sublime scenery in the countryside.
- Do some research about the most picturesque places and sites in the area you will be visiting and plan accordingly.
- If fashion or home décor are up your alley, plan around shopping and visiting ateliers. Make sure Florence is on your list for leather, Lake Como for silk, Milan for the latest designs, Naples for hand-tailored shirts and suits.
- Look for local artisans specializing in everything from wood to ceramics to fine art. Pick up a few pieces for your home. You will always be reminded of the places these works of art come from and the people who created this beauty.
- In spring and summer, attend one of the many *Infiorata* festivals that take place throughout Italy. At these annual events—in cities ranging from *Genzano di Roma* in *Lazio* to *Spello* in *Umbria* to *Noto* in Sicily—flower petals are used to create large carpets of flowers on the streets, and they are gorgeous to see.

David, Jack, Alatia, Rocky and James Bach

Interview with

THE BACH FAMILY

Enjoying a "Radical Sabbatical" in Florence

"Our *dream of Italy* was to live rich now," 10-time *New York Times* best-selling author David Bach tells me about why he and his wife, Alatia, a real estate agent with the Corcoran Group, decided to move to Florence with their school-age sons for a "radical sabbatical." David, the founder of Finish Rich, LLC, is the author of books such as *The Automatic Millionaire* and *Smart Women Finish Rich*, and has spent a career helping readers build wealth and the financial freedom that goes with it. David, Alatia, Jack and James (and dog, Rocky) planned to stay in Florence for just a year, but as of this writing, are now entering their third year living the dream.

Kathy McCabe: Why did you bring your family to Italy for a year?

David Bach: I tell my friends, your soul never forgets where you want to be. Thirty years ago, on the *Ponte Vecchio* as a college kid, I looked out on the *Arno* and thought to myself, "Someday I'd like to live here." A couple of years ago we started talking about living abroad with our family before the kids go to college. We started talking about Italy because it's always been, for both of us, one of our favorite countries in the whole world.

KM: Why did you choose Florence?

Alatia Bach: I wanted a place that we could have a much quieter, calmer way of life, but with many, many compelling things to study. I was an art history major, so coming back here and being able to study art history and be in an environment for learning, it was the only place to be.

DB: And to expose our kids to this culture. We have a young son who's really into art. Our oldest son happens to love food.

AB: This was not a hard sell.

KM: How do your kids like living in Italy?

DB: We've really seen our kids flourish in a very short period of time. We thought our kids were happy in New York. We see them much happier here. They're lighter; they've made more friends. They talk about the fact that they feel more worldly as a result of living here.

AB: They also talk about how nice the people are. From the moment they arrived, they instantly had new friends. Everyone's welcoming. Everyone is helpful. They even were commenting on how helpful the grown-ups were to us when we first came.

DB: Everywhere we go, everybody is friendly. It's not just expats that are friendly. Florentines are friendly. We've met so many fabulous Florentines. Everybody is so welcoming. Everyone's so loving and the thing about Italy, and you hear this, but it's hard to understand until you're here, is that Italy is all about family. We came here for family, but now it's truly all about family. We've been together for three months.

AB: We've never spent this much time together.

KM: What do you find easier about Italy?

DB: One of the things that makes Italy easier is its lower cost. For everybody who's thinking, "I could never do what they're doing," the first thing I would tell you is you can live an extraordinary life in Italy on a very ordinary income. It's so much more affordable. Florence is probably one of the more expensive cities in Italy, and yet if you just go five or 10 minutes outside of Florence, it's way more affordable. And still, compared to living in New York, it's half the price.

KM: So many people think their barrier is the cost. They think they cannot make their dreams come true because of money. I've been reading your book, *The Latte Factor*, and you talk about dreams.

DB: It's all about using money to free yourself to live your best life. I talk about the fact that you don't have to be rich to live rich and truly, Italy epitomizes that. We've met retirees that don't live necessarily in Florence, but they come to Florence for an art history class and they're living out in *Lucca* and they're retired, living on social security. The truth is the dream of living here can also be possible for you.

AB: We've met a lot of people who do three months here and they go back for three months. We have other friends that do six months in Italy. I think what we've learned about taking the leap to do this is that anything is possible.

KM: What's your *dream of Italy*?

DB: We're living our *dream of Italy* right now: the idea that we can be together as a family, living here in Florence. We manifested this, but now we're getting to live it and we're getting to see the effects of what it's doing to our family. And that's the greatest gift ever.

AB: The things that make this our dream, we didn't know to dream for. I didn't know that I would enjoy walking to meet the school bus and walking to run an errand, and yet those are the most meaningful experiences.

KM: What is the most surprising thing about moving to Italy with your family?

Jack Bach: The craziest thing is, you go for a walk and you can see a dozen things that are older than the Constitution. There's just so much history here and it's integrated in this modern lifestyle, which is so cool. And I love that it's so much smaller here, so I feel like it's more like close knit. I've only known some people here for like a month and I can already consider them great friends, and then I have amazing relationships with people, which is really nice.

KM: Jack, do you think you've changed since moving here?

Jack: I think I'm happier. I enjoy things more. I've always thought I was a lighthearted person. Then I came here and I realized I'm even happier than I was, because I just felt happier with myself and with my relationships with people. That's been awesome.

KM: How has your family changed?

Jack: They're not doing lots of stuff anymore. They're not out, they're here. One thing I can definitely say is they both seem a lot more relaxed.

KM: James, what's your favorite thing about Florence?

James Bach: I like to just walk the dog with my mom, and we love to look at the doors and the doorknobs. They're carved and they have all this cool artwork on them. We're always finding new stuff.

KM: What's different about traveling in Italy?

DB: Everything shuts down in August, because in August everyone in Italy goes on vacation with their family. In America we used to go on vacation for like a week. When you travel across Italy in the summertime, you see all these multi-generational Italian families together on vacation for an extended period of time.

KM: It's like a birthright and an incredible tradition in this country. August is sacred and you spend it with your family and you probably go to the same beach you've gone to for 50 years.

For more information, visit **www.davidbach.com**

Municipio, Cortona

Pace of Life

Slow down. Don't rush. That's how Italians live. "*Piano, piano*," they say. Slowly. Slowly. Italians have a different sense of time. Could it be because of their thousands of years of history? Probably. *Under the Tuscan Sun* author Frances Mayes told me that in Italy, "Time is like a river. It just flows."

That slower pace of life rubs off on visitors and expats alike. Trudie Styler says, "I think that it gives me back my sanity, this time that I have to recharge my batteries here. Just being here and going at the pace of the animals—we sit under the stars, we drink our wines, we laugh and we feel really lucky."

Most Italians enjoy a slower life where they don't live to work, but rather work to live. Family time and vacations—like the sacred August break, where the entire country seems to go on vacation at the same time—are important. Italians cherish the moments they spend together, and the August vacation is part of that.

Time is precious, especially family time, and Italians take every chance they get to savor that time—whether on vacation, at happy hour in the *piazza* or at a celebration. They live in harmony with time; they're not fighting against it or rushing.

Slower pace of life lessens stress and according to the American Medical Association, stress is the root cause of 60% of all human illness and disease.

Italians leave time for serendipity. They live in the moment and can be very spontaneous. They really do invite perfect strangers over for dinner. Italians take joy in just doing nothing. It is called *dolce far niente*, the art of doing nothing; just being.

But they also love routine, and we can learn so much from the typical Italian day. Routine calms anxiety—if you can learn to relax into a slower-paced routine and utilize your time well.

David Bach says that when he and his wife Alatia first moved to Florence from Manhattan, "Truthfully, I think we were almost nervous with this extended time. Now, the pace of life is where you're truly present. The two of us have been hardwired for speed for our entire life, and what we're learning here to do in Florence is slow down to the speed of life."

Since its founding in Italy in the 1980s, the Slow Food movement has inspired other movements to adopt its principles in pursuit of a more authentic life. Carl Honore, author of *In Praise of Slowness,* says, "It is not about doing everything at a snail's pace. It's about seeking to do everything at the right speed. Savoring the hours and minutes rather than just counting them. Doing everything as well as possible, instead of as fast as possible. It's about maximizing quality over quantity in everything from work to food to parenting to sex."

Indeed, slower living doesn't necessarily equal inefficiency. Though it may seem like it takes longer to get basic errands done, compared to the efficiency Americans are used to at home, Alatia Bach has a different perspective.

"There's a lot of efficiency here and what it is based on is an incredibly defined division of labor. For example, the cleaners do not do alterations. But it's not what we consider efficient because we're used to going to one grocery store where you can get your car fixed and you can get your prescriptions," Alatia says. "We find the perception is that something where you would have to go to five places is inefficient. It's actually really not, because each person is an expert in their field."

The Bachs have seen their two sons adjust well to the new school routine, too. Alatia notes that high school students "get out early from school and they hang out; they all go to lunch together and they all go over to *Santa Croce* and they explore. I'm not saying that they're going in and having an art history lesson, but they're spending time together and they're experiencing life and they're discovering things. And you know, the studies now show that young minds actually need down time and imagination time and just time to be. We are super driven and we came here to sort of take a deep breath."

Jack Bach, a high schooler, has noticed that "even the school sort of understands the need for free time. We still get lots of work, but they kind of understand that you want some time after school to be with your friends."

David agrees that the Italian school day has been good for not only their family life, but especially for their sons. "We came from Manhattan, which is highly competitive. It's also highly over-scheduled. I think the thing we've realized as we've come to Italy is that there's a little bit less of that. We've realized, 'Oh, you don't have to have someone plan every single day after school,'" he says.

Alatia adds, "You start to realize that your way isn't the only way."

We can all follow the slow pace and routine of an Italian day (see page 62) whether we are living elsewhere or just traveling in Italy. When planning your own Italy travel itinerary, leave time and space, both literally and figuratively, for the unexpected. The more time you have unscheduled, the more you can revel in the chance encounters you're likely to have. After all, you have to slow down and let serendipity find you. In Italy, it usually does!

THRIVE TIPS

- Follow the rhythm of the Italian day, even at home. (See page 62.)
- Slow down—do one thing at a time and be more present for everything.
- Try to "work to live," not "live to work."
- Plan time to simply do nothing—*dolce far niente*—the sweetness of being idle.
- Make certain activities sacred—everything from taking time to eat slowly while sitting down to keeping sacred the annual August vacation that the Italians venerate.
- Take all of your vacation days. In fact, you should plan a trip to Italy!

TRAVEL TIPS

- Do as the Italians do while you are in Italy and get into the rhythm of the Italian day. (See page 62.)
- Don't pack too much into one trip. Travel slowly and enjoy the place you're in before hurrying along to the next destination. Italy will always be there for you to return to and this will give you a great reason to go back and visit new places.
- Build the *pausa*, or afternoon break, into your itinerary. Enjoy the morning touring, eat a big lunch, take a nap and then get going again in the late afternoon.
- Get lost. This is the best way to discover hidden treasures.
- Leave time for serendipity. You never know what might happen.
- Consider renting a villa in the countryside and live, even if it is just for a week, at the pace of nature.
- Spend more time in small Italian towns rather than big cities. Look into the *Città Slow* (Slow City) network, which includes places that take into consideration appreciation for the environment and cultural and gastronomic traditions.

Follow the Rhythm
of the *Italian Day*

Italians are creatures of habit. Every day follows a routine of rules and rhythms. A daily routine has been proven to reduce stress and anxiety. It can be a great framework to follow at home in order to benefit from the healthy Italian lifestyle. When visiting Italy, following the rhythm of the Italian day is simply a must.

First thing in the morning, make an *espresso* in your *Moka* pot. Statistics say that 90% of Italians own one of these little gadgets to make *espresso* on the stovetop, but surely it must be more like 99%. Many Italians own several and most won't travel without one!

Stop for your second *espresso* at the local bar. Most Italians go to the bar at the same time each day and thus form a strong sense of community there. Italians drink an average of four servings of *espresso* per day. There's a mid-morning and afternoon one too. Studies have shown that drinking this amount, particularly in mid-life, leads to better heart health and lower chance of Alzheimer's disease.

Shop for fresh seasonal ingredients to prepare meals for the next day or two. Morning is best as open-air markets usually close by afternoon.

Make a sit-down meal a priority like the Italians do. A full meal is composed of *antipasto*, first and second courses and some *dolce* (dessert) or *frutta* (fruit). Eating the bulk of your calories earlier in the day aids in digestion and weight control.

Take an afternoon rest. Though not as prevalent as it once was, the afternoon *pausa*, or break, means many stores and businesses close between 1 and 4 p.m., especially in the summer. Taking a break can improve efficiency since our focus peaks at four hours. Swiss researchers have found one or two naps per week can lower the risk of heart problems. Shorter naps—30 to 90 minutes—are better for brain benefits.

Late afternoon is *passeggiata* time. This is the time to walk and see and be seen to catch up with what is going on in the *piazza*. All generations mix, providing a wonderful sense of community.

Then join friends for a pre-meal drink, an *aperitivo*. It's another great way to keep socializing, and moderate alcohol intake helps prevent heart disease, stroke and diabetes. Drinking one or two glasses of red wine per day, especially for women, can reduce inflammation, memory loss and risk of certain types of cancer. *Aperitivo* is derived from the Latin *aperire*, which means to open, as in open the stomach before dining.

Enjoy a light dinner. Follow the Italian tradition of smaller portion sizes, which are good for your health!

Interview with

ARLENE ANTOINETTE GIBBS

Designing a New Life in Italy

Arlene Antoinette Gibbs never expected to end up in Italy. She was working as a Hollywood film executive and, on a whim, vacationed in Italy. Once she was ready for a change, she felt Italy calling her, and moved from Los Angeles to Rome. Since then, she's changed careers to become an interior designer and formed a close circle of friends who feel more like family.

Kathy McCabe: What made you finally decide to move to Italy?

Arlene Antoinette Gibbs: Growing up, I was not somebody who was a big Italophile. I came to Italy in 2005 for the first time and once I arrived here, it felt like home. I went back the following year and stayed a little bit longer. I returned to Los Angeles and the feeling was even stronger. I thought maybe this is a place I could move to once I retire. I was speaking with my dad and he said, "Why don't you just move to Italy now? What are you waiting for? Nothing is guaranteed. You're not living in LA, you're just existing."

Which shocked me because my parents are from the Caribbean, from an island called St. Martin. I don't know if you know anything about Caribbean culture, but it's not a "go follow your bliss" kind of culture. I really took his words to heart. I thought about it, and I quit my job and I moved to Italy. It felt like I was getting permission.

I had a job that I loved, and I worked with great people, but I had no life. All I did was work. I had a lot of friends, but I never saw them. The film industry is a tough industry on women.

KM: What is it about Italy that feels like home?

AG: One day I was reading this book, and there was a character in the book who is like me, first-generation American. This character moved to a country that she could choose freely, that she didn't have any expectations about, instead of choosing the two countries that she had a connection to. I thought that that was really interesting, like it was a choice for me to come to Italy.

Also, a lot of the qualities that drove me nuts as a child, having these Caribbean parents, are qualities that Italians have. The family is really, really important. Also, this concept of how you're defined. For example, in America you're defined by what you do. In the film business and in LA specifically, it's really magnified and it's so much a part of you, whereas in the Caribbean, it's not who you are. I find it's the same here. I met friends here and they had no idea what I did for a living for four years. I think as far as Italy feeling like home, I think the values that I grew up with are a little bit closer to here than in the States.

KM: What gave you the push to make the move?

AG: I went to the Caribbean for Christmas. I remember looking around this table, it's like, everybody's married. Everybody has children. I was going back to LA, I didn't have a job, I didn't have a man or children. I didn't have a trip to Italy planned because I had to stay and look for a job. At one point my brother said to me, "I really think instead of going to Florence, Venice and Rome, you should pick one city and just go away for a week. We're worried about your mental health." The next day I got a check from my brother for $1,000 with a note saying, "Do not use this for bills. Go to Italy."

On this trip, I thought, "I'm just going to go to some museums and eat some pasta." And that trip changed my life. That's the amazing thing. It doesn't take even moving to a place—travel opens up the possibilities.

KM: What are Italians like?

AG: Your job does not define you. Everybody works hard but—and this is what I could not understand when I first moved here—they're working maybe more hours a week, but still find time for friends and family. Italians are more in the moment.

KM: How do you think Italians appreciate beauty?

AG: Everybody flirts here; it's not just in one direction. Here in Italy you feel like you're seen. I find men here especially notice things, whether it's a romantic connection or not. They seem more observant. Everything is presented and packaged, and I think a lot more attention is paid in Italy, but in a way that makes people feel comfortable. There's so much ugliness in the world and so much depressing news and it's wonderful to be in a place where people appreciate beauty.

KM: How has your relationship with food changed here in Italy?

AG: My relationship with food has changed quite a bit. When I was in Los Angeles, I think I was on a diet for pretty much the entire time I lived there. I was always doing some kind of low-carb diet. I've always loved to cook and I've always loved food, but I moved here and I noticed something very weird. I was not on a diet or anything and I lost weight.

KM: Why do you think that is?

AG: You have to make an effort to find the processed foods. I find I snack less here. I cook more, so I'm aware of what I'm putting in my body. Also, the things that I would buy jarred in the States, like *spaghetti* sauce, now I make from scratch. My palate has changed quite a bit, because I have a sweet tooth. Junk food is so accessible in the U.S. and here I kind of have to go out of my way, and it's not worth the effort. In the U.S. it seems it would be a luxury to go to the farmer's market, whereas here there are several near me, they're open six days a week and the prices are much lower. I'm buying seasonal.

KM: What advice do you have for people who are considering moving to Italy?

AG: You have to take responsibility for your life no matter where you are. I think people come here and they have a fantasy about what their life is going to be. I think it's important to know the good, the bad and the ugly before you move. If you don't, you might be very disappointed, because vacationing here and living here are two very different things. It's not a movie. Especially if you're an American, the bureaucracy and the red tape are real. I don't have a lot of patience, but I have more patience now and even after all these years living here, there are days when I'm frustrated with how long certain things take.

KM: How does Italy inspire your creativity?

AG: I think one thing that's interesting about Italy is that because it didn't become a country until 1861, each region has its own unique quality, whether it's food or architecture. But how does that inform my work? I would say there are two things. We do a lot of custom work. We have a lot of things made and not just for people who are wealthy. Regular people have things made for their home.

KM: Can you speak to the passion involved in how these craftsmen custom make these pieces?

AG: It feels sometimes like it's a spiritual calling. It's not a lampshade, right? It's a work of art and it's beauty. It's going into your home. You should not have anything in your home that you don't love. You should not have things just to have things. It should mean something to you, because it's your home. It's no one else's home.

KM: What does your *dream of Italy* mean to you?

AG: For me it's that I'm no longer sleepwalking through my life. I feel like I was almost like a zombie when I was in Los Angeles. I was just going through the motions. Life is short and I didn't want to live that way.

For more information, visit **www.arlenegibbsdecor.com**

Passion

The dictionary defines passion as a "strong and barely controllable emotion." In Italy, you need only look around to see passion personified at every turn. Italians have this grand emotion in spades—for everything from their families and their lovers to their favorite soccer teams, the finest wine vintage or the best recipe for a traditional dish.

In Italy, *passione* is part of the culture.

That passion has long been depicted in the movies as romantic love as well as the passionate pursuit of happiness. Think of *Marcello Mastroianni* and Anita Ekberg searching for the sweet life—and frolicking in Rome's *Fontana di Trevi*—in the masterpiece by *Federico Fellini, La Dolce Vita.* Or remember Gregory Peck whisking Audrey Hepburn around Rome on a *Vespa* as they speed by the Colosseum and *Piazza Venezia* in *Roman Holiday.*

Yes, Italy is the most romantic place on the planet, but it isn't just connection between lovers. Everyone shares passion here. As Arlene Antoinette Gibbs tells me, "Everybody flirts here, you know, it's not just one direction." It isn't necessarily romantic either; it is a way of connecting and seeing each other. The young butcher might flirt with the elderly customer.

Passion extends to every aspect of Italian life. The "Made in Italy" label is known worldwide as a mark of excellent craftsmanship, whether it's found on silk scarves or olive oil or marble sculptures. Italians are the greatest artisans in the world because they put their all into everything they do.

At *Il Palagio,* owned by Sting and Trudie Styler, the results of Italian passion can be seen throughout the estate, including the organic farm and vineyard. While visiting, I interviewed other locals about their own passion for their work, including *Alberto Salvini,* a landowner who produces *Chianti* wine and olive oil.

"For me, Tuscany is old. My roots are here because here, there is history, Italian history," he says. "We have marvelous hands that produce bags, belts, clothes—and also great wine, great olive oil. Everything we make, we make with passion and competition."

Indeed, those passionate hands—not only do all Italians talk with them, with fluid gestures emphasizing every point, but they also use them to create extraordinary works of art in every facet of life.

Dario Cecchini, the famous butcher from nearby *Panzano,* explains how Italians feel fortunate to be able to enjoy "the passion of life" every single day. "Passion, love, heart, poetry, good food, great wine, like the wines of *Il Palagio,* enjoying every moment of life," he says, quoting the Latin expression: *"Carpe diem quam minimum credula postero"* or "Seize the day; trust tomorrow even as little as you can."

"There's so much passion here," says author David Bach.

Bach first noticed that passion when he visited Italy during his youth, backpacking and staying in hostels. It's why he wanted to bring his family to live here. "Italians use their hands. They love life," he says. "They're passionate about everything. It's hard not to be passionate when you're here."

Italians approach all things with passion, and that can have positive health benefits. Studies have shown that having a purpose in life is a key driver of well-being and can decrease the risk of dying early. Researchers from the University of Michigan found that people without such a life purpose were twice as likely to die early, compared to those who had one, which held true regardless of income, gender, race or education.

At *aperitivo* in Rome with friends of Arlene Antoinette Gibbs, I ask actor *Giampiero Judica* why he thinks Americans love Italy. He says it is because Italians give them permission to be passionate about their own lives, experiencing joy and spontaneity.

"Americans just don't allow themselves to be passionate about life. So, when they encounter somebody that is like that, quote unquote, 'normal human beings,' they truly allow themselves to be passionate about life. They love that," he explains.

Throughout this book, in a series of interviews, you will meet many people who also found their passion in Italy. I love how a trip to the Amalfi Coast led Susan Gravely to start a business selling fine Italian ceramic dinnerware and décor.

My friend Becky Munson was practically hit over the head with her life's purpose. "Within 24 hours of arriving in Italy, I knew this would be my passion and my life for the rest of my life," she recounts. She returned from that trip to launch her travel business, Live Tuscan, that is devoted to sharing Italy's beauty, culture and food. "I didn't understand it. All of a sudden, I sensed it. You can't say you heard a voice because you don't hear it, you just know it," she says.

You can live your life with gusto, no matter where you are. It is just a decision to find purpose and add passion.

I don't think you have to do something special to find passion in Italy. Just be present, ask questions, and visit artisans and chefs and creators. Passion will surround you here!

THRIVE TIPS

- ▪ Celebrate what and who you are passionate about. Don't be afraid to express yourself.
- ▪ Make time for romance.
- ▪ Pay compliments—and accept them graciously.
- ▪ Allow yourself to live in the moment. Take your time, give up control and be spontaneous.

- Find pleasure in unexpected and unplanned events.
- Recommit yourself to a hobby or craft that you love—or learn a new one—then approach it with gusto!
- Make a daily gratitude list for all that you are thankful for.

TRAVEL TIPS

- Visit producers and artisans of all kinds, from those who make food products to those who create art. There is always, *always* a passionate story behind what they do.
- Plan for romance if your trip is with a lover. Enjoy an *aperitivo* with a view or relax in hot springs together.
- Smile! Flirt! Enjoy being alive.
- Ask yourself if there is something you discovered in Italy that might be part of your own life's purpose.
- Don't let physical challenges prevent you from visiting Italy as there are excellent travel companies that specialize in accessible travel for those with wheelchairs and other mobility issues. We can match you with one through the *Dream of Italy* Travel Service (**www.dreamofitaly.com/travel**).

Movement

Italy is not a car culture like the U.S. The Italian day is filled with movement, with much of that taking place outside. For super social Italians, running their errands on foot or by bicycle is not only efficient but also a chance to check in with friends, neighbors and shopkeepers of all ages. No Internet check-ins are needed in Italy. They are made in person, on the go.

Florence resident Sally Carrocino says, "In California, I spent my life in my car and the traffic, and it's a car culture. I feel healthy here because I'm walking all the time. I'm active. I'm really active. We're jumping on a bus or we're going to meet friends or we're going to the movies."

Italians in cities and towns all over the country walk just to see and be seen in the daily *passeggiata* in the local *piazza*. This takes place just before dinner and can be done on the way to *aperitivo*, though in summer, especially in the south, it might be after dinner and combined with a stop for a *gelato*. People of all ages participate.

According to a study published in the *International Journal of Environmental Research and Public Health,* those who live in highly walkable, mixed-age communities are more likely to live to be 100.

It is more than just walking; it is the movement of activities that are simply part of everyday life in Italy. You've probably heard of Blue Zones, those areas of the world where a large percentage of residents live to be centenarians. One of those Blue Zones is on the island of Sardinia, where residents have a high level of NEAT (non-exercise activity thermogenesis)—everyday activity associated with walking, yardwork, gardening and household chores. This is non-structured exercise and it keeps us young. Sitting less is key!

Regular moderate exercise, like walking 30 minutes per day, improves brain health, happiness levels, weight control and prevention of disease. Several studies have confirmed the benefits of even moderate exercise. In a study following 140,000 adults, the American Cancer Society found that walking between two and six hours per week reduced the risk of dying from heart disease, cancer and respiratory disease.

Frances Mayes loves that so much of Italian life takes place outside and that's where she gets her exercise, whether she's gardening or walking close to her home *Bramasole* in *Cortona*.

Dancing during celebrations is another way Italians move. Actually, most of them don't need a reason to start dancing—even some music in the *piazza* is a good excuse.

The lesson we can learn from the Italians is to simply *move*! We can do that anywhere.

When traveling to Italy, the country is best seen in movement. Travelers naturally do a lot of walking in the cities. Exploring on foot or by renting a bicycle makes the cities seem more personal, as you can see the roads, shops and landmarks up close in a way that you can't on a crowded bus or the metro.

Outside of the cities, Italy's stunning countryside begs to be explored on foot or bike. Get outside and get some fresh air by hiking in the mountains or along the coastline, cycle through the countryside or go skiing in winter. You can even follow the *transumanza* paths, which shepherds have used for centuries to move their sheep to greener pastures. Italians love to cycle and whether you are in the hilly north or flat *Puglia*, taking a biking tour for a day or week is a great idea. There are now e-bikes to make your journey faster.

Italy isn't just for the able-bodied, either. People with disabilities can explore cities via golf cart tours or rent special wheelchairs that can easily navigate the cobblestone streets. Everyone can move in Italy!

THRIVE TIPS

- Walk wherever you can. Replace short car trips with walks.
- Remember all steps count. While it is ideal to get in 10,000 steps per day, a recent study by the Harvard School of Public Health found that even just 4,400 steps per day reduced the risk of early death by 41%.
- Organize a *passeggiata* in your own neighborhood at the same time each day with your neighbors.
- Add bike riding to your day. If you're not biking outside, try to get a stationary bike. It doesn't have to be a Peloton to get the job done!
- Start a backyard garden. It is a great way to get exercise while you grow the ingredients to eat well.
- Dance!

TRAVEL TIPS

- Walk or hike some of the ancient routes found throughout the country. *Via Francigena* is a trail from Canterbury to Rome that passes through seven Italian regions. *Sentiero del Brigante* is a mountain path that follows the ridge of the Calabrian Apennines.
- Rent an e-bike to enjoy the scenic countryside outside the city you are visiting. These power-assisted bicycles are perfect if you are not a pro at mountain biking, allowing you to still be active.
- Make walking, hiking or biking the focus of your trip by taking an organized tour such as those from my friends at *Tourissimo*.

- Volunteer with WWOOF (Worldwide Opportunities on Organic Farms) or Workaway to work on a harvest and maintaining a farm. That kind of movement is the best for health.
- Play volleyball or soccer at the beach or at the lake; this might be the quintessential Italian experience and some kids might even join you for the fun.
- While at the beach or lake, rent a *pedalò* (paddle boat). This human-powered boat is relaxing and a great way to see where you are from a new perspective.
- Italy has a wonderful program of accessible trekking, which makes nature open to everyone.

Interview with

SALLY CARROCINO

Creating a Wonderful Life in Florence

Sally Carrocino and her late husband, John, used to vacation in Italy regularly. They dreamed of living there together, but that dream never came to fruition before John passed away. In the wake of her loss, Sally decided to make their dream come true by moving to Italy by herself with her dog, Zoe. As a retiree living in Florence, she's taken up hobbies, made new friends of all ages and is truly living *la dolce vita*.

Kathy McCabe: Did you always dream of living in Italy?

Sally Carrocino: Yes. My husband John and I traveled to Italy extensively from 2001 until he died in 2014 and we always talked about someday picking a place and just leaving California. The lifestyle is just so much more serene than in California. People have a full life. The topic of their work never comes up. It's important to them, but it's not the crux of their life. Their family is.

KM: Italy's really special to you because you were married here.

SC: Yeah, I wanted to live in Italy because it was so special for John and I that we got married here. We were together for 13 years and then we were planning a trip to Rome and we just said, well, let's get married.

KM: How did you end up living here?

SC: John died seven years ago and shortly after he died, I decided I needed to take a trip by myself. I went to Italy for a month and while I was on that trip all over Italy, places that we had been before and places that we hadn't been, I decided I wanted to come back with my dog Zoe for three months. And we spent a fabulous three months. I wasn't lonesome. Then when I got home, I was miserable. I spent lots of time trying to decide where I wanted to live in the U.S., and I couldn't find in my head a place I wanted to settle. One morning I woke up and I said, "Sally, you don't know in the whole U.S. where you want to live, but you know the exact neighborhood in Florence. Why are you wasting your time?" That was the moment.

KM: You're a longtime subscriber to *Dream of Italy*. How did it help you plan your trips?

SC: I wanted to know as much as I possibly could know about all of Italy. After we did the biggies, you know, Rome, Florence, Milan, Venice, we traveled all through the little towns, and your publication highlighted the little villages and places that you wouldn't normally think about going.

KM: You mentioned something that resonates with me and so many people: that planning a trip to Italy after your loss was therapeutic and cathartic.

SC: When John died it was the best thing I could do. I'd spend hours and hours at night going through Facebook pages and finding different cities and researching hotels. It got me away from crying. The only place I really wanted to go was Italy.

KM: You and your husband used to save up to make your travel dreams come true. Can you tell me about the account you used to keep?

SC: After our first trip, we decided that we needed a trip account.

Every month we would both write a check for $500, and by the time we were ready to go, we had the money.

KM: What do you love about the food in Italy?

SC: Going to my local fruit and vegetable market, just looking at the produce, makes me happy and I decided I was going to try everything in this new life. I was going to do all the things that I'd never done before. I changed my whole eating routine to have my main meal at lunch and just a small dinner. Zoe and I go out to lunch every single day.

The thing I love about Italian cooking is, nothing is more than three ingredients because of the quality of the produce and the cheese. You can make a *caprese* salad with just *mozzarella*, *pomodoro* and basil.

Another thing I really love is you can buy just what you need. You don't have to buy a loaf of bread; you can buy a slice of bread. For a single person, that is so important. I used to waste so much food, because if you wanted something, you'd have to buy it in quantity. Now I just buy what I want to eat that day or for two days.

KM: Do you feel healthier living here?

SC: I feel healthier here because I'm walking all the time and I'm eating really well. I'm eating fresh vegetables. I don't have to worry about any pesticides or things like that.

KM: What in Italy is more affordable?

SC: Almost everything. I'm constantly shocked at how much less I pay for food. The vet is 60€ for x-rays, for prescriptions, for a checkup. I don't have a car, so I don't have to worry about any of those expenses. I buy a yearly bus pass. It's really affordable. I came on a retired visa and it's an easy visa to get because I'm not looking for a job. They require you to have 3,000€ a month to support yourself.

KM: What can you share about healthcare in Italy?

SC: After a certain period of time I can get the Italian healthcare, but now I depend on private healthcare, and I really like the private healthcare. You choose your own doctor. The healthcare in Tuscany is phenomenal. I needed to get an ultrasound done and it was 100€. Even the private healthcare is less expensive.

KM: You're a bit of a mini-celebrity here in Florence, because I was with you and someone recognized you. Tell me how you've shared your story with others.

SC: It's been a really crazy ride. About three months after I got here, I got an email from a journalist who was doing an article for an online magazine called *Senior Planet*. She was writing about women who have retired, who have left the U.S. and moved to a different country for a new life. She asked me if I was interested in doing an interview. It was posted and it went crazy. I got letters from all over the world from women who told me I was inspiring. I mean, I never considered myself to be inspiring. I just did it to save my own life. Then about a month later, I got an email from an Italian woman who did the same sort of online magazine and she asked if she could print it in Italian. I said, of course. And when I got here, I started a blog, and with the interview and with my blog, I get lots of mail.

KM: How has Italy transformed you?

SC: Italy has transformed me I think in being a better, well-rounded person. I have so many different interests now that I didn't have before. I have more things to do and more friends than ever in my entire life, and that makes me happy all the time and I think a better person and a better friend. When you're at this part of your life, you don't think that you're going to make the best friends of your life. I have friends from 25 to 80. I have a great group of friends that are in their late 30s and these women are just so anxious to talk to me and be with me and that I have found amazing.

KM: What else has Italy taught you?

SC: Less is more, with the food, the clothes, everything. In the U.S. you had to wear something different every day. That's not important here. You can wear the same thing and wear comfortable shoes. That's what I tell people as well. Don't get hung up on stuff. Stuff is not important. It's people and relationships that are important. You have to be a little bit free to be able to come to a place like this.

One of the things I tell people is to let go of any of your paths and be open to everything. I made a promise to myself that I would say yes to all invitations and I've kept it 98% of the time because even though you might not feel like it, once you get out there, you're so happy that you did. I wanted to try everything, every type of food, every type of activity. I joined the book club and that has become really, really important for me.

▬▬▬

For more information, visit Sally's blog at **www.espressotoprosecco.com**

Community

Italians are all about people. They live in community and take care of each other. Italians are healthier and happier because they are connected and they have lifelong witnesses to their lives.

Where does so much of this connection take place? In the *piazza*, which is truly the center of Italian life, followed closely by the local café. *Under the Tuscan Sun* author Frances Mayes even wrote a book called *See You in the Piazza* about this place in every Italian town that serves as the epicenter of Italian life.

As we sit above the *piazza* in her adopted hometown of *Cortona*, she tells me, "It's intensely friendly and there's such a sense of community here and the reason for that community is this *piazza* and the *piazza* adjoining us. It's just the living room for everyone who lives around here. This is the living room and the little streets are the bedrooms, the kitchen. But this is the simple reason; it is where everyone meets everyone, does their business, keeps in touch, shops. It's the blessing of Italy."

Italians are also incredibly generous. Frances tells me, "Generally I've found the people here so generous. When I get back, I haven't been here a morning before someone says, 'Can I bring you some eggs?' or 'I've got some beautiful grapes. Would you like some?' There's this giving, giving,

giving here that just nourishes you. You feel so good when you come home and somebody left two melons on your front step."

Sting and Trudie Styler have both embraced their local community of *Figline e Incisa Valdarno* and been embraced by it. Their winemaking and respect for the land in bringing it back to its former glory has been a pivotal part of forging connections.

"I think the local community will back us up in this. They've seen what we've done, they've seen how much time, love, effort, money we've put into this thing and they appreciate that," Sting tells me.

"And we're throwing a party tonight for the locals and we'll drink some wine together. But we've always welcomed them into our world because I think otherwise it would seem strange. They would wonder what was going on here. You know, 'What are these people doing here?' So opening the gates, opening the doors and saying, 'Look, we're normal people and we want to do the right thing by this land.' That's really benefited us."

"The essence of drinking wine is to be together, to stay together," Trudie explains, "and Sting wrote a song—'We'll Be Together.' We stay together. And I think as the world is becoming in a perilous state of separation and negativity, we need to stay together more and to come and celebrate our lives and our family."

Throughout life, having close social ties and support leads to better mental and physical health, including reduced risk of cognitive decline, obesity and diabetes. Those who lack social connections have 50% higher odds of dying early than those who have community, according to a review of more than 100 studies.

Dr. *Gianni Pes*, who studied elderly residents in the town of *Arzana* in Sardinia, notes that the town doesn't have any nursing homes—because elderly people live at home with their families, which keeps them sharp. "The community is strong and gives support to old people," he told CNN.

It's not just the elderly who benefit from socializing: Teenagers who have strong peer groups are more likely to be involved in their community and government. A study by researchers at the University of *Bologna* found that "sense of community predicts social well-being and explains some of the association between civic engagement and social well-being."

For expats, the strong sense of community in Italy has enabled them to make friends and feel at home in their new country. Retiree Sally Carrocino turned to volunteering to give back to the local community.

"I found an organization called AILO (American International League of Florence), an international American women's group that is charity driven," she says. "I also started at *Caritas,* a Catholic organization that feeds the homeless and the needy. After a few months at *Caritas,* they actually put me in charge of getting the women to participate. I feel such gratitude that I did something good. If you don't have a sense of purpose, what's it all about?" she says.

Upon arriving in Florence, Sally began saying yes to every invitation to join a meetup or gathering. Through her many interests, she has found a true sense of community and belonging.

Arlene Antoinette Gibbs, an interior designer who moved from California to Rome, has found a group of friends in Italy who feel more like family. She says, "I found Los Angeles to be very lonely at times. I felt people were very disconnected." In Rome, she's been welcomed into a close-knit circle of both Italian and American friends. Together, the group celebrates holidays, milestones and everyday life.

Even Italy's big cities can feel like small towns, thanks to the community spirit interwoven into the fabric of Italian life. Coming from New York City, the Bach family didn't quite know what to expect in Florence, but David; his wife, Alatia; and their two sons have found that Florentines have embraced them as friends.

"There's a culture of learning and growth in Florence that is addictive. You want to be learning, you want to be growing, you want to be out in the community. That was really the goal, for our kids to be able to be exposed to living abroad, living in a community like this and doing it at a young age," says David.

Since Italians tend to spend more time together—whether at dinner, hanging out in the *piazza* or at a celebration—they tend to have deeper relationships with both their family and their friends. Friendships aren't necessarily work related, either, as is common in the U.S. Neighbors, family and community members are commonly all in the same circle of friends—and not only that, but friend groups are more multigenerational than in the U.S., too.

Joining meetup groups and the daily *passeggiata* will go a long way toward integrating yourself into the Italian community, but perhaps even more important is learning the language, at least at a conversational level. Otherwise, says Alatia Bach, "You miss out on having a next level of conversation and relating to all these people."

Also, becoming a regular at your local café or bar is important for those who move to or spend time in Italy. Alatia calls it "the original Internet check-in."

When we visit her in Florence, she tells me, "The same people are here, and depending on the time, I come in here at 7:30 a.m., it's the same group. If I come at 8:30 a.m., it's the same group, but it's a different group."

A study by a group of researchers at European universities found several benefits to having close-knit relationships. They found that "individuals with richer networks of active social relationships tend to be more satisfied and happier with their lives. . . . First, relationships, being key players in affirming an individual's sense of self, satisfy the basic human need for belongingness and are a source of positive affirmation. Second, the presence of social relationships has positive impacts on mental and physical health, contributing to an individual's general well-being. Finally, social relationships form a resource pool for an individual." Among these benefits: advice, help with household and economic tasks, dinner companions and emotional support.

No matter where we live, we can open our hearts and minds to others. It is both a spiritual and practical decision. Talk to your neighbors, help those in need and arrange a community event.

When you visit Italy, take steps to become part of the community even if you are only there for a short time. You can be sure to get your *caffè* and *cornetto* at the local café at the same time each morning, like Italians do, so you see the same people. Ask about any local events happening during your stay. Be curious!

THRIVE TIPS

- Become a regular at a local coffee shop or café. You will see the same people if you go at the same time every day.
- Volunteer. Spread your generosity in the community and make new connections.
- Organize a block party or another event to get to know your neighbors.
- Look after those in your community. Check in on an elderly neighbor or mentor a child.
- Get a dog. Ha! You will meet everyone in your community. (This suggestion is inspired by expat retiree Sally Carrocino, who told me her dog Zoe has helped her integrate into her new home of Florence.)
- Join a book club, even online.

TRAVEL TIPS

- Go to a neighborhood bar at the same time each morning and join the locals for morning *espresso.*
- Spend time in the *piazza* or, as Frances Mayes calls it, "the living room of Italy."
- Enjoy an *aperitivo,* a very social early evening event filled with drinks, small bites and lots of socializing.
- Visit a local market and get to know the other shoppers and vendors. You will really feel a part of everyday life.
- Fill your itinerary with local events and celebrations.
- Join the crowd at a bar or café watching *calcio* (soccer), the national beloved sport; or automobile racing, a sport widely appreciated by Italians, with team *Ferrari* having set many world records.

- Book an appointment to get your hair done, especially if you speak Italian. Hairdressers know everything going on in the community!
- Go where the people are: Look for locals at the public library, fishermen by the sea or farmers in the countryside.
- Explore the residential areas as well. You will quickly be immersed in the very heart of Italian life and community.
- Enjoy the walkability and the public transportation of Italian towns and cities. It brings you in contact with more people. Robert Putnam, author of *Bowling Alone,* says that for every 10 minutes of additional travel time by car, social connections are reduced by 10%.

Madonna delle Grazie, Castelvetere sul Calore

Celebrations

In Italian culture, life is meant to be celebrated—through faith, festivals, age-old rituals and time-honored traditions shared by everyone. Each town or village has its own celebrations, especially in the summer. You name it—a patron saint, an ancient war victory, a local delicacy—it is to be commemorated!

Francis Ford Coppola often returns to *Bernalda* for the *Festa di San Bernardino*, held in late August, where residents "make their own fun."

"On different occasions, I came with my family. Again, I always loved to see this *festa* because it's so colorful. Really people, if they could come in August to the *Palazzo*, it happens right in front of you. It's so beautiful and so exciting and so much fun," he says.

Celebrations like these are central to community, faith and family in Italy. I've been honored to take part in several big local Italian celebrations. In my ancestral hometown of *Castelvetere sul Calore*, my mother and I walked in the procession to honor *Madonna delle Grazie*, who is revered here. The celebration, which takes place twice a year on the day of her greatest miracle and on her feast day, includes bringing her statue out of her church, several Masses, a procession including a marching band and many more festivities!

In *Cortona*, Frances Mayes and I donned medieval costumes as part of an historic archery competition, called the *Giostra dell'Archidado,* a medieval festival held in late May and early June that includes falconry demonstrations, flag-flying performances and a crossbow tournament along with a re-enactment of the medieval wedding that started the tradition.

But for both of us, the parade was the highlight of our time together filming the *Dream of Italy: Tuscan Sun Special.* "That was my favorite," she recalls, "when we got in that costume room and tried on all these medieval robes and dresses, and then marched down the street behind the band. That was fun."

But it's just as important to observe personal milestones, too. Sting and Trudie Styler celebrate their wedding anniversary in Tuscany every year, an event that started small and has grown into a much-anticipated local community party with food, wine and music (including a performance by Sting) at their villa and vineyard. In fact, that party was the occasion for our visit to *Il Palagio.*

Milestones—birthdays, weddings, anniversaries—provide the perfect reason to celebrate, no matter where you are. But they also provide a reason to take a trip to mark the occasion. And Italy provides the perfect setting, often complete with food and wine, music and dancing, costumes and parades.

Study after study highlights the positive impact of these observances, underscoring that people who have more social connections age better while staying physically and mentally healthy. Scientists have found that celebrating produces more oxytocin and endorphins, which lower stress and boost the immune system. Research has found that celebrations increase a sense of well-being, regardless of socioeconomic factors, education, age or gender.

In a world where we're often focused on what comes next, research has found that it's important to allow time to review progress, be mindful, foster gratitude and savor successes, large and small alike. Take time to reflect on your journey, both literally and figuratively. In other words—celebrate!

Travel and celebration go hand in hand, so when planning a trip, look for a local *festa* that might be happening in the place you are visiting. In Italy, spontaneously join the revelry if you stumble upon a party. Italians celebrate everything, and you're likely to come across parties in restaurants, bars and *piazzas*. Stop and see what's going on—they will likely welcome you with open arms!

THRIVE TIPS

- Celebrate your own milestones. Make the food and music you enjoy part of the festivities.
- If you're religious, explore the rituals and traditions of your faith.
- Research festivals and celebrations that you would like to attend and plan a day trip or a vacation around one.
- Plan a block party to get to know your neighbors. Community is an essential part of celebrations.
- Throw a party—for no reason—just for the joy of being alive.

TRAVEL TIPS

- Plan a trip to Italy to mark a milestone in your life— honeymoon, birthday, anniversary, completing a goal, anything!
- Visit Italy during the following months to truly enjoy special celebrations:

December: Visiting Italy during the Christmas season is a charming and magical experience. To celebrate like an Italian, visit a local Christmas market where you will find handmade crafts along with delicious treats such as *panettone* and *pandoro* (traditional sweet breads) or *vin brulè* (mulled wine). You also can visit a *presepe*, a traditional nativity scene depicting where Jesus was born in a manger. Many towns and cities also have a *presepe vivente*, or a living nativity scene.

January: The feast of the Epiphany is celebrated 12 days after Christmas, on January 6, marking an end to the holiday period. While traditions vary by region, a popular celebration around this time is that of the *befana*, an elderly lady who brings gifts to all Italian children. To celebrate like an Italian, watch a *falò di inizio anno*, a symbolic bonfire lit January 5 as a sign of purification for the beginning of the new year.

February: Before Lent begins, Italians spoil themselves during Carnival with sweet treats such as *frittelle* and *crostoli*. They participate in lively parties and parades that differ from one city to another, but offer an explosion of colors, music and tradition. The world-famous Carnival of Venice, known for its beautiful costumes and masks, attracts thousands of tourists every year, but other popular celebrations take place throughout the country.

March: This is the month when yellow mimosas celebrate the *Festa delle Donne*, or International Women's Day, on March 8. Easter, known as *Pasqua*, can also fall during this month and brings its own unique Italian traditions. To celebrate like an Italian, don't miss lunch on Easter Sunday where lamb and *la colomba di Pasqua*, traditional sweet bread shaped like a dove, are served. On Easter Monday, Italians continue celebrating with *Pasquetta*, which translates to "little Easter," by gathering with friends for a picnic at the park or in the countryside.

April: This month marks the beginning of *la bella stagione*, the spring and summer season. On April 25, Italians celebrate *La Festa della Liberazione*, or Liberation Day, to remember the end of World War II. The country celebrates this historic day with parades, ceremonies and speeches.

August: *Ferragosto*, on August 15, is the most popular Italian summer holiday and the height of the vacation season, when many Italians close up shop, head to the beach or mountains, and take in spectacular fireworks displays. *Ferragosto*, or Assumption Day, is a national holiday as well as a holy day of obligation in the Catholic Church, but its roots date to Roman times.

Interview with

SUSAN GRAVELY

Bringing Italian Craftsmanship Home

Susan Gravely's first trip to Italy nearly 40 years ago was filled with seren-dipity. After arriving on the Amalfi Coast and falling in love with the intri-cate patterns on their hotel's dinnerware, Susan, her mom Lee and her sister Frances found themselves struck with passion for the handmade ceramics. When they returned to the U.S., they decided to start a company to wholesale and distribute the Italian-made ceramics to an American market, and in 1983, VIETRI was born. Today, VIETRI is still going strong selling Italian dinnerware, tableware, and home and garden décor. All of the pieces are handcrafted, authentic and made with love by local artisans and factories in all parts of Italy. Continuing her love of Italy, Susan also recently started writing holiday-themed children's books starring *Babbo Natale* (Italy's Santa Claus) and animals, who teach children lessons about love, friendship, taking care of the earth and cooking.

Kathy McCabe: What is it that is so magical about Italy and the Italians?

Susan Gravely: I've always said when I've taken people to Italy, or been with people, there are two types: those who look down and those who look up. The ones that look up are the ones who see the world and feel the world and sense their environment. And the ones that look down are missing everything. Italians look up.

You look up so that you don't ever stop loving the moment and the full picture. That's luckily what's happened in my life and to the people I work with here and in Italy.

KM: Tell me about your first trip and what impact that still has today.

SG: So the background story is that my father was in international tobacco, being from North Carolina. We had a standing globe and he'd show Rocky Mount, North Carolina, and the words as a child I always remembered are, "Look how small the world is. You're only a plane ticket or a phone call away."

My father had rheumatic fever as a little boy; he ended up dying at 60 of a heart issue. But two years later, I was in New York at the New York School of Interior Design. My sister was in design and just had her second baby, and my mother said, "I want to take the trip to Italy that your father and I planned."

During the flight, my sister went into business class to go to the bathroom and met this Italian who was from Florence. He said, "Here's my phone number; when you're all in Florence give me a call. Here's my favorite restaurant in Rome."

We tried his restaurant in Rome. We then went to *Positano*, stayed at the *Il San Pietro*.

When we ate at the hotel's restaurant, we went down through the hills, and it opened up into an enormous room carved out of the hillside with white cotton fabrics, beautiful dark towels, art everywhere and then bougainvillea all over the ceiling, opening up to the dining room with peach-colored tablecloths and all the plates with different patterns.

We were mesmerized, so we hired a driver who spoke English, went to the ceramics factory in *Vietri sul Mare* and within three days went from, "We need to buy for ourselves. We need to buy for our friends. Gosh, should we open a retail store?" to having drinks with a couple from New York who were in luxury clothing manufacturing who said, "Listening to you girls, you need to design, and you need to wholesale and distribute." And that was the seed.

So we then talked to the factory, and I still have the original piece of paper that we negotiated the price.

My sister Frances and I thought, "We can handle it." So I went back, we did all the work, we then negotiated everything. That was May. When we went back in September, *Fabio* went with us, *Fabio Puccinelli*.

KM: Is this the guy from the plane?

SG: The man from the plane becomes our agent in Italy.

KM: Wow. And the name VIETRI?

SG: We saw that word and if you reverse the syllables in Italian, *tre vite*, three lives: mama, Frances and me starting the company. The first factory we worked with was in the town of *Vietri sul Mare*. It was the perfect name and we felt like once people can pronounce it, they will remember it.

KM: You work with factories all over Italy. I know you have a special story from the town of *Nove* in the *Veneto* region.

SG: I had been told by the mayor that they wanted to give me the key to the city, and I thought that was just wonderful and I hadn't told anybody. I was just going, and I thought it was going to be at his office. My mother heard about it as did my husband and they said, "We're coming."

They closed the entire *piazza* and had opera singers from Milan. They had tables lined with white cloths everywhere. There were over 250 people there. They had this big tent in front of the art museum. I had to give the acceptance speech in Italian. My Italian is pretty good now, but it wasn't as good then.

These are the kind of memories I have after working with factories in Italy for almost 40 years and establishing relationships.

KM: How can people use products like yours to live like an Italian at home? Let's start with the table.

SG: You do not worry about perfection first and foremost. It is about creating an environment that you are comfortable in, because your table represents your life. I set the table differently every time I use it depending upon who is coming, the season and the meal. I use old and new VIETRI products. I sometimes mix the dinnerware yet keep the placemats and napkins the same colors.

Other times, I use different bowls and platters for serving. I think of our guests, or the day my husband Bill and I have had, and many times, the table setting comes from that. I love things perfectly imperfect. Yes, perfectly imperfect is what Italy and Italian homes feel like to me.

KM: What are some other tips for finding Italian inspiration in your home?

SG: Today, many American homes are very clean and white. There is a sense of orderliness and exactness to this look. Many contemporary Italians are repainting their walls to white, but I sense a bit more cream in their white color. It makes homes warmer and gives a feeling of welcome. Accent with wonderful rugs, and never forget the old books that mean something and the tokens from trips that can be put on walls as art.

Art is key—new, old, fine as well as handmade. Imperfection is perfection from an Italian's point of view. Mix what you love together on a wall, or on a table. For the table, it should be no more than three items. It is about warmth and touches of a few colors of Tuscany—wheat, saffron, some green and maybe a touch of paprika or red.

KM: I'm just curious, all these years of doing business with Italy, what has changed and what hasn't changed? What's it like being a woman doing this?

SG: I think the beauty of being a woman, which I just love, is that you're going to find difficulties if you expect them. I can only think of a couple of business situations and one time in Italy where I felt that it was because I was a woman that something happened or something did not happen. I think women are the way of the world. I think we are so multidimensional and so multitask focused, that even if we can't multi-task, we can do what we do well, and we're not afraid to give away and to support each other, and be honest with each other, so I'm all about women.

━━━

For more information, visit **www.VIETRI.com**

Bramasole

Sense of Home

The first time that I visited Italy, I felt like I was home. There was an unmistakable feeling of being back in my grandparents' family room, cozy and warm, with delicious smells wafting in from the kitchen. I have returned to Italy maybe 60 times, and it feels like this every single time.

Frances and Ed Mayes hold similar feelings for their adopted hometown in Tuscany.

"When I first came here, I got off the plane in Rome and took the bus into *Cortona*," Ed recounts. "I got here, looked around and dropped my bags and said, 'I'm home.' That was my first time in Italy. I was not expecting that to happen."

"Italy feels like home," Frances says. "I've talked to thousands of people who come here and that's what they say: 'I feel so at home here.'"

Home of course can be an actual physical structure, and not only did Frances and Ed feel so comfortable in the atmosphere of Tuscany and Italy, but when they saw the villa, *Bramasole,* they knew that would become their home.

"When we pulled up in front of this house, and I saw that kind of rosy, smeared apricot facade, I thought, 'I would like the life that can happen inside that particular house,'" she recalls. "I got out of the car, and I slammed the door, and I said, 'This is my house.' It was just one of those spontaneous decisions. I think there's a metabolic thing that goes on with people and when they are home, they know it."

When Sting and Trudie Styler first came to *Il Palagio* in 1997, they wanted to create a place to escape with friends and family, a place to rest and rejuvenate, a place of refuge at the end of a tour. In other words, they wanted to find a home.

Italian blood is definitely not a requirement to feeling at home in Italy or making a home here.

"What shocked me was once I arrived here, it felt like home, which made no sense whatsoever because I'm not Italian. Nobody in my family is Italian," says Arlene Antoinette Gibbs.

Sally Carrocino loves living in Italy because it allows her to explore every aspect of life.

"I want a really full life of charity, of friends, of entertainment, of traveling. And I can do all of that here," she says.

Home can be represented by many tangible things—a structure, a piece of land or the people. It can also be feelings, smells and sights. In recreating that sensation, some people simply want to bring the feeling of Italy into their own home, wherever that may be.

When you're traveling in Italy, look for items that will remind you of the magic of Italy in your own home. That might be antiques, photographs, candles, anything really.

There are few things more tantalizing for Italy dreamers than to imagine what their own home in Italy might look like. Take photos of places you love while visiting Italy. Spend some "dream time" scanning real estate online and pick out your "dream home."

Italy feels like home, and there's no better feeling than being in the place where you belong. I don't even need to cite a study to prove that!

THRIVE TIPS

- Smell is a particular trigger to feel "home." Surround yourself with the smells of Italy. For me, it is often the smell of coffee or lemons.

- Add images of Italy—paintings or photographs—to your home décor, especially if you ultimately want to live in Italy. It's easy to find wonderful and affordable art in Italy, from museums to street corners. Or frame your own travel photos for inspiration. Visualization makes things happen!
- You can find almost anything for the home made by Italians, from kitchen tools to luxurious linens. Visit local shops or stop by the weekly market to find an endless assortment of Italian items to outfit a home.
- Eat your meals on Italian ceramics. You can buy them during your travels or from my friends at VIETRI online.
- If you want to make your home in Italy, start researching a move to Italy!

TRAVEL TIPS

- Instead of staying in a hotel, rent your own "Italian home" in an apartment or villa. Then you can live like a local even if it isn't your permanent home.
- If you have Italian blood, you simply must visit your ancestral hometown(s).
- If a move is your dream, look at some real estate during your travels, see if you get that magical sense of belonging when you look at any places.
- Take lots of photos of your favorite views, landscapes, buildings or whatever seizes your imagination. These images will capture not only the physical places you have visited, but also the emotions they generated in your soul. When you're back home, these pictures will elicit those emotions so you can keep feeling deeply connected with your "other home" in Italy.

Interview with

WILLIAM McCARTHY
AND LIZ MAYO

Painting Italy Atmospherically

The TV special *Dream of Italy: Travel, Transform and Thrive* is also a pledge special to raise money for public television. Actor Joe Mantegna joins me to co-host 30 minutes of pledge breaks to appeal to the audience but because of the pandemic, we had to film virtually in private homes. I wanted an Italian theme for the art on both sets and posted on social media seeking out artists whose work was inspired by Italy.

Artist and artists' manager Liz Mayo reached out to me offering her paintings and that of her client, William McCarthy. I chose *Greens and Blues* by Liz to appear behind me on set in Denver, and in Burbank, Joe was surrounded by *Cypress Grove* by Liz and *Umbria* painted by Will. Both Liz and Will paint in the atmospheric style and live their *dream of Italy* by painting in Italy and hosting art workshops in the town of *Farnese* in *Lazio* twice a year. Rich with hills, lakes and trees, *Farnese*'s geography translates to dreamy landscapes on the canvas for these artists and their guests.

Kathy McCabe: Will, tell me about how and where you create your art.

William McCarthy: I use memory and imagination. Ninety-nine percent of my work comes from memory. I mostly paint in my basement studio in Connecticut, referencing drawings that I've done over the years. Little sketches. I use memory and imagination as a guide.

The only time I actually work directly from the landscape is when I'm in Italy teaching. That's the only time I actually reference a landscape and try to incorporate it into the work to show people how to interpret the landscape and show them what to include and what to think about.

KM: So most of your work is not a carbon copy of the landscape?

WM: No.

KM: It's not like it's a photo.

WM: No.

KM: It's your interpretation.

WM: Right. Very suggestive. The coloration, the shape of the trees, the grouping of trees, reticulating hills. It's all just very suggestive. I don't get into a lot of detail because it's memory based. And if you think of your memory and your dreams, they're pretty fuzzy. At least mine are. They're very rarely in sharp focus. So it adds to the type of work that I do, and I refer to my work as "atmospheric." Because that's pretty much what I'm trying to capture. I'm trying to capture a sense of place atmospherically. And that is by using color and by using imagery to suggest and to give a sense of time, a sense of climate, a sense of wonder about the landscape.

KM: How long have you been an artist?

WM: I'd always been interested in art. When I was in high school in Columbus, Ohio, I met this teacher named *Albert Daniel Mazzarella*, who introduced me to *Michelangelo* and to Italians. He took me under his wing and turned me on to really thinking like an artist. He made a huge difference in my life and got me to really start honing down and concentrating on painting.

I went to an arts school in Columbus for a couple of years. I ended up landing a job at Wesleyan University as a gallery supervisor. I had the great fortune of retiring early from Wesleyan, which is key to what happens next.

Then, I was starting to do workshops on weekends. On the second day of the workshop, this gentleman came in and introduced himself. His name was Terry. He knew about me, and he had one of my paintings he bought from a gallery. He said to me, "How would you like to bring a workshop like this to Italy?" And I said, "Yes, I would."

KM: What was his connection to Italy?

WM: His wife was Italian; her sister still lived in Rome. Her sister knew about a woman who had a villa for rent, so the woman rented it to Terry. This place was huge, and it also had a working space for artists already.

Terry had already contacted another artist named Derrick, and Derrick put together a whole bunch of people to go over to Italy and draw. Then Terry approached me and asked me if I wanted to go. I said yes. I turned to the people and I said, "That gentleman I was talking to just offered us a workshop in Italy." And all these hands shot up.

After I figured out all the expenses and how much it was going to cost me to do this, I needed one more person. So that's where my friend Walt came in. Walt was an architect. He loved Italy and had been there several times. He came with me to this little town called *Farnese* out in the country. And it was just a magical experience.

The next year, we did it all ourselves. We got a group of people to come. Walt learned Italian so we could do this. So 2010 was the first time we went, and then we went almost every year since, and then I met Liz eight years ago. It's just been an incredible experience. It's made me a better person.

KM: How has it made you a better person and a better teacher?

WM: It's made me a better teacher to be able to work with people on an intensive week. Even though we only work four to five hours a day, it's very intensive to go through that much time working together. Most of these people are novices.

KM: How have their lives changed in big or small ways?

WM: One of the participants, Diana, was in her mid-fifties. She was struggling with where she was supposed to be in life. And she came there, and she fell in love with that part of Italy. It was her first time there, and she fell in love with it. She liked the simplicity of it. She ended up living there for almost two years. She made all the arrangements and ended up moving to the town of *Bolsena*, which is probably four times the size of *Farnese*.

KM: Is she a painter?

Liz Mayo: She paints. She was a jewelry artist, primarily. She had painted years earlier, and she went back to painting with this workshop.

KM: Liz, before you met William, had you been to Italy?

LM: I first visited Italy in 1984. It was magical. I literally had dreams about hillsides in Italy for the next 20 years until I went back, and I still do. I don't know exactly what hill I'm dreaming of, but I dream of it.

I used to be more photorealistic in my painting, a lot more detailed. I took a workshop with William even before I went to Italy with him, and I really loosened up how I paint. I said, "Why am I trying to make it look a certain way that I think it's supposed to be? I need to make it the way I want it to be, and how I think it should be. It may not be exact, but that's okay."

And William really helped me loosen up and not use so many tiny brushes, and tiny details. And it really changed how I paint completely.

KM: What inspired you to paint *Greens and Blues*, which is behind me in the special?

LM: What inspired me is when we are driving towards *Lake Bolsena* and we come down over the hill and in toward the crater, and seeing the blues and the greens of the fields, and the blue in the background. It's just that feeling of being in the landscape, being part of the beauty of the beautiful lake and the beautiful fields and the beautiful trees.

KM: And what about *Cypress Grove*?

LM: There is not exactly one place that I remember seeing them lined up like that. Like William says, it's our memory of seeing cypresses at some point in some place, turning a corner driving down the road. And those cypresses, just like the umbrella trees, you see them and you know where you are, you're in Italy, right?

———

For more information, visit **www.artfullymanaged.com** and **www.williammccarthyfineart.com**

How to Travel to Italy in a More Meaningful Way

Travel is the first step to transforming our lives. That's the premise of the TV special *Dream of Italy: Travel, Transform and Thrive* and this book. Exposing ourselves to new sights, sounds, smells, tastes, textures, people, conversations—all lead us to new perspectives and possibilities we could have never imagined in our everyday lives. While I contend you can certainly travel to Italy virtually, especially in these times, there's something about your feet feeling the cobblestones of Rome, your nose smelling the freshly made *espresso* or your eyes seeing the intricate detail of a Renaissance painting just feet away that expands our horizons.

I encourage you to make the real journey when that is possible. Not surprisingly, making travel a regular part of your life has mental health benefits. A recent study in the publication *Tourism Analysis* found that those who travel frequently are 7% happier than those who don't travel at all.

When first visiting Italy, it is easy to end up with something of a hit-and-run itinerary to quickly see the major sites that have long been on your bucket list. No one can blame you for this. In some ways, it can be a great introduction to figure out where you want to go in Italy on your *next* trip. Italy, though, calls for time, time to breathe, space. This is the home of slow travel. Whatever the pace of your trip, there are ways to make your travels in Italy more meaningful and to travel deeper. Here are some ideas:

Read, Plan and Build Anticipation

You may or may not be surprised to learn that much of the joy in life is in the anticipation. The French novelist Gustave Flaubert said, "Pleasure is found first in anticipation and later in memory." The journal *Applied Research in Quality of Life* found that those who were taking a vacation experienced the most happiness in the weeks *before* a trip.

One way to build anticipation is to read as much as you can about your intended destinations—fiction and non-fiction. Italy has been the muse for countless writers. If you're looking for suggestions, join the *Dream of Italy* Book Club on Facebook.

While daunting, planning an Italy itinerary is so much fun. Save the places you dream of in your online bookmarks, Pinterest board or both. If you need suggestions of where to go, what to do, what to eat, who to meet and more, all over Italy, visit **www.dreamofitaly.com/magazine** You will find thousands of my best ideas and those of the many writers who have contributed to the award-winning travel magazine *Dream of Italy* over nearly two decades!

Get to Know the Locals

While of course Italy is one of the most beautiful places on Earth, it is the Italian people that encompass the true beauty of *il bel paese*. Italians are some of the most hospitable people in the world. I can guarantee you that some of your best memories will be when you interact with the locals.

While you will certainly meet locals who work at restaurants, shops, museums, hotels and the like, you can also make an effort to meet more. Definitely ask your friends if anyone has "a friend of a friend" or can recommend people they have met on their travels.

Absolutely hire a local tour guide in each destination, even if you might feel like you don't need one. Tour guides in Italy are highly trained and must take a very difficult test to be licensed. You will learn more than you could have imagined and definitely make a new friend.

Take at least one cooking class or other classes given by artisans. This is another great way to meet locals in a more intimate setting. Stay at an *agriturismo* or small bed and breakfast, as most are family-run and you will likely meet the entire family!

Learn the Language

Learning Italian, even the basics, is a key that will unlock friendships and connections with locals in both cities and small towns. While English is increasingly spoken in large cities—indeed, in places like uber-touristy Venice, it seems you can't escape English—it is still scarce in small towns and rural areas. No matter where you are, a little Italian will go a long way.

In cities, knowing a bit of Italian will enable you to venture off the tourist track and discover new things; in rural areas, language will empower you to chat with your lodging hosts and local shopkeepers. You may even find yourself taking an Italian-language tour of a local site.

It has never been easier to learn Italian on-demand. I definitely recommend downloading a language-learning app like Rosetta Stone. You can get a grasp of the basics and learn some words in even the small time that you are waiting in line at a store. I also like to play YouTube videos that teach Italian. Another wonder of the modern age is online language exchanges where you can connect virtually to help an Italian practice English and help you learn Italian.

You might also consider attending language school in Italy. It is a great option, especially for solo travelers. Often the schools can help you rent an apartment or stay with a local family. You might attend language lessons in the morning and have time to explore in the afternoon.

Food Is the Passport to Italy

Why else would you visit Italy if not to try the food and wine? In our food chapter, we discussed the basics of what makes Italian food special. Yet food is also a passport through time and the history of the Italian peninsula. Food tells a story. A bit of trivia: The first known cookbook *De Re Coquinaria* (Of Culinary Matters) was written by Apicius in Rome in the 4th century AD.

You can learn so much about the history of each corner of Italy by its food and traditional recipes. Were the people poor? How was food stored and preserved? What were the major industries? Was there trade? What were some of the religious or spiritual traditions here? Was this area invaded and who were the invaders?

A history lesson in every bite!

See Touristy Sites From a New Perspective

I truly believe you need to see with your own eyes the places you've dreamed about in Italy, from the Colosseum in Rome to the Leaning Tower of *Pisa* to the canals and gondolas of Venice. Touristy sites are part of what makes Italy a favorite destination for millions of people. Enjoy them!

A big part of the mission of *Dream of Italy,* though, is to help you experience the touristy places from a new perspective. In the TV series, I travel down the *Arno* in a classic *renaiolo* (sand digger) boat and see the famous *Ponte Vecchio* from a rare vantage point, from below. I learn more about the history and purpose of gondolas by taking a lesson in how to row a gondola. I also explore the canals of Venice and the relationship between the Venetians and the water by taking a special ecology tour led by a scientist.

I've been to Rome so very many times but my most recent visit was one of the most interesting. Why? I got to see the Eternal City in a total new way—in the sidecar of a *Vespa*. The most amazing part of our tour was tilting my head back and looking *up* at the bottom of the famous Roman stone pine trees that line the *Via dei Fori Imperiali* leading to the Colosseum. New perspective!

Appreciate the Diversity, Off the Beaten Path

Keep in mind every region, city and village is slightly different in Italy. Enjoy the new discoveries from place to place. You probably already know some of the basic differences among the big cities—Milan is the fashion and design capital, Florence is known for art and Rome has a wonderful concentration of ancient ruins—but there are so many more nuances to discover. As we've mentioned, each area has its own culinary special-ties, traditions and even dialects. You could live several lifetimes and not uncover all the layers of Italy, but it is fun to begin the process!

Some ideas:

- Head to the little-discovered region of *Molise* (from where many Italian-Americans hail), which has become a destination to enjoy hiking, kayaking and the outdoors.
- If you're partial to urban life, explore a lesser-known city like Turin (known for *Piemontese* cuisine and gorgeous architecture), *Trieste* (the coffee capital, which was once a Habsburg city) or *Lecce* (a Baroque city known as the "Florence of the south").

- If you're big on beaches, there are so many choices. Perhaps venture to the coastline of *Calabria*, Sicily or Sardinia for a southern coastal adventure.

Leave Time for Serendipity

Italians live in the moment and, while you're in Italy, you should too. If you're the type to plan out every hour of your vacation, go against your instincts and leave chunks of at least a few hours here and there. This may seem counterproductive, but trust me on this. In Italy, you simply must leave time for serendipity.

If you're more inclined toward spontaneity in the first place, you're in luck. Italy has a way of presenting opportunities at just the right moment—after all, when you're in Italy, you're always right where you're supposed to be. If you need help planning your dream trip to Italy, visit **www.dreamofitaly.com/travel**

Interview with

BECKY MUNSON

Dreaming to Live Tuscan

How many people can say that they met at a cocktail party hosted by Frances Mayes at her iconic villa, *Bramasole*? Well, my friend Becky and I can! We were filming the cocktail party in October 2018 for the *Dream of Italy: Tuscan Sun Special* for PBS and Frances invited *Vittorio Camorri*, who brought his American business partner, Becky. Becky is the founder of Live Tuscan, which offers 7-day, 10-day and 14-day immersive trips based in *Cortona*. (She recently added the Amalfi Coast to some itineraries.)

Becky has a joyful and calm spirit and we hit it off immediately, not only for our common love of Italy, but also for our mutual interest in meta-physics. You might say neither of us think that it was an accident that we met. A few months later, Becky extended a gracious invitation for my (now late) father and I to join one of her weeks in *Cortona*. My father, who was nearing the end of his life, came alive that week, and those memories and Becky and *Vittorio*'s kindness will always be deeply etched in my heart. Becky found her *dream of Italy* in a most interesting way. She now splits her time between North Carolina and *Cortona*.

Kathy McCabe: How did you fall for Italy and Tuscany specifically?

Becky Munson: Well, my whole life has been Italy because my mother is 100% Italian and her father was born and raised in Rome and that's all she knew. We were raised to believe that being Italian was a gift. We were really, really blessed to be Italian.

I was always Italian but never had a dream of starting a business in Italy. That fell on me. Destiny pushed that onto me on my very, very first trip to Tuscany.

I had been to Italy before, but that was to Rome. But I was invited to a cooking class in Tuscany with six other women that I knew. We went to cook with the incredible chef Faye Hess. She lives in the tiny town of *Mercatale di Cortona.*

Within 24 hours of arriving, I knew this would be my passion and my life for the rest of my life. I didn't understand it. All of a sudden, I sensed it. You can't say you heard a voice because you don't hear it, you just know it. It is a knowing. It is a boom. "You will do this for the rest of your life."

KM: This wasn't your dream all along?

BM: This was no plan for me. People say, "Oh, you made your dream come true." It is a dream. It is mine and it has come true. But I have to tell you that it wasn't something I set out to do. It wasn't a goal. It happened to me.

That's when I met *Enzo.* He picked us up that next morning. I already had the vision of what I wanted it to be and it's exactly what I have now. But I sat in the front seat; I asked him a million questions. I'm still in the front seat asking him a million questions.

We got back to the house and everyone else was writing recipes and I'm writing a business plan, which I have never done in my life. I never owned a business. I was home with my kids.

KM: How did you meet your other partner *Vittorio*?

BM: Well, I got back to the States and I spent hours upon hours on the computer looking for what I saw in my head. I needed a house that suited many, many, many specifications for the American traveler, also for my vision of what I wanted it to be.

When I called about that house, *Vittorio* picked up the phone. I said, "I'm Becky and I am going to start a business in Tuscany and I would like to see this house." We had a meeting and he told me, "Whatever you can dream, I can create it."

Ten years later, it is the three of us. We all are just firmly committed. There's a purity in what each of us bring to it.

KM: I've experienced your magnificent hospitality for myself and I've been traveling in Italy for 26 years and I've never experienced anything quite like it. The dinners at *I Pagliai* are beyond anyone's imagination—mind-blowing table settings, delicious and creative food (I'll never forget the sunflower-shaped bread), live music. What do your guests experience during their time with you?

BM: They feel awe. They feel moved. I have people in the vans every day who cry. They get teary-eyed because I have the music playing for the specific scenery that's going by outside. Every sense, all five senses are engaged all the time. So you are on a high, a sensory high the whole time.

They fall in love again. They are changed. They expect something very topical, but it becomes very personal very quickly. I believe that people come to me for a reason. That they are drawn to me.

Somebody told me a couple of years ago, we were "the *Camino* of Tuscany," meaning the *Camino de Santiago*. You get so much emotion and bonding with each other.

KM: Going back to how you came to this work, have you been struck so hard by something before?

BM: I have never had anything happen to me like this before. I have never had a powerful intuition or voice or knowing. That's why I was able to start a business in a country where I didn't even speak the language. I just was fearless. I just thought, "I'm doing this. The way will come. The way will appear. I'm only going to keep taking the steps."

The first year I only had one group. I launched my website six months after I came back from the cooking class.

My first year and a half, I cooked for all the groups. The second year, there were no guests. It was like a hot air balloon that was just bumping along the ground, it wasn't getting any lift.

My prayer was always and still is, either encourage me or redirect me because I am open either way. Encourage me or redirect me. It never failed. I got encouragement almost immediately. I'd get another booking . . . I knew the path was clear.

I was pretty fearless. It is a learning curve. The learning curve never stops. I still have a learning curve when I go. It has been 10 years. I still will find out something and be like, "Oh my gosh, this culture is going to kill me. Seriously, this is what we have to do to do this?" Or, getting a ticket being parked here because that's something I didn't know about.

I remember the first time I went to the grocery store and I didn't put gloves on and I squeezed a peach.

KM: Oh dear God . . .

BM: Yeah. She was yelling at me for touching the fruit, squeezing the peach. I brought my bag of peaches to the front and I didn't weigh them and put the number on them. And I was just like, "This is just so much."

KM: When did you end up deciding not just to travel back and forth but to live in *Cortona* part-time?

BM: It was in mid-2016. When I left *Cortona* over the years, it became harder and harder to leave. Then eventually it became like Velcro ripping apart, it just ripped me apart and my family would say, "You can't be trusted. Just whatever you say or do for a month when you get back, you can't be held accountable." Because I wasn't myself. I was just like, "I need to be there."

That January I went back and I thought, "OK, I'm staying for six weeks. Two months max. I'm going to learn the language. I'm going to study the language every day. Every day I'm going to get up and I'm going to walk a different street in *Cortona* so I can see every street."

I was there in the rain and the gray. I fell in love with *Cortona* when no one was there. I got to know so many people. I got a lot of street cred because I was there in the winter.

KM: How easy or hard is it to live in *Cortona*? What has that been like for you?

BM: I should have been a lot more afraid than I was. I was so brazen even with my language. I'm not afraid to make mistakes. Eventually, it's going to get to the point where there are none, but I'm not afraid of being embarrassed. Moving to *Cortona* was not easy in that there were a few tough nuts to crack in town, which I did manage to crack. Some of them took a couple of years. Culturally, there was curiosity on both parts. They were curious of me and I was curious of them and of course I wanted to absorb everything. I'm fortunate in that I have two business partners who are Italian and who want me in the Italian culture. I'm invited to Italian events. I'm invited to places where I'm the only American.

Every time I go back, I realize the learning curve is not steeper, but it's still there. It never flattens. It's still a different culture, but it's my culture.

KM: What about advice for people who might want to live in Italy or *Cortona* part-time? What do you wish you had known?

BM: I would say, for somebody who is thinking of moving to Italy, they shouldn't hesitate. They should do it. If you're in a small town where they don't speak English, they need to find a place, at least at first, that has some English.

For more information, visit **www.livetuscan.com**

Kathy's grandmother *Marie Cuzzone* and great-grandmother *Caterina Scrima*

Exploring Your Italian Ancestry and Claiming Italian Citizenship

More than 16 million Americans are descendants of Italian immigrants, the majority of whom arrived in the U.S. between 1876 and 1924. The threads these immigrants have woven through American families and American life are undeniable. Their legacy touches so many aspects of life, from the simple family recipes shared at the dining room table to holiday traditions passed down through generations to the staggering accomplishments of Italian-Americans in everything from the arts to medicine.

If you have even a small amount of Italian blood, you might want to find out more about your Italian roots. Not only can genealogy research help you plan a trip to your very own ancestral corner of Italy, but tracing your ancestors could also help you claim Italian citizenship, giving you an Italian passport and an easy way to move to Italy or the European Union should you choose. It is a unique opportunity to make your *dream of Italy* come true.

Finding Myself Through My Roots

Rediscovering my ancestral hometown in 1995 led to a complete transformation of my own life—including the birth of *Dream of Italy*. I tell much of this story in the introduction to this book, but I will add some of the background and detail here.

My great-grandfather *Generoso Nargi* first came to New York from *Campania* in 1888. He got a job working on the railroad in New York and sadly, he gravely injured his arm. The doctor insisted that it be amputated. He said, "No. I'm going back to *Castelvetere sul Calore*, and I will be healed there by the *Madonna delle Grazie*." He returned to his hometown in Italy and indeed was miraculously healed. Then, in 1890, he returned to the U.S., never to set foot in Italy again.

I first heard the poetic name of the town *Castelvetere sul Calore* around the dining table at my parents' house in Springfield, New Jersey. Sometimes during Christmas or Easter dinner, usually over dessert, my grandfather Louis would wax poetic about this town his father *Generoso* left behind. You would have thought my grandfather had seen this town himself, as he would always get misty-eyed talking about it. My grandfather would also share how, in the 1960s, he and my grandmother stopped in Naples for the day on a cruise and asked a cab driver to finally take them to the mythical, mysterious and miraculous *Castelvetere*. They ended up in the wrong *Castelvetere* 40 miles away—so close yet so far. He would always end the story by saying wistfully, "Well, they (his relatives) would have never let me leave."

My grandparents never returned to Italy.

My Italian-American grandparents were my daycare, as both of my parents worked. Their house was full of warmth and the occasional raised voice by my grandfather, as he did have that Italian passion and temper. I was very close to my grandfather, so when I had to do a year-long project in high school, I decided to write a biography of him. That's when a distant cousin sent me some translated birth certificates from *Castelvetere sul Calore*. These documents were so detailed, explaining who each person was, where they lived and what they did for a living. I was fascinated.

My dad took me to the New York Federal Records and Archive Center (part of the National Archives), which was at the time located in Bayonne, New Jersey, to find my grandparents' and great-grandparents' census records, and we pored over the microfiche files to learn more about where they lived in the early and mid-20th century. Census records are a treasure trove of genealogy information, as they often tell if the person recorded was naturalized as an American citizen or "alien."

When my mom and I planned our first trip to Italy in 1995, I knew we had to make a pilgrimage to *Castelvetere sul Calore* to fulfill my grandfather's dream. He was 93 and living in a nursing home at the time, so he couldn't join us. At the time, the Italian Tourism Bureau in New York City had phone books from nearly every area of Italy. I stopped by their office and photocopied the directory for my ancestral hometown, keeping an eye out for the name *Nargi*, of which there are many listed in this very small town.

The day we arrived, we met so many people who looked like my mother's family and who were actual family—distant cousins like *Manfredo* and *Livio Nargi*. They shared that the name *Nargi* only came from this town and that yes, the *Madonna* was as miraculous as we had heard. Again, as I recall in the introduction to this book, my mother felt like our one day there was something out of *Brigadoon*. It was like *Castelvetere* came alive once in a hundred years. It was the fact that my grandfather died suddenly back in the U.S., about 36 hours after my mother and I fulfilled his dream, that tied me to this place for eternity.

When I wrote to *Manfredo* to tell him of my grandfather's death, he wrote back to me to say, "Your grandfather only left this earth when he knew your mission was complete." I visited my beloved *Castelvetere sul Calore* several more times, started *Dream of Italy* in 2002 and returned to film an episode of *Dream of Italy* for PBS in 2017.

All of this because I started to research my family tree back in high school!

Finding Your Roots Could Transform Your Life

I'm not alone in my quest to find my Italian roots and the life-changing results such a journey can have. Like me, Hollywood film director Francis Ford Coppola and actor Joe Mantegna also traveled to their ancestral hometowns in their 20s, which left a lasting impression on them both.

As I've shared, Coppola sought out *Bernalda* after growing up hearing his grandfather's stories about his ancestral hometown. After the success of *The Godfather* made him *Bernalda*'s most famous progeny, Coppola returned year after year to visit. In those visits, he began to feel like he was truly returning home. Not only had Coppola become a world-famous director and built a successful wine business in Napa Valley, but he had also curated a number of boutique hotels, now called the Family Coppola Hideaways. Some friends in *Bernalda* convinced him to buy the historic *Palazzo Margherita* and turn it into a nine-room boutique hotel as an homage to his ancestors.

Actor Joe Mantegna, who graciously joined me as my co-host for the pledge breaks in the pledge version of the TV special *Dream of Italy: Travel, Transform and Thrive,* has a similar story. When Joe first traveled to Europe in 1975 while touring with a theater company, his grandfather asked him to be sure to visit Italy to meet distant relatives. He and his wife, Arlene Vrhel, ventured down to *Acquaviva delle Fonti* in *Puglia*. "I did it as a favor. I told my wife, 'We'll go, we'll knock on the door. I speak pretty good Italian. We'll have coffee, we'll take a few pictures, we'll go on to wherever,'" he says.

After an incredibly warm welcome from his relatives, however, "We stayed for 12 days. We loved every minute of it. It was like discovering a whole family who had always been there. It was monumental," he says. As his career evolved, Mantegna continued to visit his relatives, and even brought them a bottle of wine from Coppola while filming *The Godfather 3*.

My friend Valerie Fortney, genealogist and owner of *My Bella Basilicata,* moved to her ancestral region three years after first visiting—a direct result of diving deep into her family tree. Valerie and her husband now live in *Trivigno*, near her ancestral hometown of *Anzi*.

Valerie says researching her ancestry has "given us a greater appreciation of our ancestors and what they went through to emigrate to the U.S. Coming to *Basilicata* for the first time to see the towns my family came from also revealed relatives I didn't know we had here, and that link brought us back time and again, until we felt the pull to move here. We've lived in *Basilicata* for more than a decade now, a sort of 'reverse immigration' that kind of brought my family full circle."

Many of us have more than one line of Italian ancestors. My entire maternal side is of Italian descent. On another trip to *Campania* in 2012, my mother and I decided that because we had seen her father's ancestral hometown, it was time to visit her mother's. Her mother's parents, *Generoso Cuzzone* and *Caterina Scrima,* were born and married in *Ariano Irpino.* They had several children in Italy before moving to America, where my grandmother was born.

Ariano Irpino, a small city of 22,000, is about 25 miles north and more than 15 times the size of *Castelvetere sul Calore.* We had less information to go on, but our friend *Gaetano Petrillo*, who is both a wine expert and a genealogist (he's also known as The Wine Bus Man, and you met him in the *Castelvetere sul Calore* episode of *Dream of Italy*) said he would help and picked us up on the Amalfi Coast to take us to the hilltop town.

Asking the locals is often the best way to find what you are looking for. We stopped at a restaurant for lunch and *Gaetano* quizzed the staff on the part of town the *Cuzzones* were from. They didn't know. Then he asked about my great-grandmother's maiden name, *Scrima*—bingo! They knew. When I got up to go to the bathroom, I saw a piece of art on the wall of the restaurant that said, "*Ariano di Puglia.*" When I asked *Gaetano* about it, I discovered that *Ariano* used to be part of the region of *Puglia*, which meant I am actually part *Pugliese*! I've been obsessed with *Puglia* ever since I first visited in 2004. I now think my blood is the reason. We were able to visit our ancestral corner of *Ariano* and even say a prayer in the local church our ancestors must have frequented.

Yes, both of my Italian great-grandfathers were named *Generoso*, which means "generous." They became friends in the U.S., and family lore has it that *Generoso Cuzzone* introduced *Generoso Nargi* to his future wife, *Maria Ciano*. *Maria* was a friend of *Generoso Cuzzone*'s wife, *Caterina Scrima*. My grandparents, Louis and Marie Nargi, played together as children but lost touch after the Nargis moved to New York. They re-met later at a wake—yes, a funeral wake. So when my mother was in her early 20s, my grandmother would take her to all the wakes to maybe meet her match! But in the end my mother met my Irish-American father in a bar of all places, while wearing a lucky bell from Capri. It represents a legend of St. Michael, who supposedly gave a bell to a poor shepherd boy on Capri and said, "Take this bell and always follow the sound of it to keep you from danger."

Locating Records

Finding your ancestors might require a lot of methodological research mixed with a bit of luck. The most important pieces of the puzzle are names, approximate dates (e.g., birth years, immigration years) and hometown.

Even when you think you might have the correct information, you could be surprised by your new findings. When my mother and I visited my maternal great-grandfather's home town, *Castelvetere sul Calore,* we came to discover that *Generoso Nargi* was born on September 8, 1864 (two years earlier than what was declared in the U.S. documents) to a family of farmers and small landowners who most likely worked the rich land still used today to produce wine.

Melanie Holtz, professional genealogist and owner of *Lo Schiavo Genealogica*, says, "Begin in gathering what your family has, as far as documents. Maybe your grandmother knows they came from such and such a town or knows they were *Napoletani*. Ask your relatives: Do they have photos? What information do they know about the immigrants?

There's always going to be families who are, say, four or five generations down. There's no one alive who really remembers much about them, but in those cases, we can research. They're traceable."

This is, of course, assuming you know precisely where in Italy your ancestors came from. Relatives will often say, for example, that they are from Sicily, but omit the town in Sicily they came from, leading to some confusion as the majority of records are stored in each town rather than in the province or region. Military records are the exception and can be found at the state archives (*archivi di stato*). These records can often be key to finding what town your ancestor was born in when you only know the province.

"A lot of times, if you look at the immigration manifests for certain time periods, for place of origin it asks where they last resided, which may not be the same place as where they were born. Oftentimes, when they went to immigrate, they would spend two weeks, four weeks in *Genova*, in *Napoli,* in *Palermo*, as they waited for the ship and had a ticket for it to arrive. So, sometimes they would put that they last resided in *Palermo*, but they really were from *Messina*," says Melanie.

A couple things may help: Italian military service was required for all men after 1875 and, unlike birth records, military records are the responsibility of the national government. Further, look at ship's manifests from around the time and place you believe your ancestors left from Italy.

You might also plug the names you know into **Ancestry.com** or **FamilySearch.org** to see what you can find. FamilySearch is an organization run by the Church of Jesus Christ of Latter-Day Saints, which sends representatives around the world to microfilm and digitize genealogical records for religious purposes. Anyone can use their records, as you don't have to be a member of their church. In 2012, they reached a new agreement with the main Italian archival organization to be allowed to digitize all civil records held in all of the state archives in Italy, which is still in process. Due to their efforts and those of other organizations, many Italian records are available to research from local Family History Centers and the Family History Library in Salt Lake City. As part of this agreement, FamilySearch will give copies of these digitized records to the main Italian archive to place on their website, *Antenati* (**www.antenati .san.beniculturali.it**).

FamilySearch also has some military, parish and notarial records available for research, while some Catholic diocesan archives have or are digitizing the parish records in their collections and putting them on their websites. In the last few years, the Italian Parish Records project has been helping expand access to these records.

Other ways to find the town of origin are through the baptismal records of the first few children born in the U.S., property deeds, wills/ probate records, World War I and II draft registration cards, and naturalization records.

If you've exhausted these methods and are still stumped, try hiring a professional like Melanie. "Those immigrants that came from southern Italy and Sicily were often more hesitant to give authorities identifying information because of their history with the Italian government. They were kept quite poor with excessive taxation, social policies that favored the industrial north and lack of educational opportunities," she says, explaining why some records may be incomplete or missing.

Valerie advises those looking for records to familiarize themselves with both the Italian language and the format of most Italian records. By learning a few Italian words and how to interpret common documents, which generally use the same template, you can more easily glean information. Italian records will tell you more than you might imagine. Birth certificates, for example, sometimes list the paternal grandfather's name, each parent's age and occupation, where the family lived at the time of the birth, whether the father reported the birth and whether the father was away at the time of the birth. Parish records follow a certain template and are written either in Latin or a mix of Latin and Italian, though they often don't list the mother's full name.

Once you know who your Italian ancestors were and where they came from, you can begin to search for official documents. Many people indeed venture to their Italian hometown—an ancestral pilgrimage, if you will—to find birth, death and marriage records, which are available in the local town hall (*municipio*) and/or churches. But if you are unable to fly overseas for such a mission, you can certainly write to your ancestor's town hall and request copies (the more specific information you give, the more likely the town clerk is to reply). Let's face it, this is Italy, so it can be hit or miss. The most foolproof way—and quickest, especially if you are in the U.S.—is to a hire an ancestry research service to procure the documents.

When civil records were created in Italy depends on where your ancestors came from. In general, in the north, there was civil registration between 1806 and 1815, then it began again in 1865 and continues today. In those missing years, the church kept the vital records of the Italian people. In southern Italy, you'll usually find that civil records began in 1806 and in Sicily in 1820. Normally, for citizenship purposes, the government wants to see civil records, but will accept parish records in situations where all copies of a civil record have been destroyed or if the date of the event occurred within that time period in the north when the church maintained the records.

Name Changes

While it's true that Italian names are often misspelled in U.S. records, a common misconception is that these names were changed upon the immigrants' arrival at Ellis Island or its predecessor, Castle Garden, the country's first immigration depot in New York. In fact, Ellis Island did not create the passenger manifests; rather, officials there checked off names on the manifest (which was created in Italy or the country of origin) as passengers disembarked.

"The passenger manifests were created at the point of origin by someone who spoke that language. Now, that doesn't mean that they didn't hear wrong. The ship official who was writing down the name of the passenger could have heard wrong, but the names were not changed at Ellis Island," Melanie explains.

More commonly, immigrants changed their names themselves to better fit in with English names—for example, *Giuseppe* becoming "Joseph" or *San Giovanni* becoming "St. John." Italian women kept their maiden names throughout their lives and still do, so you should look for maiden names as well. Once they came to the U.S., though, women usually took on the American custom of taking their husband's surname.

Surnames especially also evolved over the centuries in Italy. One of the most surprising things that I found when I engaged a genealogist from *My Italian Family* (you met *Giovanni DeSimone* in the *Castelvetere sul Calore* episode of *Dream of Italy*) to search for records in both of my ancestral hometowns (*Castelvetere sul Calore* and *Ariano Irpino*) is that *Nargi* is only the latest incarnation of my ancestral surname.

Giovanni started in the municipal records and then made his way back to the church archives. *Castelvetere sul Calore* started keeping baptismal records in 1594. Though the Nargis, who were Norman invaders, have been in Italy for much longer, in terms of documents, he traced my family line back to *Savino de Nargio* (meaning "son of *Nargio*"), who was born in 1625. Somewhere in the 1700s, the name evolved to *de Nargi* and, soon after, the "*de*" was dropped to become just *Nargi*.

Claiming Your Italian Citizenship

Learning about your Italian family and visiting the places where they are from might make you wish you could be Italian yourself. Obtaining citizenship may be closer to reality than dream, as the spirit of Italian hospitality is evident in the country's citizenship laws. Italy considers descendants of Italians to be born with Italian citizenship unless their Italian parent naturalized before their birth or before June 1912. That is, your family's Italian citizenship may have passed through the generations, lying dormant and waiting for you to claim it.

This is the rule of *jure sanguinis*, meaning "right of blood" in Latin, which indicates that those who have Italian blood running through their veins, no matter how diluted, are Italian. That is, if your grandfather was born in Italy and moved to the U.S., never naturalized to become American or naturalized only after the birth of his American-born child (your father), then it is likely that you were born an Italian citizen no matter the country of your birth, and your family never lost their Italian citizenship.

On the surface, the rules for claiming Italian citizenship seem simple: Your ancestor must have been born in Italy and must have lived after the country's unification in 1861 (as Italian citizenship could not have existed without the formation of Italy). Unlike some other European countries, Italy allows descendants to claim citizenship no matter how distant their ancestor—you may be eligible through, say, your third- or fourth-great-grandparent. However, there are some areas of present-day Italy that did not become part of the country until after World War I and there are special laws surrounding immigrants from those areas.

Attorney *Michele Capecchi*, whose international law firm *Capecchi Legal* (**www.capecchilegal.com**) specializes in helping people acquire their Italian citizenship, admits that many people underestimate the complexity of recreating the Italian line of blood, especially when the Italian roots go back three or four generations (given that you have to collect documents that are more than 100 years old). All the documents you must use to prove that your Italian-born relative was really a member of your family must be authentic (no photocopies) and must be legally certified either using the legalization services of the Italian consulates or, for U.S. documents, using the *apostille* procedure. If you plan to apply at an Italian town (*comune*), there's an extra certification that must be placed on the translations by Italian authorities.

Capecchi reiterates the importance of collecting the documents related to the naturalization of the Italian-born ancestor. Melanie suggests this be the first step because if the person naturalized (i.e., relinquished their Italian citizenship) to become, for instance, American, you need to determine if the naturalization was granted before or after the birth of your immigrant ancestor's child. Additionally, you will need to consider several elements such as the age of the children at the time of the naturalization of their parents, whether the children were born in Italy or abroad and when such a naturalization occurred.

Dig a little deeper, though, and as with all things Italy, you'll find the guidelines are not quite this simple. In addition to the complexity of recreating the Italian line of blood, there are also a few cases of the *jure sanguinis* rule that commonly affect citizenship seekers:

▪ If your Italian ancestor naturalized before 1912, or (even after 1912) they naturalized before the birth of their child who is your direct ancestor (e.g., your father or grandfather), you are not eligible for citizenship. In becoming an American citizen, your Italian-born ancestor gave up his Italian citizenship and thus severed ties with his homeland.

▪ If your Italian ancestor naturalized before 1912, even if they naturalized after the birth of their child, then the line of blood is interrupted. In fact, based on the interpretation provided by many Italian consulates, if your ancestor became a naturalized U.S. citizen before June 14, 1912, you are not entitled to the Italian citizenship if the son was a minor on the date of his father's naturalization, even if he was born before your Italian ancestor's naturalization.

▪ Italian nationality law states that only men could pass citizenship to their children during any time period (assuming no other part of the nationality law disqualified them). However, the law is not the same for women. According to the interpretation provided by the Italian Constitutional Court (*Corte Costituzionale*), women could hold Italian citizenship but could only pass that citizenship to her child if the child was born *after* January 1, 1948. However, in 2009, this part of the law was declared unconstitutional and discriminatory by one of Italy's highest courts, the *Corte Suprema di Cassazione*. This declaration now allows for citizenship cases where there is descent from a female born prior to 1948 to be brought before the *Tribunale di Roma*. Thousands of these cases have been won.

Capecchi, who represents hundreds of "1948 cases," highlights that one of the benefits of these court applications is that you will not need to wait for an appointment with the consulate and, most importantly, you will not need to travel to Italy for the hearing. Your Italian attorney will represent you, as well as the other members of the same side of the family who want to join you, as your legal proxy in front of the court. Additionally, several members of the same Italian ancestral family (even if they live in different states and countries) can gather their Italian claims in one single application, using the same attorney.

The U.S. does not explicitly recognize dual citizenship, but will not dispute it. Plainly, it's a sort of "don't ask, don't tell" situation—if a U.S. official asks, you are free to state that you have dual citizenship, but you will still need to enter and exit the U.S. with your American passport.

Italy now recognizes dual citizenship but did not before 1992; all Italians living abroad before 1992 had to choose between their Italian and new country's citizenship. Whether and how you can reclaim your Italian citizenship if you naturalized before 1992 is discussed in the citizenship section of each Italian consulate's website. This is a complicated situation, and it is often best to consulate an Italian citizenship attorney before taking any steps.

My Citizenship Story

It seemed at first that it would be easy for me to claim Italian citizenship through my great-grandfather *Generoso Nargi*, who was born in *Castelvetere sul Calore* and immigrated to the U.S. When his son Louis, my grandfather, was born in Monson, Massachusetts, in 1902, his father was still an Italian citizen and hadn't naturalized. Slam dunk, right? Because my grandfather was born Italian to an Italian citizen. Well,

Generoso did eventually naturalize in 1905, and this is the problem. The 1912 law states that any Italian who naturalized in another country prior to 1912 gave up rights to Italian citizenship not only for themselves but also for their minor children (my grandfather) at the time. Dead end to claiming citizenship.

I then turned my attention to my other great-grandfather, *Generoso Cuzzone*, father of my grandmother Marie. He emigrated to the U.S. before my grandmother was born, also in 1904, and he never naturalized. Great, right? But the line has to trace all the way to me, and we are going through women. My grandmother Marie gave birth to my late mother Kathleen before 1948. According to Italian law, because of this, my mother could hold but not pass on her Italian citizenship to me. Another dead end—or is it?

Fortunately, many people in my situation have worked with attorneys like *Michele Capecchi* to challenge this discriminatory rule and claim their Italian citizenship based on these Italian Supreme Court (*Corte Suprema di Cassazione*) precedents before the Civil Court in Rome (*Tribunale di Roma*). It is at the discretion of the judge but is usually successful.

Capecchi says that once the court recognizes my Italian citizenship, my name will be placed on the registry of Italians living abroad (AIRE) and my vital records will be registered, as an Italian citizen, in the same birth registry of *Ariano Irpino*, where *Generoso Cuzzone* was born.

"We have to recreate a chain that goes from *Generoso* to you. You never lost your citizenship. You have always been Italian, even for three generations. Basically, your entire family was raised and grew up and was born in America. But the gift of citizenship that *Generoso* gave to his daughter, Marie, and then Marie gave to your mother Kathleen is still there," he says.

Capecchi clarifies that once all the documents (all the vital records of my Italian side of the family, namely marriage and death certificates) are collected, he will submit the lawsuit before the *Tribunale di Roma*, asking the judge to recognize my Italian citizenship pursuant to the aforementioned interpretation of the Supreme Court.

Once the application is submitted, the Registry Office of the Court will assign the case to a specialized judge in Rome, and within a month we should know the date of the hearing. The case will be heard approximately 14 to 16 months later. While the ruling is up to the discretion of the individual judge, I am advised that there is a very good chance that the judge will acknowledge my Italian citizenship.

To be able to go through my mother and my grandmother and to honor them that way is really beautiful. I come from a line of strong women.

Why Claim Italian Citizenship?

There are numerous benefits to also holding an Italian/European passport, including:

- **Education:** Your children can go to a European university, which costs much less than college in the U.S. You can also pursue an advanced degree in Europe for a lower cost.
- **Healthcare:** Healthcare in Italy is much more affordable than in the U.S. As a citizen or permanent resident, you can join the national public healthcare system and receive care free of charge or at a low cost. If you go to a private hospital, you may have to pay, but the costs are marginal. Some medical procedures or medicines are legal in Europe but not in the U.S.
- **Moving to Italy:** The most common reason, and some would say the biggest benefit, of having Italian citizenship is that you can retire, live and work in Italy without any visa renewals or restrictions. Citizens also receive privileges such as the right to work, live and receive healthcare visa-free in countries throughout the European Union. In the last few years, Italy has begun offering tax advantages when purchasing property and programs that help you remodel an old Italian house.
- **Travel:** If you don't want to live in Italy, you can travel

throughout the whole EU without visa restrictions—and you'll get to stand in a shorter immigration line at European airports! You can stay in the EU past the 90-day limit for non-Europeans, too. Though you aren't issued a passport upon receiving citizenship, you can apply for an Italian passport just like you would a U.S. passport.

- **Voting:** Italian citizens living abroad can vote in Italian local and provincial elections with an absentee ballot, and those living in Italy can vote in national elections as well.
- **Investments:** Purchasing property and setting up a business are much easier if you are an Italian citizen. You also have the opportunity to make certain investments that are only available to European citizens.
- **Family:** Italian citizens can pass down their citizenship to their descendants. Non-Italian spouses can also apply for citizenship, though they must take an Italian language test at a conversational level if they married after 1983, which is not required for Italian-Americans. However, the Italian descendant must obtain citizenship before their spouse can apply. If you move to Italy as a citizen, your spouse can apply for a family reunification visa to enable them to live there with you.

First Steps

First, determine who your most direct Italian ancestor is, when they left Italy and whether they naturalized to become a U.S. citizen.

"The key point is to determine if there is a naturalization, and whether it was before or after the child you descend from. If it was before the birth of the child you descend from, then that breaks the chain of citizenship, and no descendants down that line can gain citizenship by blood. If the naturalization took place after the birth of the child and after June

14, 1912 (and if the child was born in a country that grants citizenship *jus soli* [right of soil] like the U.S.), then that child received the Italian citizenship of their parent. As long as there's no other breaks to the chain through naturalization in the subsequent generations, then you're able to get citizenship through that line," says Melanie.

If you believe you might qualify for Italian citizenship, you will then need to make an appointment at the Italian consulate that serves the state you live in. Because proof of eligibility isn't required upon booking the appointment, you can make the appointment and then gather your required documents.

How Long Does It Take?

1. Through the Consulate: Unpredictable due to the backlog at the consulates. The most common way to apply for citizenship (i.e., if your application is based on the masculine line of blood or on a female relative born after 1948) is by submitting the request at the Italian consulate in the U.S. that has jurisdiction for the area where you reside, where you will make an in-person appointment and submit your documents. There are nine Italian consulates in the U.S. (Boston, Chicago, Detroit, Houston, Los Angeles, Miami, New York, Philadelphia, San Francisco) in addition to the Italian embassy in Washington, D.C. You must make your appointment at the consulate that serves your state.

Wait times vary drastically across the consulates: Some book up 18 months in advance, while others have an eight-year waiting list. The embassy's wait time is about three months, though it requires an extra step in verifying the accuracy of translations. Following your appointment, legally the consulate has to either approve or deny your citizenship application within two years, but backlogs are common and that time frame is sometimes extended. A new appointment-making system is currently being installed in the Italian consulates in the U.S., which should make the appointment process easier and perhaps quicker.

2. In Court: Up to two years. For those like me who are trying to claim their citizenship through a female ancestor born before 1948, the court process typically takes about two years. You will not have to travel to Rome and you are not requested to appear in court in person, unless you want to, of course. Additionally, *Capecchi* notes that, while the application before the consulate is individual (you can only file for yourself and your minor children under age 16), the court application is much more flexible and allows an entire family (adults only), who have the same common Italian ancestor and the same parents, to apply together regardless of the state or country where they reside. Imagine the case of a mother, whose grandmother was Italian and can apply (via the "1948 exception") together with her three adult children and their respective two adult children, for a total of 10 people. The entire family will be able to apply together!

3. In Italy: About a year. The third way to claim citizenship is to become a resident of Italy. Those who are eligible to apply for citizenship through the standard procedure at a consulate can instead skip the consulate backlog and apply while in Italy. This process takes 12 to 18 months in bigger cities, but much less in smaller *comuni*, and requires the applicant to live in Italy for the entire duration of the application. By establishing your legal residency in Italy, the *comune* acquires jurisdiction over your application. In this case, if your citizenship application takes more than three months, it is possible to request, via the local immigration office, a special permit to stay called *permesso di soggiorno per attesa cittadinanza* (permit of residence while awaiting citizenship), which legally prohibits you from working while in Italy, even remotely, but allows you to remain in Italy for the entire time of this application.

You must show proof of at least a six-month rental agreement (or sometimes a one-year contract), and typically an Italian official or police officer will visit your apartment shortly after you submit your residency application to ensure you are present in the country. If you plan to rent an apartment, clarify to the owner that you need to establish your formal residency in that apartment for the whole duration of this process. Be prepared that not every owner is keen to let you fix your residency in their apartment because they are taxed at a higher rate when it is a long-term contract. You need all of the same documents as you would if you were applying through the consulate. However, your documents also have to be apostilled (similar to a notary but authorized for use in a foreign country) and translations have to be certified at an Italian courthouse.

To apply in Italy, you do not need to live in your ancestral hometown; you can choose any city in Italy. In fact, you might not want to apply in person in your ancestral hometown, because sometimes the volume of applications can overwhelm small towns and create a backlog. Citizenship applications are submitted to the *anagrafe* (town registry office), and you will need a fluent Italian speaker to accompany you.

Melanie's company, *Lo Schiavo Genealogica*, helps aspiring Italian citizens apply on the ground in Italy. She operates in the northern Italian province of *Bergamo* and helps clients through the whole process no matter what happens. Even in the middle of the Covid-19 pandemic, she was able to get two clients' citizenship processes finalized. To get more details on what is included, visit her website at **ItalyAncestry.com**

What Records Do You Need?

You will need birth, marriage and divorce records from both Italy and the U.S. Whether or not you need other records is determined by the consulate: "There is nothing within Italian nationality law that requires death records, census records or social security applications, all of which are sometimes asked for by the consulate to more accurately display the family unit," says Melanie.

Don't send in the original documents, as the Italian consulate will keep them—send certified copies instead. Please note that every vital record that you collect abroad and submit to the Italian consulate or Italian *comune* in Italy must be accompanied by an Italian translation and by the *apostille* legalization (in countries where the *apostille* does not exist, the documents must be legalized before the consulate). On average, expect to spend six to nine months getting your documents together, depending on how many generations are between you and the immigrant.

The consulate will also determine if your documents need to be legally amended due to misspellings or other errors. Melanie explains, "Each consulate has some leeway as far as how exact you need to be. In general, all documents for a direct ancestor must be consistent as far as the name of the ancestor, his birthdate and the names of his parents. Everything must match the ancestor's birth record. The laws in the state in which the record was issued will determine if a record can be amended, if it can be done through their vital statistics department or if a court case is needed to amend the document."

How Much Does It Cost?

The consulate charges about 300€ to apply for citizenship, although this amount is always changing. You will have to pay fees when you request documents from both Italian and American agencies. For a four-generation project, document costs would amount to about $1,000 if you do it yourself.

Genealogy and citizenship services can simplify the process for you by helping with translation, digging up elusive records, amending documents, contacting U.S. and Italian agencies, visiting Italian towns and guiding you through each step. If you use a citizenship service like *Lo Schiavo Genealogica*, expect to spend $3,000 to $5,000, depending on how far back your records need to go.

Attorney fees for the court process for the 1948 rule cases vary. If the law firm is also used for genealogy investigations, collection of the Italian and foreign documents, review of the application and translation, fees are generally around 6,000€ per case, depending on the number of generations included—so if you, your sister and your mother are all trying to get citizenship, you could split the attorney fee among you. If the law firm is used just for the application in court (while you handled the whole collection of the documents without their help) the cost is around 4,000€. In this case, on top of that, expect to pay around $3,000 to obtain documents.

Applying in Italy costs about $8,000, not including the documents, but including three month's rent and utilities, if you go through a company like *Lo Schiavo Genealogica.*

Citizenship Through Adoption

If you were adopted as a minor, either into or out of an Italian-American family, you may be eligible for citizenship. Because Italian culture and nationality law both heavily emphasize family connections, adoptees can also obtain citizenship, provided they have the same documentation and eligibility as non-adoptees.

Quintessential Italian
Sayings and Proverbs

It is always wonderful to know how to say as much as you can in the Italian language. I asked my friend *Maria Pradissitto* to share some of the most meaningful phrases, sayings and proverbs from her native Italy.

La dolce vita
This Italian saying refers to the sweet life; a life of pleasures, luxury and ease. This is the stuff of all of our dreams.

Dolce far niente
This means "the sweetness of doing nothing." It refers to the joy of relaxation without making plans.

Fare bella figura
This means "to give a good impression" and can be applied to many aspects of life. It is simply the fact of behaving, in a given circumstance, in such a way as to deserve praise for one's positive qualities. Depending on the context, these can be physical qualities (for example, you can dress to look good at a party), but more often they are moral qualities or abilities.

Natale con i tuoi, Pasqua con chi vuoi

This saying suggests who to spend the holidays with: Christmas, by tradition, is spent together with the family. Easter, on the other hand, can be spent together with friends and acquaintances.

Vivi e lascia vivere

Live and let live, which of course means to face things with tolerance.

A tavola non si invecchia

This phrase is used to say that, at the table, one feels good; that by eating, one does not feel the weight of the years.

Al cuore non si comanda

The heart always wins over the head because rationality cannot prevent you from experiencing certain sensations or emotions.

Anche l'occhio vuole la sua parte

This means that the eye is used to admire the aesthetic beauty of things. The expression is used with regard to the furnishing of rooms but also to the ornamentation and decoration of many other things such as table settings or the layout of a book.

Non è bello ciò che è bello, ma è bello ciò che piace

There is not absolute beauty; beauty is often relative. In English, this is often said as "Beauty is in the eye of the beholder."

A caval donato non si guarda in bocca

One must always be grateful for the gifts received, even if their value is not exactly what was expected. This is the Italian equivalent of the English saying, "Don't look a gift horse in the mouth."

Interview with

MICHAEL CIOFFI

Creating an *Albergo Diffuso*

Italian-American attorney Michael Cioffi grew up in Ohio, where he was the first in his family to graduate from college. Little did he know that *his dream of Italy* would take the form of creating an *albergo diffuso* (literally translated as a "scattered hotel") in 17 buildings in the town of *Castiglioncello del Trinoro* in Tuscany's stunning *Val d'Orcia. Monteverdi Tuscany* started with Michael buying just one house for his family.

Kathy McCabe: What were your impressions of Italy the first time you visited?

Michael Cioffi: The first time I visited Italy was after college. I was a liberal arts philosophy major, and of course, classically over the last couple of 100 years, if one could do so, you went to Europe and sort of did the grand tour after college. Through my education, I fell in love, but it was a little bit like computer dating. You don't really see them. So I had to go meet this love of mine. I spent a lot of time in Italy in the year between law school and undergraduate school.

For my 50th birthday, I decided to go and spend 50 days in Italy to sort of rekindle. When I came back at age 50, she was even more beautiful than I had originally thought. I fell in love with this particular village, *Castiglioncello.*

KM: Was your original intention to establish a hotel?

MC: No, not at all. I'm a lawyer and I'm not a developer or a hotelier. I bought the first house with the idea that I would restore it and then it would be a place for me to go, and at the time my father was alive and his parents were both born in Italy and immigrated from Italy.

Then another building needed to be restored and saved. Then eventually it occurred to me that it was expensive to restore these things. I had to come up with a business plan and model, and eventually landed on this idea of having a boutique hotel that's infused into this medieval village [an *albergo diffuso*]. If you walk through the village you cannot tell there's a hotel there. It truly is infused into the bones of this medieval village, which is about 800 years old. The oldest structure dates back to 1117.

KM: What sort of connection do you feel to Italy?

MC: It is an incredibly beautiful place because of the geography. In the middle part of the 20th century, these French philosophers, who were urban designers and planners and post-war philosophers, created a term called psychogeography.

In other words, from the land itself comes this incredible feeling. And it's real; it's palpable. It makes you ecstatic and happy when you see it. I think one of the secrets of the greatness of Italy is that when you look at it as just a piece of land and you go up and down the coast, and then up the mountains, almost every square mile of Italy is fascinating. There's no wasted space. It's all incredibly beautiful, and it's that beauty that's given rise to this civilization over the centuries that goes all the way back to Neolithic man.

One of the things I love about the *Val d'Orcia* is that there are caves there and *Monte Cetona*, which is a mountain that is visible from many of our rooms in the hotel and is right across the valley from *Castiglioncello.* In that mountain were cave dwellers and cave painters. There's this connection to those people who were seeing the same landscape that we see now and reacting to it by creating art. That was three millennia ago.

KM: Psychogeography. That makes so much sense.

MC: Everything comes from the environment. Everything comes from this geography, which is why we have to struggle to protect it. Everything in a society, in a civilization comes from the environment: religion, the socioeconomic structure, how people grow food and disseminate food. Their whole value system is all tied to the environment. The environment is fundamental to everything we do as human beings. And part of it is what you said, like intuitively when we see this incredible land that is Italy, we react to it in a strong way.

It's much bigger than me and it's much bigger even than Italy. This is something you want to preserve for humanity. This is something that people need to see centuries in the future. People have done that in Italy throughout the centuries and people have preserved things for centuries.

You feel this connection, not just to the geography, but to everything that's happened in that location. First of all, one thing that makes it so powerful is that the building is unchanged. The *Val d'Orcia* looks the way it looked to the Etruscans and the way it looked to these cave dwellers. This has remained pristine geography, pristine land.

KM: You grew up Italian-American. Where were your grandparents from?

MC: They were from *Caserta*, which is in southern Italy. It's in the central part of the country; very poor. We're the sons and daughters and grandsons and granddaughters of poor people. My grandfather had a girl-friend; they were both about the same age. I think he was 17 or 18 when he left to go to America. My grandfather came here, got a job in a factory and then went back and got his girlfriend, my grandmother, and they got married.

My dad, who was born in the U.S., also worked in the factories of Procter & Gamble, and it is not unusual for the first generation child of immigrants to not graduate from high school. He was a laborer his whole life, but he had a premium on doing whatever he could to give his kids a better life. Education was a premium.

KM: What have you learned about doing business in Italy?

MC: Hire a really good lawyer, because the laws are different. They're not quite the same as in the U.S. The bureaucracy is much more difficult to deal with. Then, it's really important that the people around you, whether it's your little flat in Florence or it's a farm, see you as a person who is doing your business for love or because you want to be part of that society and that culture, and that you're not an ugly American coming to sort of change everything.

KM: What was the perception of your hotel and renovations among the locals?

MC: It was very negative at first, even though I knew my intentions were purely altruistic. You just have to stay the course, and now *Monteverdi* is the largest employer in the region, providing 70 full-time jobs and supporting a lot of families. It's about investment of capital and restoring the village in a way that's authentic. You hire local workers, local architects, local engineers and historians. One of the very first things I did goes back about 10 or 12 years ago. *Castiglioncello* sits on a little extinct volcanic peak. *Castiglioncello*, roughly translated, means "little castle in the sky." There was always this folklore that there was a castle there at one time.

I eventually bought the very top of the hill as part of the purchase of another piece of property. A lot of the locals, including some architects, said, "You should just build a great house there. It has this incredible view of the *Val d'Orcia*." I said no.

I wanted to do a real authentic archaeological dig to see if I could uncover the remnants of this alleged castle. I really thought it was important to tie the village back to its roots. They said, "No, you can't do that because if you discover something, then the government will shut you down and it'll become a museum." I said, "I don't care. Then the whole top of the village will be open to the public. It will be an archaeological park." We did uncover this wall and the remnants of a tower and all the stuff inside, like wells and storage areas.

All of that's now preserved and it is an archaeological park. It is open to the public. I hired an archaeological team from the University of *Siena* and funded it completely by myself. When I did that, as opposed to building some crazy house, everyone thought, "Whoa, okay, this guy's heart is in the right place." That really helped to cement my relationship with the locals. It was about reconnecting this village to its history, to its past, because the castle walls had been buried over time.

KM: You're an opera fan. What does opera mean to you, and how has it connected you with Italy?

MC: Opera is this art form that captures this whole range in a very provocative Italian way, which is incredibly dramatic. I think the Italian operas are the best. It's an art form that I think, more perfectly than any other art form, captures the whole range of human emotion and weds it to music. I called my hotel *Monteverdi* after *Claudio Monteverdi*, who is the father of the modern opera.

Also, there's a little bit of a pun, because *Monteverdi* means green mountain. So the hotel sits on top of this green mountain surrounded by these forests. When *Claudio Monteverdi* was writing to the Pope for patronage, he would refer to himself as the green mountain.

▬▬

For more information, visit **www.monteverdituscany.com**

How Do We Actually Transform?

In the TV special and throughout this book, the stories of people who were inspired by Italy to transform their lives jump off the screen and the page.

What they all have in common is a *dream*...big or small, long brewing or spontaneous, ever evolving or incredibly specific.

During the pandemic and as I was finishing the editing of this special and writing of this book, the TV series *Dream of Italy* became enormously popular to binge watch on Amazon and other streaming channels. I received more emails and social media messages than ever from viewers about how my adventures on-screen and the stories in the episodes were helping them imagine life beyond lockdown and opening them to the possibilities of finding their roots or moving to Italy or just taking a risk to live a deeper, more authentic life.

"I thought I was in the Italy business; now I realize I'm really in the *dream* business and giving people *permission to dream*," I told a friend during this time.

"It has always been both, Italy and *the dream*," she said. "And just giving people permission to live."

This is your life. You are ultimately most accountable to yourself, not to other people, for how you spend it. As you consider your own dream and transformation, remember that you *don't* have to ask anyone for permission to dream and pursue something that makes your heart sing.

If you *do* feel like you need actual permission from someone besides yourself, drop me a note and I will send you an official *Dream of Italy* permission slip signed by yours truly! I'm not kidding. (Now, I need to create one.)

Dream It, Define It

Do you remember how much you dreamed as a kid? Tried on different possibilities for what you might do when you grew up? As we age, our dream making often diminishes. This is what I discussed recently with Sheri Salata, former executive producer of *The Oprah Winfrey Show* and the author of the best-selling memoir, *The Beautiful No: And Other Tales of Trial, Transcendence and Transformation*. Talk about someone who has sat at the feet of the masters of our time in making meaningful change.

"You've got to make an active effort to stir the dream pot, because you're not raised to keep doing that to the end of your days. You have to retrain yourself, reformat your life, so that dreaming, and creating and rut busting, and trying new things and bringing yourself fresh joy, is as important to your calendar as anything else you'll do," Sheri explains.

Sheri (**www.sherisalata.com**), who is also the founder of *The Support System*, a membership platform for women, and *Write Your Story | Transform Your Life*, a 12-week transformational course, stirred her own dream pot and discovered a *dream of Italy* in "getting paid to travel to Italy."

"It is *my dream* to spend deep, soul-full weeks in Italy on journeys of intention with like-hearted friends. Diving into new experiences. New sights. New energy. Stirring the dream pot. Feeling the rush of fresh joy. Taking my life experience to a new level of awe and wonder and appreciation," she colorfully explains.

Defining your dream, putting it into words, is powerful. Write down your dream. What words describe it best? What does it look like? What does it feel like?

Nearly every expert in manifesting and creating new lives agrees that one of the keys is to feel the emotion—gratitude, satisfaction—of already having achieved it. You have to feel it to believe, so write down what it feels like and practice that feeling.

Does your dream resonate with your purpose?

That's important, says TV host Debbie Travis. "Ask yourself what's your purpose. Many, many people come and stay with us because they think they've lost their purpose. My purpose is to have a property on a hillside in Tuscany," she adds.

Through her Tuscan retreats and writing, she also helps others, especially at mid-life, focus on what's next. Her book *Design Your Next Chapter: How to Realize Your Dreams and Reinvent Your Life* is a must for anyone looking for something new (**www.debbietravis.com**).

Visualization is also important in defining and manifesting a dream. Sarah Centrella (**www.sarahcentrella.com**), master life coach and mani-fester, found "seeing" a dream for herself on Pinterest helped her truly believe the place she had dreamed about all the way back to her difficult childhood was surely within reach.

"I would go on there and look at pictures of Tuscany. What did people do in Tuscany? What do the markets look like? What does harvest look like? If I spent an hour doing that, my brain was transported. I was able to kind of let go of all those constraints about reality, like who, what, where, when, how, why, and just say, 'Wouldn't that be amazing? I want that,'" she says.

Sarah uses this tool with her clients and in making "future boards," about which she has written a book, *#FutureBoards: Learn How to Create a Vision Board to Get Exactly the Life You Want.*

When I first connected with 10-time *New York Times* best-selling author David Bach (**www.davidbach.com**), I excitedly told him I had watched him many years ago on *The Oprah Winfrey Show.*

During our TV interview I said, "I remember watching you on *Oprah* and then when I finally met you and we were having lunch, I said, 'Did you always imagine you'd be on *Oprah* or was it a surprise?' And you said, 'I imagined that 300 times in my head, maybe 3,000 times, before it happened.'"

"We manifest our life," David reiterates. For David, imagining the dream happening again and again has been a most powerful tool.

Taking Responsibility

One thing that expat retiree Sally Carrocino and I discuss when we meet in Florence is that other people often express envy for her life and tell her how "lucky" she is.

"When people tell me I'm so lucky to live in Florence, I correct them because it's not luck," Sally says vehemently.

"Luck is going out and finding a bus. I'm fortunate because I created this to happen and it just didn't happen overnight. It's work and you've got to be committed to it and have a passion for it. I feel incredible gratitude and fortunate that I had the gumption to do it. I didn't want to wake up some day and think, 'I wish I did,'" Sally adds.

When someone assumes that another person's achievements are mostly the result of luck, it can let that person off the hook from striving for their own dreams, if he or she doesn't feel "lucky."

I understand how Sally feels being told she is simply lucky, when her new life is really the result of her actions. I receive many very well-meaning comments about how "lucky" I am to do the work I do with *Dream of Italy.* Yes, I feel so very grateful. But I created this brand nearly two decades ago and put so much blood, sweat and tears into it. Plus, I made many sacrifices while creating my own opportunities.

I believe(d) in myself and my dreams.

I also went through enormous personal challenges in the years I was building *Dream of Italy,* something I haven't discussed much. Any one of these challenges would have been a viable "excuse" for not moving forward.

You can't achieve transformation if you're an excuse-making machine. All of the people you see as successful also likely had many things that could have derailed them, but they wouldn't allow it.

Taking a big step towards doing something new or transforming also requires you to trust yourself, which is a skill you can build, Sheri tells me.

"You have to coax yourself into becoming the trustworthy steward of your own well-being," Sheri explains.

"You have to understand that all of those things, the bigs and the littles, drinking eight glasses of water a day, are most definitely tied to loving yourself and your feelings of worthiness."

"So, all the little practices that I call 'esteemable practices' are things where you're respecting yourself, you're treasuring yourself, you're cherishing yourself, you're taking care of yourself. Next thing you know, your esteem has risen, your feeling of worthiness has risen, and then it all gets easier."

Telling It Loud

What good is your dream or even your full-fledged plan if it is your little secret? Even a secret you hide from yourself?

Sarah says making a declaration of her dream to travel to Italy with her kids the first time, even as a struggling single mom, was a powerful sign to the universe that she was serious, and after that things lined up.

"Four days after this declaration, I get an airfare alert saying that flights to Italy had dropped by 50%. And because I'd been getting them for so long, I knew what prices normally were from my city. I knew it was dramatic. I was like, 'Oh my God, this is crazy.' I also knew it was a direct sign and it was directly testing me to see just how in I was," she explains.

"I thought, 'Okay, I'm about to take pretty much every dollar I have and buy four tickets to Italy with no plan.' And I did. It was very scary, but it was the most amazing thing that we ever did. And, of course, the rest of it worked out. That's how it always happens once you act on faith and take the opportunities that are in front of you. The kids and I spent three weeks in Italy," says Sarah.

My friend Glenn Main, founder of The Main Point (**www.themain-point.com**), helps private business owners with strategic problem solving, particularly after reaching success. Even though they've "made it," they often face new blocks and challenges that Glenn coaches them to overcome.

Little did I know when I told him about my new special *Dream of Italy: Travel, Transform and Thrive,* or TTT for short, that he also has a T3 philosophy. His is "tell the truth," which means talk to others about your dream so you can have accountability and others keeping you on track.

Of course accountability is a wonderful byproduct of spreading the news of your dream far and wide, but talking about it can also bring in unexpected connections and help.

"I also think it's like that old prayer. It's that old thing that says when you pray, move your feet. It's all about taking action," says Alatia Bach.

"I called everyone I knew that had any connection to Italy and I was like, 'I'm moving to Florence,'" she shares. Through that process she found a friend of a friend in Florence who not only helped her find a real estate agent but also helped with the plans for the boys' international school. Later this even helped her with their visa. The funny thing is some of these people were mutual friends of ours.

A mutual friend also connected me with David, whom I didn't know before, and that's how he and his family ended up in this TV special. It is a small world and talking about your dreams can bring you the assistance you need.

Pick a Date

"If your heart is telling you right now that you'd like a radical sabbatical, that you'd like to move to Italy, start by picking a date. Literally pick a date. It could be three years from now, four years from now, five years from now, and then you work backwards," David tells me.

This is one of my favorite quotes from the TV special because the advice is so simple, yet powerful, and applies to any goal.

Glenn agrees that picking a date is a must. He has another 3-pronged mantra: D3 or D-cubed stands for "deadlines demand decisions."

"Let's pull out our calendars, and let's mark a date and decide what's going to happen on or before that date," he says, noting that "some people get decision tremor, which is, 'Oh my God, what if I can't get it done by then?' And I say, 'Move the date.'"

Though you may need to be flexible, the important part, Glenn says, is "you're deciding to do something, and you're being accountable to a deadline."

All planning flows from the date for accomplishing the goal. The plan can be broken down into steps that seem more manageable than going from 0 to 100 in one fell swoop.

Preparing Financially

Of course, David's career has been devoted to teaching others how to create the financial freedom to live rich lives.

"What you need to do is open a dream account, an account that literally you put money from every paycheck into that account," he says.

This is exactly what Sally and her late husband did to fund their travels to Italy.

"After our first trip we decided that we needed a trip account. Every month we'd each write a check for $500 and we would look forward to writing that check. By the time we were ready to go, we had the money. You know, we didn't have to worry about a huge credit card bill because we had the money," Sally says.

I think it is also important to keep in mind something Glenn believes strongly.

"You own your future. The future is your property. So if you understand your future as your property, how do you handle it? How do you treat it? What is it that you're going to do with your own future?" he says.

Glenn's C3 philosophy, which is "cash creates confidence," also helps would-be transformers concentrate more heavily on what they have to gain from fulfilling their dreams.

"Cash doesn't have to mean money, but it does a lot of times. It means that you can point to a reward, an accomplishment, an achievement or a monetary gain. Something actually happened as a result of all the effort that you went through to tell the truth, set deadlines, make the first decisions and act upon them," he notes.

What Stops Us?

Fear is probably the greatest enemy of transformation.

"I think the number one point for anybody who's got a dream or a vision or a seed of an idea is fear. But when you write a list of fears, then you start seeing they will all be negative. Then you have to decide what is a real fear and what is an excuse," Debbie explains.

Debbie also encourages her readers and retreat goers to make a list of positives of your dream coming to fruition.

Every decision we make in life is usually to the exclusion of something else we could choose, and that can be daunting.

"Change represents loss," Glenn explains.

"Change doesn't represent gain. We want to think of it as gain, but we always see the loss. Even positive change usually means loss," he adds.

Glenn's C3—"cash creates confidence"—actually "helps to maintain this ability to lose or accept loss," he says. You must remember that there are both practical and meaningful rewards on the other side of transformation.

Interview with

DEBBIE TRAVIS

Designing Her Next Chapter in Tuscany

Debbie Travis' stunning *Villa Reniella* in *Montefollonico*, Tuscany, might be one of the most beautiful places I have ever seen in Italy—and I've been everywhere. The views alone! Debbie, a self-taught interior decorator who was featured numerous time on *The Oprah Winfrey Show*, hosted one of North America's first home decorating TV shows, *Debbie Travis' Painted House*. Together with her husband, Hans Rosenstein, she now heads a television production company. Debbie also runs retreats in Tuscany geared toward women as well as vacations at her villa with food, wine and wellness themes. She's the author of the books *Design Your Next Chapter: How to Realize Your Dreams and Reinvent Your Life* and *Joy: Lessons From a Tuscan Villa*.

Kathy McCabe: Why did you want to buy a place in Tuscany?

Debbie Travis: We were filming in the *Cinque Terre* and we suddenly looked down at one of these little villages, which was known as a painted village. As we were filming, out of a doorway across the road came a woman in maybe her 60s and started shouting at us in Italian. What she was saying was, "What are you doing working? It's lunchtime." We said, "Well, we're from North America. That's what we do." And she said, "You come and have lunch. You come in my house."

So we went inside. There was family and friends, and they were on a balcony looking over the sea, the Mediterranean, and I think I had the best meal I've ever had.

One evening, at the end of this trip, the crew had gone off somewhere and we were sitting in a bar. And we were just watching the world in a *piazza* go 'round and my husband said those magic words: "What if?"

I knew exactly what he meant: "What if we bought something in Italy?" That was the nugget, the goal, the dream that started to come into fruition. It began with looking for a property as a family home that we could maybe use as a holiday house, and we didn't know where to go.

We honed in on an area, and my husband decided to go to language school. While he was at language school, I went for a walk and I saw this old dusty villa. In the meantime, like many of us when we have a dream that is a seed of an idea, it tends to get a life of its own.

Then I was being interviewed on the West Coast—I often do public speaking to women in business and I was talking to about 1,500 women— and the interviewer said to me, "What is next for Debbie Travis?" I don't know where this came from, but I said, "Well, I am going to be inviting women of all ages from all around the world to stay with me at my villa in Tuscany and we'll do yoga in the lavender field; we'll hike through the olive groves."

KM: You have said you don't speak Italian very well. How did you work the system?

DT: Well, my husband does. But they're very, very open, the Italians, and they like the fact that you like their country. I find that different in other countries; you feel like a real intruder. In Italy, it's the other way around. They are so welcoming. They apologize to me for not speaking

English, which I find remarkable. I'm very embarrassed by not speaking Italian. I just don't have the brain.

I believe that if you have this idea of purchasing something in Italy that like any project or any next chapter, you can talk yourself out of everything. If you go into this going, "Oh, I don't speak your language. Oh, I don't want to work with permits. I don't want to work with that kind of bureaucracy," then you're never going to do it. But if you go in going, "Look at the weather, look at the food, look at the wine, look at the people," then that stays with you all the time. Nowhere's perfect, but you have to dwell on the stuff that you love.

KM: That is great advice. What was the hardest thing about moving to Italy?

DT: Most of us see Tuscany in the photographs and it's blue skies and cypress trees and fabulous swimming pools. Well, the first shocker was February, and sleet and snow. I was camping with these guys in this property and that's when I think the first breaking point was, when I was alone and the weather was damp and dismal and the novelty was starting to wear off.

Also, when you rent, especially in Tuscany, you can rent these magnificent places that are 25 minutes down a dirt road—amazing when you're renting. Not when you're living there. Our property turned out to be a really good find because it's an eight-minute walk from the village. You've got everything in this beautiful medieval village, but you're out of it enough without the gossip and everybody knowing what underwear you wear.

KM: When people go on retreats with you, how does their life change?

DT: I think it's a mixture of things. First, I designed this originally 10 years ago mostly for women—we have men as well—but a place where women could come on their own because a lot of women don't have anybody to go away with. When you go on holiday alone, what does a woman do? It can be lonely.

I said to myself, "I want to solve that problem." So, Tuscany is famous for the long tables. It's the dream: everybody eating together, shouting at one end of the table, food being passed up and down. So I organized the trips so people could come by themselves and meet other people.

KM: What do you love about Italians?

DT: I think there's a sense of happiness. But it's not the over-the-top happy. So when somebody says to me, "Hi, how are you doing?" I'll say, "Do you really want to know? Because I'm having a really bad day and I feel like crap." And they back away from you. But in Italy, they ask and they tell.

You have to fit that into your lifestyle because you go to the post office in America, that's one of 20 chores you've got for the day. Forget it in Italy. Three weeks ago I was standing in the post office and there's a guy there with his chicken and he starts telling me about his chicken. A real chicken on a string, and it's a very precious chicken, apparently. And then this goes on, and on, and on, and then he asks me if I want to come back and see the other chicken. How do you say no? So I go back and then I end up having a cup of tea or coffee and then I ended up having dinner there.

All our devices have saved us during the lockdowns and this miserable time we've had, and what do we crave? We crave people. We crave community. That is what happens when you go to Italy, because the Italians are the nosiest people on the planet. An Italian will ask you who you are, what you're doing, how much you earn and why you're there. That's the way they are.

—

For more information, visit **www.debbietravis.com** and **www.tuscangetaway.com**

So You Dream of Moving to Italy?

It's easy to get lured in by the dream of taking the leap to move to Italy. Who hasn't entertained the thought of ditching the rat race to live a painterly life in Venice or a retiree's fantasy in the Tuscan or Umbrian countryside? Or the Ligurian coastline, the frenetic-but-fascinating center of Rome, an off-grid corner of *Calabria*—you get the idea.

The inspiring guests featured in the TV special are living proof of the dream's benefits and the perks of either taking what David Bach called a "radical sabbatical" or making a more permanent move. With grit, patience, careful research, saving and some strokes of good timing, your dream can come true, just as theirs did. But before you book a one-way ticket and pack your bags, armed with little more than the seductive promise of *la dolce vita*, dedicate some time to determining whether an Italy move is, in fact, what you really want.

You don't need me to tell you that Italy is a country of untold beauty, culture and history. But any time we stay somewhere longer than we would on vacation, even when it's against an idyllic or intellectually stimulating backdrop, we will still have to pay bills, pick up the dry cleaning, deal with freak plumbing accidents, navigate health scares, dispute credit card transactions and line up in DMV-like public offices. Are you prepared to confront these more mundane elements of everyday life in a land that isn't your own? While speaking a foreign language? Without the built-in emotional support systems you've cultivated over years in your own community?

People in Italy may enjoy a slower pace of life overall, but they don't live problem-free. Are you willing to deal with how the slower pace translates in business settings? Bureaucratic appointments? Transportation?

Beyond the fact that daily inconveniences don't disappear in Italy, it's also important to consider the psychological and emotional challenges that any international move can involve. For many, these challenges are part of the appeal, and great growth can indeed come from them. But ask yourself if you're prepared to work through them when they inevitably arise.

As Arlene Antoinette Gibbs puts it, moving to a foreign country won't magically make any personal issues you have in your home country disappear. "You have to be realistic about why you're moving here," Arlene says. "If you have to work here, if you don't have a trust fund or even if you're moving because you met this amazing Italian man, you might think you won't need to figure out what you're going to do day to day. But you need to think about it. You need to have a sense of purpose."

Sally Carrocino, who keeps herself busy in Florence even amid retirement, echoes Arlene's sentiment: "If you don't have a sense of purpose, what's it all about?"

It's not to say that everything must be 100% figured out before you take the plunge. Any change of this magnitude requires some level of risk and uncertainty to reap its rewards. Considering the implications and the nuts-and-bolts practicalities of making a "dream move" happen can feel daunting and discourage you from even trying. That's not what we're here to do. But give it real thought, even when it may be uncomfortable. Weigh your options and take the planning process one day at a time. As Sally reminds us, "I'm not 'lucky' to live in Florence, I'm fortunate. It took work! It didn't happen overnight."

Go to Italy For a Trial Run

One way to get a clearer sense of whether the day-to-day Italian life-style might work for you over the long term is to enjoy a three-month trial run. American citizens are allowed to enter the Schengen zone of the European Union, to which Italy belongs, for up to 90 out of every 180 days as a tourist, with no visa required.

That means you could potentially spend six (non-continuous) months in Italy annually, paperwork-free. You can take courses, enjoy community events and begin building a network of personal connections and even initial professional contacts. The key thing you are prohibited from doing as a tourist is conducting official business.

"It's a good approach if you're not sure yet," attorney *Michele Capecchi*, managing partner at *Capecchi Legal*, explains. "See if you like it before committing to all the paperwork. If you just come as a tourist, as long as you stay here within that specific limit of time, you don't have to worry about documents or pay taxes."

If you make a three-month trial run, resist the urge to plan out a detailed itinerary or to overexert yourself with sightseeing. This period should be about getting a sense of how locals live and how you might feel as one yourself. Expat coach Damien O'Farrell (**www.damienofarrell.com**), who has worked out of Rome for three decades and has coached 10,000 people on moving to Italy, is a major advocate of the trial run when done right.

"Ninety days, if you really live the life in Italy, is good for allowing you to see if you could do it over the long term," he says. But "living the life" doesn't mean frolicking around the *Fontana di Trevi*: "I tell people, go to the post office," Damien adds. "If you haven't been given patience, karmically, this is going to teach you patience. See what it's like to line up for an hour and take two hours to pay three bills. Rent a car and see what it's like to find parking! Do all the things that you would do living here, really testing the waters."

Testing the waters of local living is key, as a garden-variety vacation to Italy is much like the first blush of romance: Every day is new; every activity and conversation is exciting. But in the honeymoon phase, you haven't seen how your new partner behaves under stress and how attentive he or she is to the laundry, so to speak. Before you make a long-term commitment to Italy, take off your rose-colored glasses and learn what she's like when the going gets tough. A three-month trial stay will help with this. Sally reminds us, "If it doesn't work, it doesn't work! You can always do something else."

The period is short enough to be rather low-stakes, but long enough that you will be able to get a sense of how you manage the language barrier, how you handle yourself when your hot water heater gives out mid-shower (and it happens to everyone eventually) and where, geographically and socially, could realistically fit you and your needs. What might this look like in the practical sense?

John Henderson, a retired journalist in Rome, has thoughts about what you should prioritize doing during your trial run. "Do a fact-finding or a recon mission," he says. "Pretend you're looking at apartments and answer ads, just to get a sense of how it works and what the market is like. Take a pen and paper and write down all the things you need to live here. Go to the grocery stores, see how much the food costs; go to the public transportation centers, see how much the transportation pass costs. How much does a movie cost? A theatre or a gym membership? Italian lessons? Get all the basics and get a number on how much you're going to need to live each month."

If you get halfway into your trial run and already have a clear sense that returning permanently is what you want, it might be strategic to move beyond pretending to inquire about apartments or other properties and instead to start searching in earnest. Use word of mouth; take note of *Vendesi* and *Affittasi* (selling and renting) signs outside buildings; and explore your local listings, filtering your search parameters to properties that fit with the timing of your potential move. (Accept that this can be complicated for renters, as most landlords, once they publicly advertise their properties, are looking to get them rented, well, yesterday.)

Take down contact information and communicate openly about your projected timeline. After all, if you're not an EU citizen, proof of suitable accommodation is a requirement for issuance of virtually all visas, to be discussed in a subsequent section. It's often one of the more complicated boxes to check off, since property searching from afar can be risky. In other words, take advantage of your time on the ground! (But to ensure *you* aren't taken advantage of, have a trusted Italian speaker look over any agreements before you sign anything.)

During your trial run, it's crucial to remember that the "Italian lifestyle" is not monolithic. Your circumstances—as a retiree, a freelancer, a lifelong learner enrolled in a course of study—will greatly influence your day to day, just as your geography will. Food, wine and beauty may be constants up and down the Boot, but Italian life looks very different in downtown Milan than it does in, say, rural *Campania*.

Damien walks people through these kinds of considerations before giving tailored guidance, encouraging his clients to take a hard look at their five-year Italy plan. He says candidly that he sees many people underestimate the difficulties they will face if they don't speak, or commit to learning to speak, Italian. The importance of asking yourself what it is you want out of your Italian life, and being pragmatic and self-aware in your answer, really can't be overstated.

To illustrate, Damien recalls working with a New York couple on sorting out immigration logistics for a move to small-town *Calabria*. These were "real New Yorkers," he said, who fed off the excitement of nights at the theatre and new restaurant openings before burning out on big-city life and deciding they wanted a major change.

But Damien remembers checking in about nine months after the couple made the move and learning that they both felt isolated and unstimulated. The husband was at a loss as to how to support his wife, who was suffering from a sudden onset of depression. "It comes down to what you are looking for," Damien says, and being honest with yourself about your needs. No one makes a major move because they want their life to look exactly the same, but you will still be you in Italy. What are the things that you currently enjoy, that feed you? Does the Italian setting that you are looking at moving to give you space to recreate them in a new location?

City Versus Countryside

Not everyone who moves to a rural setting may struggle in the same ways the New York couple did. "If you want a quiet, bucolic lifestyle, simplicity, maybe Internet that comes and goes, in a small town; if you don't feel that you need much in terms of entertainment, or maybe just sitting in the *piazza* is enough entertainment for you, then I think you could be very happy in a more remote setting," Damien says. But even then, consider: Are your language skills up to snuff for chit-chatting in the *piazza*? If not, "that could be a very isolating way to live," Damien puts it bluntly.

Perhaps you're a social singleton or a couple who looks forward to inviting new friends into your home for dinner. Have you taken a hard look at the demographics of the towns you're considering? It's not easy to play host or hostess when the local population might be made up of reserved types who've known the same people for decades, and who spend most of their social energy on their immediate families or their grand-children. Family is everything in Italy, and while family can certainly look any way one wants it to, it might be easier to build those connections and find a circle of friends in a city with a dynamic mix of foreigners and internationally minded Italians, the way Arlene did in Rome.

Arlene notes that in Italy she feels less pressure to couple up and less of a stigma around being a childfree woman than she did in Los Angeles. "That may surprise people, because family is so important in Italy, but the concept of family is different. There are many ways to define what it means," she says. Arlene's experience is not unique; many expats describe a similar sense of freedom and lifestyle validation in their new home. But it's best taken in context: The truth of being able to define family how you want might be easier to live out in a metropolis than in *Molise*, for example.

Moreover, even if you can get a group of new friends gathered around the table in small-town *Calabria* or a remote corner of *Basilicata*, you may find that relating to one another is challenging. Here you are, an outsider from a faraway place who's made a radical life change, sharing a meal with folks who may have a more provincial outlook.

Both sides can benefit from each other's perspective, and you've presumably come to Italy seeking something that you can't get in your gatherings around the table stateside. Still, it's important to honestly assess whether those sorts of social connections will be satisfying over the long term.

Realistic balance and having a sense of what works for you is the key to success in your Italian dream. David and Alatia Bach's Florentine fairytale speaks to this. David emphasizes how he and Alatia had spent the bulk of their lives in major cities, and so knew they wanted to be in a city, but a "quieter, more manageable and maybe even friendlier" place than New York.

Alatia gets real about the urban versus rural choice that the family debated. "We did think about being up in the hills and living this pastoral life, but being from Manhattan, we got a little nervous, so we came down to the city," she says. "Florence is small; there's only about 300,000 people here, but it attracts a wide range of intellectuals, not just college kids. And you meet [lifelong learners] from all over the world."

If, like the Bachs, you thrive on meeting new people and exploring a place's cultural offerings—or if, like them, you want those kinds of experiences for your children—you're probably better suited to one of the big-ticket towns than to farmhouse living. Plus, in a city, you're more likely to find an international school for your children to attend.

Beyond social and cultural stimulation, there are practical issues of access to consider when you're thinking about remote locations. While Italy's public healthcare system is renowned, if you decide to age out of place like Sally is doing, you need to ensure that you're within easy reach of a major hospital and other medical infrastructure.

What's more, within both the public and private healthcare systems in Italy, you're likely to find English-speaking medical professionals and

Anglo-friendly resources in areas that have heavy populations of international students, transplants and tourists. But even in Florence or Venice, a nearby English speaker is never a guarantee in any given emergency. Think about how much that will be compounded in an ancestral village in *Abruzzo*!

Cost of Living Considerations

Whatever your motivation for moving to Italy, cost of living is always a top concern when making the transition. For many, life in Italy is more affordable than life in the U.S. But that's not always the case. Healthcare (and happy hour cocktails) may burn less of a hole in your pocket than they would in most U.S. cities, but savings in some areas come with upticks in others (household utilities like gas and electricity, all the administrative fees associated with making the move and so forth).

Keeping these factors in mind, here is a loose overview of what a retired couple might reasonably expect to spend in an average month, in two very different parts of the country. At the time of publication, the conversion rate for 1€ is $1.18 but be sure to check the current exchange rate at **www.xe.com**

FLORENCE

Naturally, the cost of living in a big city like Florence will be higher than in rural areas.

Rent: Average 16.10€ per square meter per month (central Florence); 15€ per square meter per month (outside center). Nice two-bedroom apartments can be had for 1,500 to 1,800€ downtown.

Healthcare in the national system (*Servizio Sanitario Nazionale*): Holders of elective residence stay permits can opt for the *iscrizione volontaria* (voluntary enrollment) option in the public healthcare system, paying an annual contribution of 7.5% of their previous year's income (for incomes up to 20,658.28€) or 4% for higher incomes.

One-off medical checkup at private practice: Around 70 to 100€

Utilities: 185€ (averaged monthly: gas, water, electricity)

Groceries: 300€

Car insurance (referred to as *polizza RCA*, or *responsabilità civile auto*): 41€ monthly

Gasoline for car: 1.80€ per liter

Public transportation pass: 35€

Dinner for two at a low-key *trattoria*: 60€

Dinner for two at a more upscale restaurant: 120€

Coffee and *cornetto* at a casual bar: 2.50€

CASERTA PROVINCE IN CAMPANIA

This pricing is for life in the countryside; living in the city of *Caserta* itself would be a bit costlier.

Rent: Average 6€ per square meter per month; two-bedroom apartments in countryside towns like *Casertavecchia* can be found for 250€

Healthcare in the national system (*Servizio Sanitario Nazionale*): Holders of elective residence stay permits can opt for the *iscrizione volontaria* (voluntary enrollment) option in the public healthcare system, paying an annual contribution of 7.5% of their previous year's income (for incomes up to 20,658.28€) or 4% for higher incomes.

One-off medical checkup at private practice: Around 70 to 100€

Utilities: 185€ (averaged monthly)

Groceries: 220€

Car insurance (referred to as *polizza RCA*, or *responsabilità civile auto*): 77.50€ monthly

Gasoline for car: 1.50€ per liter

Public transportation pass (all of *Campania*): 42€

Dinner for two at a low-key *trattoria:* 40€

Dinner for two at a more upscale restaurant: 80€

Coffee and *cornetto* at a casual bar: 1.20€

Don't Dismiss Part-Time

Not sure a full-on move is right for you? Of course, many Americans get their annual or semi-annual fix on vacation, without needing to totally uproot themselves. There are even some who take it a step further and make half time in Italy, half time at home their annual reality.

The Bachs never considered part-timing a viable option, since they have children in school, but they have met many in Florence who have made it work. "We've met people who do six months out of the year here, six months out of the year there, even one couple that does three months in Florence, three months in *Puglia*, and they've done that for 25 years," says Alatia. (It's worth reiterating: Those are two separate three-month stints, not one continuous six-month stay, which would require a visa.)

Being a part-timer in Italy has many of the benefits of being a regular without the bureaucratic complications of being a resident. As a regular presence in your Italian location of choice, you will develop relationships and favored spots, and will enjoy many of the benefits of being a "local" who sticks around longer than the average vacationer, while also becoming part of a large, far-flung community of people who love Italy around the world like so many in the *Dream of Italy* audience.

"I think personally that this can be a good balance for some people," Damien says. "They enjoy the 90 days in Italy but then they're happy to go back to the U.S."

Michele Capecchi reminds us that it's entirely possible "to come to Italy just to enjoy it" while keeping the creature comforts, conveniences and familiarity of the U.S. within reach.

Kathy and attorney *Michele Capecchi*

Obtaining a Visa to Live in Italy

Immigration law is the nail in the coffin of many a move-to-Italy dream. But it's not impossible to navigate with the right amount of determination, a lawyer ally in your corner and the patience to deal with some inevitable setbacks. Those reading this and contemplating a move will generally fall into one of three categories: (1) those "unicorns" with an Italian or European Union passport at the ready, (2) those with a viable path to Italian or EU citizenship and (3) the majority, those with no current path to citizenship who will have to consider what visas will make their dream possible.

If you already hold citizenship in Italy—or any country within the European Union—then you can take a large amount of elbow grease out of the equation. Italian citizens have the right to reside indefinitely and to work not only in Italy, but also in any EU member state. With an international move, there will of course still be kinks to iron out, but those with an Italian or EU passport are primed for a much smoother path.

Note: The information contained in this section gives a general overview of these processes and visas, but is not intended to be comprehensive and does not constitute legal advice.

Arlene Antoinette Gibbs, for example, holds a French passport and says that many Americans quiz her about how she pulled off her move, immigration- and work permit-wise, not realizing that she holds the automatic right to work as an EU citizen.

"I know nothing about the process of getting a work permit, sorry!" she admits with laughter. But people in her circles do, and Arlene raises an important point about steering clear of an entitled mindset. "There's still a little bit of this attitude of, 'Oh, I'm American, I'm not really an immigrant.' Well, yeah, you are. Are you Italian? No? You're an immigrant."

Arlene explains that while there may have been more of a free-for-all approach to borders and international jobs in decades past, today, overstaying the 90-day tourist allowance for American citizens is not tolerated and, beyond the obvious legal and ethical problems involved, hanging out without any access to public systems or benefits is simply no way to live sustainably. "The authorities really do keep track," Arlene says. "So figure out your visa situation; where there's a will, there's a way."

Now, that may sound easy coming from an "EU unicorn." But plenty of non-unicorns have figured it out with time and commitment: Sally Carrocino fell into category three above and was able to obtain an elective residence visa.

No matter what type of visa you ultimately procure, it's important to note that once you're on the ground in Italy, the visa itself is no longer valid as a stand-alone document. Instead, the visa is the precursor to the *permesso di soggiorno* (permit of stay). Within eight working days of your arrival in Italy, you must go to a post office in the *comune* (municipality) where you're residing and ask for a kit to apply for your *permesso*. The permit of stay will denote a purpose for your time in Italy, which will be identical to the purpose for which your visa was issued (study, work, elective residence and so forth).

In simple terms, the visa is what gets you into the country, while the *permesso* is what keeps you there. After you submit your application and supporting documents via the post office, your kit will be sent off to the immigration authorities. You will eventually receive a summons, either via SMS (text message) or registered postal mail, to an initial appointment in the *ufficio immigrazione* of your local *questura* (the immigration office of your local police headquarters) for fingerprints and photos. If everything is in order, you will later (often many months later) receive an SMS indicating that your *permesso* is ready to be picked up.

In most cases, your *permesso* can be renewed as long as you continue to meet the requirements that you met when it was issued. In some cases, your *permesso* can be converted into a longer-term visa—an example of this is transitioning it from a student permit to a work permit. Florence-based journalist Mary Gray, who arrived in Italy as a student but later converted to worker status upon getting a job offer, explains, "My original visa is from 2013. But I have been renewing my *permesso di soggiorno* for the past near-decade, and just recently obtained my long-term residence permit." From a practical standpoint, this also means that once you are on the ground in Italy, the Italian consulate that issued your visa has done its job. Therefore, any *permesso*-related queries you may have should be directed to the immigration office of your local *questura* or to an attorney.

Here is a general, noncomprehensive overview of the main types of visas that can get U.S. citizens with ordinary circumstances into the country for stays of longer than 90 days. All can be requested at the Italian consulate that has jurisdiction over your current city, state or territory of residence. Check which consulate has jurisdiction over your area at **www.bit.ly/italianconsulates**

Visa Types

STUDENT VISA (*Visto per Studio*)

Although nothing is ever guaranteed, student visas are, on the whole, one of the more straightforward types of moving-to-Italy paperwork one can obtain. That said, if it has been decades since you were in school, consider that you may have a more complicated time trying to obtain one than someone who has a clear need to study Italian or Italian culture for their job, or who is continuing their education after previous, related academic experience.

To obtain a student visa, generally you need to be able to demonstrate that you are enrolling in a university or an accredited private program that entails at least 20 hours per week of study commitments.

Not all study programs are created equal and not all study programs will provide a pathway to a visa. As fun as it may sound to take cooking classes with a Neapolitan *nonna*, small or private courses of that sort generally won't suffice. Whether you're looking at a private language school, a cinema course, an in-depth culinary class at an accredited institution or pursuing a graduate degree of some kind, you need to ensure that the school you're applying to is formally recognized by the Italian Ministry of Education (abbreviated as MIUR in Italian).

Reputable programs will be familiar with the process of issuing acceptance letters for you to present in your application for the student visa. Your visa will only be issued for the length of the course or program(s) you've enrolled in. The acceptance letter generally also states the level of commitment the course requires (it should be 20 hours/week at least). Some consulates may also need to see that you have paid for the courses in full.

One potential obstacle to issuance of the student visa is the finances you have on hand. You need to be able to show that you have enough money in the bank to support yourself for the duration of your stay. Be aware that study abroad programs that run over 90 days, full Italian university programs, independent courses on Italian language or culture and training programs will all have different economic requirements. Check the website of the consulate where you will be applying, which may give you an idea of the minimum amount.

Keep in mind, also, that base amounts offered as a guideline realistically may not be enough for most adults to live on, at least not in attractive university towns like *Bologna*, *Pisa*, Florence, Venice, *Perugia* or Rome. The minimum is likely given with traditional twentysomething students in mind, many of whom have parental support or live in shared housing.

You will also need to show proof of suitable accommodation for the length of your stay. Florence-based attorney *Michele Capecchi* notes that this is one of the main hurdles to overcome in getting a visa of any kind. Consider that study programs with more hands-on approaches might be able to help with this, as some of them offer assistance with finding housing or setting their students up with host families.

It is a good idea to start the application process for your student visa at least three months ahead of your planned arrival in Italy. Processing times can vary considerably.

ADVANTAGES OF STUDENT VISAS

- Taking a course (or several) is a perfect way to dive deep into the Italian language and culture and to enrich your understanding of your surroundings. The student visa option is also a clear favorite for long-stay but not permanent residents who want to make the most of their time in Italy.
- Italian language schools, in particular, cater to students of all demographics, nationalities and motivations. You're likely to quickly meet an interesting group of people upon arrival and have a welcoming community to plug into as you settle into Italy.
- Many schools will be willing to help you with getting a handle on everyday life logistics.
- When you're in Italy on a student visa, you are permitted to work for up to 20 hours per week (for a total not exceeding 1,040 hours per year). If you're lucky enough to find a part-time gig, this can mitigate the cost of studying while offering a glimpse into what Italian work culture is like.
- If you're hoping to later convert your student permit to a work permit, using this time as a student to network, put out feelers

and perhaps even prove yourself indispensable to one particular company through part-time work might give you an advantage.

DISADVANTAGES OF STUDENT VISAS

- Private programs and language schools can be expensive and time consuming. Do not go down the student visa route if you're doing it primarily as a means to an end; make sure that you're actually excited about and intrigued by the course(s) you're signing up for, as you will need to attend regularly. *Capecchi* cautions that consulates will be wary of applicants who appear to want a student visa simply as a way of staying in Italy longer than 90 days. He also recommends that students independently attending a course should be prepared to show the purpose of the course they plan to attend and to demonstrate how it is connected to their previous studies or professional background—why they "need" to come to study in Italy versus taking a course in the U.S. Applicants should also always be aware that submitting all the required documentation never guarantees the issuance of any particular visa.

- Renewing a *permesso di soggiorno per motivi di studio* (study permit) can also have its complications. Generally, you need to be able to show the immigration office of the local *questura* of your town of residence that you are advancing in some way. This could mean indicating you've passed an exam if enrolled at an Italian university, or that you're progressing to the next level of Italian study at a language school, for example. You also cannot change institutions or programs, with only rare exceptions provided for.

- There is a finite amount of progress you can make in any given study program, and indeed, student visas can't be renewed indefinitely.

Even if you have an undergraduate and graduate degree, having those doesn't preclude the possibility of obtaining another (far more economical) degree at an Italian university. Teaching formats and university life in Italy are remarkably different from college life back home. You won't be living in a campus bubble with dormitories and Greek life, clubs and coeds. The campus as we know it in the U.S. doesn't exist in most Italian university contexts. Different buildings for different *facoltà* (departments) are instead dispersed around their host cities. Residential life is virtually nonexistent—think of all Italian universities as commuter campuses.

At the outset, applying to an Italian university in the hope of obtaining a *titolo di studio* (degree), such as a *laurea magistrale*, requires more bureaucratic hoop-jumping and linguistic prowess than applying to a for-profit language school or similar program, which is a bit more straightforward.

But patience with this process can have its payoff in the long run: (1) advancing toward a degree might help ease the process of renewing your study *permesso;* (2) costs of Italian university are, on the whole, considerably lower than in many private programs; (3) if you're hoping to stay in Italy after your program ends, some privileges are afforded to non-EU citizens who earn degrees from Italian universities on Italian soil, including the possibility to convert your study *permesso* to a work *permesso* outside of the annual quota system for foreign workers, a concept explained in the section on work visas.

If you wish to enroll at an Italian university, you will need to obtain a *dichiarazione di valore*, literally translated as "declaration of value." This is a lengthy document that attests to the validity of your U.S. degree(s) on Italian soil and elaborates on the content of the courses you took. (Fair warning: This process involves procuring transcripts from your undergraduate university, and even your high school in some cases.) The procedure can be carried out with assistance from your Italian consulate and by corresponding with the *sportello per studenti stranieri* (foreign students' help desk) at the university where you wish to be admitted.

ELECTIVE RESIDENCE VISA

You do not necessarily need to be a retiree to take advantage of the elective residence visa option. Sally Carrocino, the retiree featured in the TV special, is a textbook example of an elective resident. This particular document is for anyone who can show proof of self-sustaining income not generated through work. As described by the Italian Consulate of Los Angeles, the option is available to "retired persons, persons with high self-sustaining incomes and financial assets—who have chosen Italy as their country of permanent residence and who are able to support themselves autonomously, without having to rely on employment while in Italy, whether as dependent employees, as self-employed employees or employees working remotely online."

Expanding on this, attorney *Capecchi* says, "Even if you're not retired, if you're a person who is willing to stay here and if you don't need to actively engage in business activity, it is likely that you can do so, as long as you're able to show through the documentation that needs to be submitted that you have sufficient passive income to stay without working."

The point about not working, even remotely, is particularly important. The elective residence visa is not a free-for-all license for digital nomads (whose best option, though also far from a free-for-all, is the *visto per lavoro autonomo*, discussed in the next section). Elective residence visa holders are not just prohibited from seeking on-the-ground employment or other work in Italy. Instead, they need to be able to prove that they have steady income outside of any form of employment: from Social Security benefits, rental properties, income-generating assets through a trust fund or other means.

"What's important is that you have passive income where you don't have to proactively be doing business while you are in Italy," *Capecchi* explains. "Regardless of the stories you can find online, elective residence visas are one of the trickiest types to obtain," he adds, "because of the complexity of putting together the proper financial and bank documents to be used to prove to the officer of the consulate that your income is sufficient. The number of clients that arrive to us in tears after rejection from the consulate is impressive. Ask for legal support before embarking on this type of visa application."

What's the number that Italy considers acceptable? There is not a universal magic minimum, but at the time of publication, the Italian Consulate of Los Angeles lists 2,596€ coming in monthly (about $3,375) as its base estimated rate for a single individual. Numbers will be higher for those with spouses or dependents accompanying them. *Capecchi* further clarifies, "If the funds that you have in America are sufficient to cover expenses that you have in Italy—and that's something that has to be seen case by case—there are great opportunities to stay here."

There are no specific restrictions on precisely when you can apply for an elective residence visa. But for planning purposes, *Capecchi* shares that when he's working with clients pursuing this route, if they are hoping for a June or July move, he suggests starting to collect the relevant documents in January.

Some are predicting that, in light of the Covid-19 crisis, change may be afoot for the elective residence visa. There is some talk that regulations may become more stringent as Italy and countries with similar schemes recognize that attracting so many retirees can carry consequences for the national health infrastructure. In general, always keep in mind that the nuts and bolts of immigration law and policies are frequently changing as the world changes.

WORK VISAS

Work visas, whether for employment (*lavoro subordinato*) or autonomous work (*lavoro autonomo*), have a reputation among expats in Italy as being notoriously tough to obtain. This is particularly true if you're not being recruited or transferred from abroad by a multinational company or an NGO, but are trying to go it alone as an entrepreneur or hoping to get hired by a small or family-run Italian company with limited resources.

Work visas have earned their thorny reputation largely because having a solid offer of employment or a viable business idea aren't enough, on their own, to procure this paperwork. Instead, work visas are issued within a strict quota system, based on a governmental decree, the *decreto flussi*. Translated as "flow decree," the *decreto flussi* is commonly (but not always) published around December on the Ministry of Internal Affairs (MIA) website (**www.interno.gov.it**), and states how many non-EU citizens will be allowed to enter Italy in the relevant year for work purposes, along with how many non-EU citizens already residing in Italy as students will be able to convert to worker status.

Put in simple terms, the *decreto flussi* is the doorway to working in Italy, and you can only get in while it's open. When the government publishes it, the door swings open for a finite number of entrants, and people race to get in line. Once that finite number of viable entrants is reached, the door is shut to foreigners entering for work reasons until the next round—the new decree.

Besides the MIA website, details and predictions about the *decreto flussi* can be followed via reputable Italian news sources (*ANSA* is the wire service; *Corriere della Sera* and *La Repubblica* are two key national daily newspapers). Both the flow decree itself and the time period in which it is announced can vary considerably from year to year. Additionally, the quota numbers can be misleading if not broken down properly: The cap on non-EU citizens entering the country for work purposes in the most recent *decreto flussi*, which was October 2020, was 30,850.

Maybe that number is higher than you thought. Your odds may seem good, particularly if you're highly educated and fluent in Italian, right? Not so fast.

The majority of those spots were reserved for short-term seasonal workers in the agriculture and service industries from a select bloc of countries. Only 12,850 spots were reserved for non-seasonal employees, autonomous workers and student-to-worker conversions. And of those 12,850, some 6,000 spots were reserved specifically for workers in road haul transport, construction and tourism/hotels from only a handful of countries with high migratory flows to Italy. Each flow decree tends to come with lengthy specifications like this.

This isn't to say getting into the quota is impossible. But what makes getting a work visa much more logistically complicated than other visas is the fact that so many variables need to line up at the same opportune moment: the timing of your search, the publication of the decree, the collection of all the documents involved. Once the *decreto flussi* is published, hopefuls have to move quickly with their applications to get in line. That means people who already have a job offer or a business plan with all the relevant documents already collected will have a huge advantage over people who scramble only once the quota is announced.

The catch-22: It is tricky to get Italian employers to put a job offer on hold for a non-EU citizen, even a brilliant one, and to convince them to wait around for the *decreto flussi* to open when they could instead opt to hire an EU citizen, or someone else on the ground in the country who's already authorized to work, or someone with whom they already have an established relationship.

Mary, who converted from student to employee status, explained that in her experience, it wasn't that the application process for the conversion itself was so complicated; it was everything in the lead-up to it. "We took the first formal steps after the flow decree was published online on the Ministry of Internal Affairs' application portal, which was straightforward enough," she says. "The part that was more complicated, both for my then-employer and for me, was in the months prior to that, when I was a part-timer, working the 20 hours per week allowed by my student permit. It took a while for us to reach a mutual agreement that I would be hired and come on board full-time when the *flussi* opened, since neither of us knew exactly what the time frame would be. The company was wonderful to take that gamble on me, but they probably wouldn't have if I had not already been working for them part-time for about a year prior to doing the conversion," she adds.

This is an example of how, during your studies, using your time to network or to begin building relationships through part-time work can be a stepping stone. The reality is that most traditional, small Italian companies are not going to go out on a limb for someone who's submitted an application from across the ocean, but they might do so for someone they already know and trust, and whose work they value. Notably, too, the quotas in recent years have been friendlier to in-country student conversions, with next to no allowances for office and white-collar workers being hired from abroad.

As Arlene notes, "It might be different if you, say, worked for Calvin Klein in New York and then *Armani* hires you to work in Milan. A company with that clout might take care of it," if you've got proven experience in the field, killer credentials, international contacts and clear advantages over domestic hires. A small Italian tour operator looking for an English mother-tongue copywriter is just not going to have the same resources or incentives to make a complicated international hire.

Believe it or not, there are some pros to the work permit. One major upside of securing one of either type is that you don't necessarily lose your work permit if you decide to change jobs (though you're likely to feel some measure of loyalty to any organization willing to muddle through the confusing process with you). Additionally, it doesn't keep you bound to a particular type of work.

Say, for example, you initially obtain one as an employee, but down the line decide you'd like to start your own business. You can get your business registered with a VAT number (*partita IVA*) or create a company through the *Camera di Commercio* (Chamber of Commerce) where you reside. When your work *permesso* is due for renewal, you need to indicate that you are changing from subordinate worker to autonomous worker (or vice versa). In your postal application, you must include the relevant documentation of the type of work you are now doing. One thing you don't have to worry about when renewing is the annual quota system.

So, what happens if you finally obtain the coveted work permit, but end up losing or having to leave a job? It complicates things, but fortunately, it does not constitute a valid reason for the *questura* to revoke your work permit, which will remain valid until its original expiry date. The *permesso di soggiorno per attesa occupazione* (awaiting employment or job seeker's permit) can also be issued if you find yourself needing to renew without a job. Note, however, that an entry visa for job seekers does not exist—the permit is only for those who have held work in Italy for whom complications arise.

Converting a Student Visa to a Work Visa

NOTE: *In recent years, the* decreto flussi *has made little to no allowances for traditionally white-collar or office-job workers applying for employment visas, instead denoting numbers for positions in agriculture, transportation, seasonal work and the like, or entrants from countries with whom Italy has cooperation agreements. Highly skilled workers might want to investigate the* EU Blue Card **(www.apply.eu)** *as an alternative option for seeking employment in Italy.*

The general process described below applies mainly to student permesso *holders on the ground in Italy who might be able to convert their status upon receiving a job offer.*

If you're lucky enough to have a valid, standing job offer from an employer when the *decreto flussi* is open, your prospective employer will need to submit an application for the *nulla osta*, your initial clearance document, on the MIA portal (**www.nullaostalavoro.dlci.interno.it**), along with supporting documentation, some of which will need to be collected from you and some of which will elaborate on the type of contract being proposed.

Ideally, the application for the *nulla osta* should be put in motion as quickly as possible after the *decreto flussi* is published. Some employers can manage this on their own, but many firms, particularly larger companies, will have a *consulente del lavoro* (labor consultant) or another party to whom they outsource this step. If the application falls within the quota, the employer will be summoned to provide further

documentation and you will make a series of trips to bureaucratic buildings like the *prefettura* (prefecture) and *questura* (immigration office of
police headquarters).

Self-Employment Visa
(*Visto per Lavoro Autonomo*)

If you have a burgeoning business idea or are a self-employed person or
freelancer thinking of moving to Italy, you're unfortunately not exempt
from the quota system, unless you apply for the investor visa (**www.
investorvisa.mise.gov.it**), a new two-year visa for non-EU citizens who
choose to invest in strategic assets for Italy's economy and society.

However, under more standard conditions, and for normal self-employed workers, you will need to keep an eye on news about the *decreto
flussi*. Unlike with, say, the elective residence visa, where the specific
timing of the application is flexible, as *Capecchi* puts it, "If you know you
want to move your business, or you want to be a freelancer here, I tell my
clients that we need to start collecting documents right away, so that
when the gates of the quotas open, we are ready to submit the application."

When submitting your *nulla osta* application, you need to be able to
produce the license or authorization documents for the business you will
be conducting. *Capecchi* notes that if you are in your home country when
you plan to apply for this type of visa, you definitely need to appoint a
legal proxy (with a formal power of attorney) to collect the relevant documents from the Italian side (at the Chamber of Commerce, the labor desk
or the *comune*, to name a few) that show that you are allowed to set up or
continue your business in Italy.

For these reasons, *Capecchi* advises his potential clients to get in
touch as soon as they are ready to move forward with a business idea
without waiting for the quotas to be out, given the amount of time that
the collection of these documents can take. By the time your paperwork is
collected, it is likely that the new quotas will already be published!

Note that the indications the *decreto flussi* makes—about nationalities, industries and so forth—can extend to specifications about what
distinct types of independent professional and entrepreneurial figures are
permitted to enter Italy at a given time, and place caps on each category
(for example, translators or tech consultants). If you have substantial
resources, you may be better off exploring the new investor visa instead of
the self-employment visa.

The "Perma-Permesso"

After five years of continuous residency in Italy, you become eligible to
apply for the *permesso di soggiorno UE per soggiornanti di lungo perio-
do* (EU permit of stay for long-term residents), which does not need to
be renewed from an immigration perspective, but simply updated in
the same way you'd have a driver's license or other form of ID renewed
periodically. For those five years of residency to be considered continuous, you need to have been renewing your *permesso*, not returning to
the States to have new visas issued for new purposes.

Summing It Up

Visas and *permessi di soggiorno* can be vexing, but no red-tape riddles
should stop you from taking the leap to Italy if it's what you really want.
As expat coach Damien O'Farrell puts it, "I don't think people should limit
themselves. I don't think they should be put off by the visa or anything
like that that can be worked through." Just keep the realities of working
through it in mind before you hop on a plane hoping your paperwork will
magically manifest. As with most things concerning Italian bureaucracy,
individual situations will vary case by case, rules and laws are constantly
changing and it's best to work with a legal intermediary and/or a relocation consultant when you have questions.

Marina Pascucci and John Henderson

Interview with

JOHN HENDERSON

Retiring in the Eternal City

American journalist John Henderson dreamed for years of moving to Italy before he eventually retired in Rome. His move came in phases starting with a sabbatical from his sports-writing career. John is one of the few American men we know who have made the move to Italy on his own. He now shares his life with his Italian girlfriend, *Marina Pascucci.* Now that he's living in the Eternal City, he has learned to deeply appreciate Italian life: good food and wine, friendships with locals, soccer and the unexpected beauty tucked away in every little corner of the city.

Kathy McCabe: I know a little of your story, but how did you come to fall in love with Italy?

John Henderson: It goes back to the year 2000. I had just covered the Sydney Olympics, my first Olympics, and really loved it but was really burned out on sports writing. In our contract with *The Denver Post*, you can take a year sabbatical and have your job guaranteed when you get back. So I talked to this guy and he told me how great it was spending six months traveling around Italy.

My girlfriend at the time was a radio reporter and she was also burned out at her job. We set out for November 2001 to move to Rome, and then 9/11 hit. We went there for a year; we loved it so much that I got two extensions on my sabbatical.

I ended up staying 16 months, and then the U.S. invaded Iraq in March of 2003 and the dollar started to drop against the euro. We fell in love with Rome so much that when we left, we vowed we would return forever.

Well, I couldn't find a job, and in 2010 my girlfriend and I broke up. And I said, "Okay, I'm just going to save my money and retire." In the meantime, during all these years, I kept going back and forth to Rome to visit, to see old friends, just to improve my Italian, to get a feel for living there some more as it changed economically. In August of 2013 I reached my financial goal, in December 2013 I got my visa and in January 2014 I moved.

KM: Do you have the elective residency visa?

JH: It is *residenza elettiva*. That gives you permission to live in Italy for a year. After a year you need a *permesso di soggiorno*, and that's when you've got to show proof of financial stability, insurance and housing contract. It's basically permission to live here, as long as I don't work.

KM: You just knew when you were in Rome, you wanted that city life, right?

JH: Yeah. There are so many more museum openings and wine tastings and politics. The pulse.

KM: But you plan to stay?

JH: Oh yeah. I will die here. I can't think of any place else I'd rather live.

KM: Tell me your impression of the lockdown in Italy. What does it say about Italian culture?

JH: I remember after the first week, people were getting on their balconies and holding candles and singing Italian songs. That was moving. I mean, everybody came. I really felt like I was part of the Italian people, part of the Italian culture that everybody was really coming together to make each other feel like, "Look, we're going to get through this."

KM: What is it that you have discovered about Italians?

JH: I generally do think Italians care more about each other than Americans do. I think they are willing to sacrifice more than Americans are. I think all of Europe is like that. I always tell people in Italy, in America you learn to work, in Italy you learn to live.

KM: Which is beautiful. What ways do you think Italians live?

JH: They love their spare time; they love to go out. Even parents. They love their food and wine; they love to sit outside and drink and talk all night. And they love their two weeks in Sardinia in August. It's spare time, food, wine and beauty. Those are the things they value.

KM: Tell me about beauty.

JH: The beauty is in the architecture; in the cities. Living in Rome is like living in an outdoor museum—everywhere you go, you see artwork. You're in a rainstorm in the *Piazza del Popolo*, and you're running into the *Basilica Santa Maria del Popolo* and you see three *Caravaggio*, authentic ones.

KM: You moved to Italy as a single, American man. We don't hear a lot of stories of that. Why do you think that is?

JH: I think American women are more adventurous than American men. I think they're more willing to take chances. American men get settled and they're more identified by their salary and their position, and they don't want to lose that. I'm also unique in that I never married. I have no wife, no ex-wife, no kids. So that helped a lot. I know a lot of men who asked me how I did it and that's what I tell them, and it pretty much disqualifies them on all four counts.

KM: What about making Italian friends?

JH: I found that pretty easy as I found Italians very open. That's my experience. I got welcomed into homes.

I'm a big soccer fan. I've got an *A.S. Roma* key chain, and I show this around town and they say, "Oh, *forza Roma!*" I even get discounts in the public markets. This gives me a way to bond with the locals.

And be humble about the U.S. All cultures want respect. Treat them as equals, be curious, they will always answer your questions, learn.

Then don't be afraid to throw a party and invite every Italian you know and have them invite a friend. I joined the Italian food and wine lovers' group where you try different *trattorie* and wine bars. Another way to get into the culture is to go to the museums where there are art exhibits.

Go to a *scambio* (language exchange), where you'll meet Italians who want to learn English. There's a website called **Conversationexchange .com** and you put your bio there, and then Romans who are trying to learn English contact you and you go out for coffee or a glass of wine.

KM: Do you think living in Italy, living in a new culture helps you age better, cognitively?

JH: Yes. Well, cognitively I've also learned, and this is true, if you're learning a new language it is a great way to keep your mental capacity going, you're always learning.

Also, living in Italy as an expat, you never feel like you're getting old because every day you see that you have a new experience, you pass a new restaurant you want to try, you read about another town in Italy you want to visit and everything is so close. I always have something to look forward to. You never feel like you're in a rut living here.

KM: What has surprised you the most?

JH: My biggest surprise was how much harder the Italian language was than I thought it would be. I thought if you moved here, you'd learn it fast, really fast. The accents are different from region to region and very few people speak English. It's very humbling, embarrassing, frustrating and scary sometimes.

—

For more information, visit **www.johnhendersontravel.com**

Work Life in Italy

It is important for anyone who wants to move to Italy, who still has to work for a living, to educate themselves on what employment culture and the job market in Italy is like, and what they have to offer it that's unique. (Spoiler alert: English skills alone won't cut it!)

There isn't a one-size-fits-all description, but broadly speaking, the Italian economy was facing an unemployment crisis, most heavily affecting young people, even prior to Covid-19. Before the pandemic, there was already a pronounced brain drain trend, which, according to the national Chamber of Commerce *Confindustria*, was costing Italy up to 14€ billion (roughly $17 billion) annually. Some Italians abroad boomeranged back home in light of the Covid-19 crisis, with many continuing to work remotely for their companies or clients in other countries; time will tell if Italy manages to retain this wave of talent.

Challenges of the Italian Work Landscape

The reasons for brain drain of the country's best and brightest are many, but in a nutshell, it's about lack of opportunities, low earning potential, apparent indifference toward meritocracy and, for would-be entrepreneurial types, bureaucratic obstacles to setting up profitable businesses. When it comes to concrete prospects, there's a stark divide between the less-developed south and the more industrialized central and northern regions (the north in particular). According to a 2021 report by *Statista*, the average annual gross salary is 7,000€ higher in Lombardy than it is in *Basilicata*, but that doesn't take into account cost of living, which is considerably higher in metropolitan areas, where most of the jobs are in the first place. The same *Statista* report indicates that the average annual gross salary across Italy hovers around 30,000€.

Anecdotally, it's not uncommon to hear of highly educated expats who speak two or three languages working on short-term contracts (*contratti a tempo determinato*) with no guarantee of renewal, or netting 1,200€ or so monthly after taxes. While that may be enough to survive or even thrive on in somewhere like the outskirts of *Caserta*, if you're a higher-educated professional, you're probably more likely to set up life in a place like Florence, where renting a two-bedroom apartment can easily cost you that much per month.

When you consider the scarcity of jobs and the precariousness of the overall work culture, it's no wonder that many people tend to stay in their positions for years on end, often with little to no advancement or salary growth, once they acquire a coveted *contratto a tempo indeterminato* (permanent contract).

If you're an independent business owner or freelancer with some hustle muscle, an urge to prioritize passion over profit and a knack for thinking outside the box, there are opportunities to be had or created in Italy (if not necessarily billions of euros to be made). If you're someone who craves stability and an office, and who doesn't mind working in the same job for some time, permanent contracts are out there. But if you fall under a third category where your main priority is consistent upward mobility and financial growth, you are probably not cut out for traditional Italian work culture.

The bottom line is that many bright, educated Italians already struggle to find sustainable long-term employment, so foreigners have an uphill battle to fight and must find a way to distinguish themselves if they're to be competitive in the job market. Additionally, Italy's family-first and favors-for-friends culture, while charming in most personal settings, can have major downsides in the professional world: namely, nepotism and a culture of *raccomandazioni* (recommendations).

Keys to Success

While networking, word of mouth and who you know are important in any nation's work culture, Italian business seems to run disproportionately on face-to-face relationships. Certainly there are perks to this, which might include enjoying a more humane pace to business deals, or taking a full lunch break at the bar with colleagues rather than scarfing down a store-bought salad at your desk. Expat coach Damien O'Farrell says that in professional exchanges, "Of course it's still about business, that's a given, but in Italy, there's a very human side." The drawbacks to that same human side might potentially include watching your résumé land in the slush pile so a position for which you're highly qualified can go to someone from the boss' inner circle.

Faced with realities like this, orchestrating a move to Italy could involve a career pivot for many people, as it did for Arlene Antoinette Gibbs, who of course made the change from Hollywood film executive to interior designer. If you're thinking about making a shift, don't underestimate the power of your own network—both the pre-existing one and your growing connections in Italy. When Arlene was beginning to think about the viability of her interior design path, she sought advice from a writer friend who covers design. "She introduced me to an interior designer here in Italy and I thought it was going to be just an informational meeting. But at the end this designer said, 'Okay, you know what? I have a showroom; you should come do an internship,'" Arlene marvels.

A key in pivoting: Be intentional. As Arlene tells it, "A lot of expats find themselves falling into doing things for a living as opposed to having a passion for that thing. So there's a lot of frustration and then they end up taking it out on the country."

Though it's a fruitful and rewarding option for some people, teaching English in particular is one area where this "falling into it" often seems to apply. The major positive about teaching English is that lessons led by mother-tongue speakers—whether privately held in homes or businesses, given as part of a curricular or extracurricular program at an Italian elementary school or *liceo* (high school), or offered through a private, for-profit institute—are always in high demand.

Speaking and Teaching English

If you are one of few English speakers in a given area, you may even be able to corner the market. But many Anglo transplants to Italy make the mistake of thinking that being a native English speaker on its own is enough for a company or school to want to hire you. Sometimes, they're proven right—but usually that's a red flag that you're not dealing with a very serious organization.

Be wary of some private language institutes that have a high demand for mother-tongue teachers but lack the resources or willingness to invest in proper teacher-hiring practices. For better or for worse, English teaching is often seen as the default job for foreigners looking to fund an extended stay in Italy, and some schools tend to take advantage of this on multiple fronts, hiring a revolving door of inexperienced and underqualified teachers, and then offering them little in the way of legal paperwork, proper above-the-table compensation or on-the-job training. Ultimately, this borders on exploitation and does a disservice to both the teachers and the students, who may be wooed by the promise of mother-tongue instructors, then disappointed to find that their teacher has no formal qualifications.

Perhaps even worse still, those same teachers may very well be working alongside far more qualified professional teachers who are nonetheless getting the same treatment and pay. This of course is not universal across private language institutes, but as Mary Gray puts it, "The 'shady English teaching gig' is a common enough rite of passage among expats, especially those in the 20s to 40s range, that any offer one gets from a school or a private individual should be examined pretty thoroughly."

Most English-speaking expats will also find that once they start making local friends and connections, requests for language exchanges, private English conversational lessons or referrals for private English tutors become rather commonplace. Casual but focused conversation in exchange for a little pocket money here and there can be a fun way to find your footing and meet new people early on in your Italian life, but not a particularly stable way to live, nor a career path to carve out.

There's always a demand for foreigners who are willing to treat English teaching as a serious profession rather than a simple means to an end. There are safe and sustainable ways to teach, earn a decent living and make a meaningful difference in students' lives. If you want to operate as a legitimate teacher or tutor, a better strategy than "showing up as a native English speaker and hoping for the best" is to invest in obtaining a transferable education certificate or an English language-specific instruction certification, such as the CELTA, or the Certificate in English Language Teaching to Adults, which is internationally recognized and often specifically requested in Italian job board announcements.

There is also the more general TEFL, Teaching English as a Foreign Language. Many variations on the TEFL exist, however, and not all are created equal: A $200 online certification course is not going to look the same way on a résumé as an in-depth, in-person training program lasting a month or more. Some programs like this are even offered on the ground in Italy and provide resources and networking opportunities for grads and alumni (note that, in most cases, a TEFL certification course on its own won't count as a viable option for issuance of an entry visa).

Location Matters

While there's much to give one pause, the work situation in Italy isn't categorically bleak or bad; it's just important to be aware of the larger context and the limitations. Use them to realistically assess which opportunities and markets might fit with your skill set, priorities and lifestyle needs.

Arlene describes how, in an exchange on social media, a curious American makeup artist once reached out to her about wanting to move to Italy. "I said, 'Great, you should go to Milan because that's where the fashion business is based.' I mean, there's film here in Rome, but for her type of work, I thought Milan would be better. She says, 'No, I really want to live in Florence and Rome.'" At that, Arlene shrugged: "I said, 'Well, I don't know. . . . There are Italian makeup artists in Rome who are not working consistently because there's not as much work.'" In other words, dream big, but think pragmatically about your day to day. You might need to tweak your vision to make a living.

In that same vein, Damien recalls helping with relocation services for a middle-aged client who was still highly professionally focused, but intent on moving to the Umbrian countryside. Fortunately, after a trial run, the client saw the writing on the wall. "We talked it through; she was still very focused on career and business growth, and this was just not going to happen in this town in *Umbria*," Damien adds, noting that now, this client can take regular train trips to the Umbrian countryside when she wants a getaway while enjoying the benefits of a busy and dynamic professional life in Milan. "She thought realistically about what was important to her," being honest with herself about her hopes for a five-year Italy plan, "and so her life in Italy has been very successful."

You may want to look in your own backyard first—the U.S., that is—while thinking ahead to how your career could translate to Italy. For example, seek out openings at multinational or Italian companies with U.S. outposts that could potentially facilitate a transfer for you down the line. (And recall your reflections on whether or not a move is what you really want; perhaps a job with clear ties and regular trips to Italy could offer enough of an Italian fix.)

Turin is a busy industrial center, as the headquarters of household-name Italian companies like *Fiat* (automobile manufacturers) and *Lavazza* (coffee products). Consider Rome and try thinking beyond the saturated tourism and hospitality sectors, turning your attention instead toward international companies and NGOs. Film and television could also be viable markets: Netflix, which recently invested 200€ million in original Italian productions, is set to open an office on Rome's *Via Veneto* (the main drag of the gloomy glitterati in *La Dolce Vita*) as of 2021.

The *Caput Mundi* is also home to several major United Nations organizations that pay competitive salaries and of course contribute to important missions: the World Food Programme, the Food and Agriculture Organization and the International Fund for Agricultural Development. And Florence is home to the Italian headquarters of UNICEF, hosting its *Innocenti Research Centre.*

Interestingly, as an outgrowth of the Covid-19 crisis, Florence and other Italian cities are launching initiatives to encourage digital nomad and start-up types to set up extended stays, recognizing the social and economic benefits that such workers could bring.

As this guide was going to press, for example, the Florence Convention and Visitors Bureau, together with the City of Florence, was preparing to launch BE.LONG, an online platform designed to help those parties with bureaucratic questions, housing matters and integrating into the fabric of the city, and ultimately aiming to revive the historic center and its medium- to long-term rental market. However, it remains to be seen if these sorts of forward-thinking municipal government and tourism board initiatives will ever be accompanied by real reform to the lengthy process of applying for and obtaining a work visa, which is generally the main barrier, alongside tax concerns, to moving to or setting up shop in Italy.

About Taxes

Any transplant to Italy, particularly those who are self-employed (i.e., autonomous workers) or who hold assets in multiple countries, should never try to navigate the tax system alone. Remember that even if you reside permanently outside the U.S., all American citizens are still required to file a tax return. Your specific situation in Italy will vary depending on a number of factors, but long-term residents in Italy will generally need to file a *dichiarazione dei redditi* (tax return).

A good *commercialista* (accountant) is a crucial element in any Italian expat's life, and there are many English-speaking ones who cater specifically to the expat demographic.

Reputable Italian chartered accountants—*dottori commercialisti*—are professionals with degrees in economics, business, tax or financial disciplines. They will be registered in a special professional association, the *Ordine dei Dottori Commercialisti*. (Italy has a dedicated *ordine* for licensed professionals in each of many mainstream sectors—think architects, lawyers, journalists.)

The *commercialista*'s principal tasks are comparable to those of a U.S. accountant: They perform services and offer counsel to companies or individuals concerning tax compliance, compilation of tax returns, bookkeeping and preparation of financial statements, corporate law, bankruptcy law and labor concerns.

Ashley Bartner, who runs the *agriturismo La Tavola Marche* with her husband Jason, emphasizes that the right *commercialista* for you will depend on your specific needs. Some may be better versed in the finer points of your trade than others, so that's worth asking about. Ashley's accountant's specialization in agriculture, for example, has meant that his role goes beyond just helping the pair keep their books in order. "Our guy specializes in agriculture, and so he is looking for different types of grants and EU funding, and things like that. So some accountants can be your eyes and ears for all of that because it's just too much at times to process or understand how to digest it all. So then, you can go to him and ask, 'Is there anything we should be looking at or doing?'"

Not all accountants will have offerings of this scope, so be sure when you are shopping around to get a clear view of what services each firm provides and how far those extend.

Unless you're working with a highly specialized international accounting firm, you shouldn't rely on tax professionals in the U.S. for information about your filing and payment obligations in Italy. "One of the things I always tell people is that you really need a good accountant and a good lawyer," Damien shares. "A lot of people try to do it on their own now. That's fraught with problems. You need to work with a lawyer and an accountant, particularly if you're running a business. And then as I said, you get your dream team and once you've got that, your life is basically set up."

Damien also shares that in putting together a dream team, it's helpful to ask around for referrals from, as he puts it, "people who seem to know what they're doing." Echoing this, Ashley says, "Whatever business you're going into, ask people in the specific area or region, 'With this type of activity, do you have experience with someone you trust?'"

Commercialista referrals and the like are common conversation topics in online expat forums. Rather than simply settling on the first recommendation you get, aim to have informational interviews with a range of accountants before deciding on the one that's right for you and your needs.

Navigating Healthcare

Whether you're working in Italy or moving there for retirement, healthcare is a vital concern. "Obviously as you get older, healthcare is a main concern," Damien O'Farrell says, "and in Italy, even if you opt for a private policy, it's still a lot cheaper than it is in other markets." Damien, who himself makes use of private healthcare, pays around 1,200€ per year.

Healthcare is one of Italy's big advantages. Italy grants its legal residents access to a world-renowned nationalized system. The country frequently ranks in the top 10 healthiest countries on the planet, with a high life expectancy for its residents. Sally Carrocino gushes about how even with her sunny California origins, she feels healthier in Italy, and attributes most of it to lifestyle changes: "It's because I walk all the time. I'm not sitting in my car and I'm eating everything fresh. And in California, I always thought I ate a lot of vegetables!"

Affordability

But it's not just about fresh produce and pedestrian-friendly downtowns. Adjusting to Italian healthcare can be a shock to the system for an American—in a good way. As O'Farrell puts it, having been in Italy for

31 years now, "When I hear what some people pay for health insurance in other markets, I almost keel over." David Bach, who has made his name offering financial advice, echoes this sentiment with his broad overview of lifestyle costs in Italy. "Let me just be very candid: One of the things that makes Italy easier is its lower cost [...] We're constantly surprised," he says.

As this translates to the healthcare realm, going bankrupt from medical expenses or relying on crowdfunding outlets like GoFundMe to pay for major surgeries—a practice that's now commonplace in the U.S.— is unheard of in Italy. The Italian Republic enshrined the right to free medical care in its constitution and established the nationalized system, known as the *Servizio Sanitario Nazionale* (SSN), in 1978.

Broadly speaking, while Americans tend to hesitate to go to the doctor until something is unmistakably wrong, often fearing high costs, Italians and residents of Italy more readily embrace the need for regular healthcare. Emergency services, including ambulance rides (national tel. 118), are always free of charge and are considered a basic right, even for undocumented residents, visitors and those not registered in the national healthcare system. Culturally, the system is set up to take care of you, not work against you.

Retired journalist and "elective resident" John Henderson is a testament to this truth. He was floored by his early experiences with the Italian healthcare system before he was ever registered with the national public service (SSN). Prior to signing up, he had health insurance out of Belgium, but notes that it covered very little. A few years ago, John says, he contracted an optical nerve disease. "I got treated at my local public hospital. I remember my first day I went in and they analyzed it, they tested me, gave me advice and medicine. I walked out and I said, 'Where do I pay?' And they said, 'Nowhere,' and they looked at me strangely," he remembers.

In the months that followed, John did have to undergo additional treatment and see a specialist to better identify the specific problems. "I got treated for four or five months. I got a laser surgery, more tests, more advice, and they nailed down what the disease was. I went to two or three places. My total costs were about 650€. I itemized those and checked what it would be in the U.S., and it would have been around $16,000. And this is for somebody who was *not* part of the national health service," John explains.

Since then, John has enrolled in the SSN, but his story illustrates that healthcare costs are typically not debilitating even if you aren't enrolled. If you are not an Italian or EU citizen, which will be the case for the majority of readers, your enrollment (*iscrizione*) in the national healthcare system will depend on the type of *permesso di soggiorno* you have. Generally, resident workers (holders of *lavoro autonomo* or *lavoro subordinato* permits) have a right to enroll in the national healthcare system (*iscrizione obbligatoria*) free of charge, though of course they can elect to opt for private care when the need arises. Elective residence permit holders and students, depending on the region, may instead be able to enroll via the *iscrizione volontaria* (voluntary enrollment) option, paying an annual contribution of 7.5% of their previous year's income (for incomes up to 20,658.28€) or 4% for higher incomes. "Annual" contribution refers to the solar year, or the period between January 1 and December 31. At the time of publication of this guide, the Ministry of Health states that the minimum cost of annual voluntary enrollment is 387.34€.

For all non-EU citizens, your *tessera sanitaria*, the healthcare card issued to you when you enroll in the SSN, will be valid for the length of your permit of stay, and will need to be renewed. (Anecdotally, though, an expired *tessera sanitaria* isn't going to mean you're refused medical care if and when you urgently need it.)

While healthcare is a national right, medical services are administered regionally, and then by districts within each region. This means that the care one receives in the *Val d'Aosta* may differ significantly in quality and access from the care in *Calabria*. The regions of Tuscany, *Emilia-Romagna* and *Veneto* are consistently classified among the best in Italy for essential access. Due to decades of economic disparity between the north and south, regions in southern Italy tend to lack the same quality of infrastructure, a gap that became increasingly evident amid the crippling Covid-19 crisis.

How It Works

Italian residents can opt for medical care at private or public institutions. While public institutions provide excellent quality of service, you shouldn't expect shiny floors and the spa-like atmosphere that pervades some U.S. hospitals. Public hospitals provide grade-A medical care with little to no added luxuries, allowing doctors and nurses to focus on their jobs. As John puts it, "They're clean, they're just old and dingy. [...] But in Italy, they take care of their sick. You don't see people going bankrupt for medical costs here."

Anyone registering for the national healthcare system will need to choose a *medico di base* (family doctor or general practitioner). This will be your go-to person for check-ups, referrals and issuance of prescriptions. When you go to obtain the *tessera sanitaria* (healthcare card) at the ASL (*Azienda Sanitaria Locale*), or local health authority in your area of residence, the clerk will provide a list of doctors who may or may not be accepting patients.

Often, the selection process is a matter of choosing whoever is available and within easy distance of your home. While a name on a page may not inspire much confidence, don't agonize too much over your general practitioner at the outset; the important thing is to get your *tessera sanitaria* processed and your data into the system. You can always switch your *medico di base* later. All that's required to change is another visit to the ASL, which is generally much smoother than other high-stakes institutional buildings like, say, the *questura*.

If you need a doctor outside the normal office hours of your general practitioner, but your condition doesn't feel urgent enough to warrant bona fide emergency room treatment (*pronto soccorso*), you can visit the

Emergency Medical Service (*Guardia Medica*) in your area, presenting your health card.

Advantages of Private Healthcare

So, if the public system is so renowned, what are the advantages of going private? While Italy's public system boasts equity of access and quality of care, it is also notorious for long wait times. General practitioners often do not offer the option of appointments, instead operating on a first-come, first-served mentality based on whoever is in the waiting room that day. Additionally, general practitioners have a capped number of how many patients they can take on at a given time, so the highest-in-demand doctors will frequently have long waiting lists. This has allowed a market for the private sector to develop and flourish.

For some expats, the ease of access and the higher likelihood of finding an English-speaking or even native-English-speaking doctor make the private sector appealing. (Note, however, that in major cities and tourist destinations most public doctors and medical staff will speak enough English to properly inform patients who lack a high level of Italian. And while your local ASL probably won't have a dedicated document indicating which doctors in the public system speak English, American and Anglo consulates and embassies in Italy tend to keep running lists online for the residents they serve. Tapping into other expats in your area for intel on English-speaking medical professionals, either in person or online, can also be helpful for this.)

Another private sector pro is the lack of a middleman when booking specialists. The middleman/woman in the public system, of course, is your general practitioner, to whom you must go for referrals, and then wait for the next available appointment with the specialist he or she recommends, paying a nominal co-pay. You can forgo this sometimes-slow SSN process when you opt for visiting a private specialist, but you will have to pay out of pocket; keep in mind, however, that even in the private sector, costs are rather contained compared to what you might be used to. Although figures can vary, a one-off visit to a specialized private clinic is much more likely to set you back somewhere between 70€ and 100€, rather than, say, 700€ and 1,000€ as you might expect stateside.

Overall, instead of viewing public versus private healthcare as a strict either/or choice, it might be easiest to enroll in the SSN and then opt for private when certain treatments call for it.

Medications

Often, people come to Italy with medications prescribed by American doctors and psychiatrists. Most times, these prescriptions aren't valid in Italy and require an Italian doctor (your new *medico di base*) to write a new prescription. The best course of action to take is usually to first go speak with a pharmacist who may be able to tell you if (1) they can fill it directly without a prescription, (2) a doctor needs to draft a new prescription in Italy or (3) if the medication cannot be filled in any Italian pharmacy.

Remember: Not all medications prescribed in the U.S. are allowed into Italy. This is something to discuss with your doctor in the U.S. before departure. In certain instances, the Vatican Pharmacy can fill international prescriptions as long as they are in line with Catholic teachings. Italian pharmacists are a wealth of knowledge and Italian pharmacies are teeming with inexpensive over-the-counter options.

Medicare

A major concern for movers of a certain age is how an international jump will affect Medicare coverage. The short answer: Medicare does not provide coverage in Italy. As individual situations vary, you will want to contact the U.S. Social Security office to discuss your individual case and ensure you're in line with current policies and regulations. That said, there are some concepts that apply broadly. If you're already receiving Medicare benefits when you decide to make your Italy move, you should be able to remain enrolled in Part A (hospital insurance), which most receive premium-free.

Weighing the costs and benefits, you will have to decide whether or not to continue to pay for Medicare Part B (medical insurance) based upon the frequency of return trips you make to the U.S. It is important to note that each individual and couple has different situations when it comes to receiving Social Security, both in the U.S. and farther afield. You may find it is worth looking into different travel medical insurance options that would be valid for the length of time one wants to spend in the U.S. each year.

Emotional Health

Your mental and emotional state are also key components of living a fruitful and healthy life. As David Bach shared of himself and his family early on in their radical sabbatical, "We're all more present in our lives right now than I think we've ever been. We're less distracted. We're more here right now and I think that's giving all of us more of a lightness, a sense of joy."

If Italy's a "heart home" for you, you will likely find that too, particularly in the early stages of your move. But for all the wonders and excitement that a new life in Italy can offer, expats may find themselves facing unique challenges that can adversely affect their mental health, particularly if one already lives with depression or anxiety. According to one study, expats have a tendency to feel more anxious and trapped than their U.S. counterparts. In cities with large expat populations, you will find psychiatrists, psychotherapists and psychologists who may cater specifically to that community and its concerns.

Dr. Mary Ann Bellini in Florence, for example, works primarily with the student and expat population and particularly with the unique needs of cross-cultural couples. Moving on an international scale is never easy, and when dealing with everyday tasks in a different language and perhaps feeling *othered* in ways you may not have experienced before, a sense of feeling unseen or unheard can set in. Dr. Bellini emphasizes how the "excitement and hyperactivity of the new lifestyle" can lead some transplants to neglect their mental wellness. In all the hustle and bustle, she says, "One can easily forget the important tools of a successful transition: communication, personal growth and change and cultural awareness."

While you may be thrilled to make the leap to Italy, don't fall into the trap of thinking that the beauty of the country will ensure round-the-clock gratitude and existential satisfaction. Don't chastise or bully yourself for having off days or extended periods. You're still human: At some point or another, it's common for expats, even those who overall feel satisfied, to question their decisions or ruminate on things.

New stimuli and modes of thinking and even ways you're perceived in your new country can be thrilling, but they can also create mental anguish, particularly if you're not giving yourself adequate space to adjust, rest and process challenging emotions. Keep an eye on your feelings and thoughts and don't neglect them as part of the holistic health equation. Seek professional care when necessary.

Sally Carrocino and friends

Finding Your Community

A huge part of staying of sound mind is making meaningful social connections. And there's no question that learning Italian—and studying before you go—will immeasurably enrich your ability to connect. Today, technology and social media, as well as language learning resources like Rosetta Stone, can be incredibly helpful pre-departure tools to help get you set up for a thriving social life with both Italians and fellow internationals.

Connect Virtually

A staggering amount of people who have lived, currently live or want to live in Italy share their experiences on online forums, email listservs, Facebook groups and more. Relocation expert Damien O'Farrell created the Facebook group Ultimate Italy, whose more than 14,000 members aim to share "solely positive, uplifting and inspirational messages, stories and news about Italy," as well as trade tips and practical information. Another group of his, Business Italy Marketplace, is a crowdsourced collection of employment offers, classes, special deals, property listings and numerous other opportunities of interest to international folks in Italy.

Joining virtual expat groups (see the Resources chapter at the end of this book) is a great way to start forging new connections, both with locals and other foreigners—and is a habit you can continue cultivating once you land and find in-person groups to join. While Internet forum advice is no substitute for sound legal counsel or direct consultation with an expert, having a space to sound out others and share experiences is invaluable and can help you feel less isolated when encountering road-blocks. Social media has helped in cultivating a strong and supportive expat community nationwide.

Jump In

Just remember when you join to channel that same energy into offline interactions, too! Presumably, you're not taking the leap to Italy only to spend most of your time posting and reading threads. Sally Carrocino jumped into social life in Florence with both feet, letting go of precon-ceived notions about the types of people and activities she might have been interested in, at least at the beginning.

Of the advice she gives other Italy transplants or dreamers, Sally says, "I tell people to let go of any of your past ideas about 'I don't want to do this or that,' and to be open to everything. I made a promise to myself that I would say yes to all invitations, and I've kept it 98% of the time. Because even though you might not feel like it in the moment, once you get out there, you're really so happy that you did."

Don't Blame Italy

When you're community-building in both virtual or in-person spaces, it's important to be mindful of the fine line between expat *solidarity* versus shared *bitterness*. Avoid adopting a "blame-Italy" mentality about your problems; it can be easy to fall into that trap. Surrounding yourself with empathetic expats who can understand your unique challenges and support you is uplifting; surrounding yourself with constant complainers and co-dependents won't add much to your new life beyond resentment.

Arlene Antoinette Gibbs recalls a difficult period between 2016 and 2018 when she started to internalize the more cynical mentalities of some expats in her circles. "I realized I had to change my attitude because I was starting to fall into this bad habit of repeating to myself what people were saying to me. Things like, 'You're not gonna make it as an interior designer or decorator in Italy, because you're a foreigner, and you don't have an Italian husband who can introduce you to people that can hire you.' I think I started to believe those things and to feel very frustrated," she shares candidly.

"And I started saying, 'Oh, the reason why these things are not happening is because I live in Italy.' But I realized I had to get back to basics and think about why I moved here. And it comes back to creativity and beauty."

Takeaway: Just as you're likely to have loved ones or acquaintances stateside who question the plausibility of your dream of living in Italy, or who try to talk you out of it, you're likely to meet people in Italy who project their own experiences and disappointments onto you. No place is perfect, and sour apples can be found all over the world! While some measure of pragmatism is essential to surviving in Italy, being surrounded by pessimism can trap you and infiltrate your inner monologue. Be mindful of the company you keep and the online forums you frequent.

Volunteer

Fortunately, creativity, beauty and a can-do spirit of positivity and purpose are all found through many community organizations and volunteering opportunities. In most major cities, there are plenty of opportunities to give of your time (in English or Italian) with local nonprofits, soup kitchens, religious organizations and charities, some of which may be particularly welcoming to, or indeed in need of, English speakers.

Sally, for example, finds a lot of satisfaction by giving back to the community through the American International League of Florence (AILO), a charitable organization that has members from not just the U.S., but also from Italy and other nations. AILO organizes cultural events, community gatherings and fundraisers for local and regional charities throughout the year—perhaps most famously the Christmas Bazaar, a mega-marketplace where 100% of proceeds are donated to charity. If you're interested in finding similar organizations in your new home, try searching using the term "ONLUS"—the Italian acronym for *Organizzazione Non Lucrativa di Utilità Sociale* (nonprofit organization of social utility).

Gender Gap

One glaring reality of life among American expats in Italy—which plays out in social settings, community organization focuses and, for singles, dating dynamics—is the pronounced gender gap. Whether you're socializing with mostly Italians, mostly expats or a balanced mix, you will quickly notice that American women in Italy, whether single or married/ partnered with an Italian or a fellow expat, tend to far outnumber American men.

John Henderson has a few theories about why that is. "I think American women are more adventurous, more willing to take chances," he says. "American men get settled and are more identified by their salary and their position, and don't want to lose that. I think a lot of guys find it harder to pull the trigger, especially if they have kids, even if they're single or divorced."

While that's by no means an assertion that American men should refrain from taking the leap, it's something for men (or for their partners) to keep in mind, especially if they hope to find fellow male expat friends on top of their Italian connections. They're out there, but be aware that there's a higher prevalence of expat women-targeted interest groups and forums, so it's often simpler for expat women to find each other.

Finding Activities

No matter your gender, making friends in a new place is a process with ups and downs. One specific challenge for expats is the tendency to fall into black-and-white thinking about who they want to meet. While it's smart to avoid a bubble-like, expat-only existence, resist the urge to state categorically that you want to "only make Italian friends" or "only make expat friends." Instead, seek to vary the spots and crowds you frequent, and see who you connect with organically. Everyone wants to feel seen and heard for who they are; no one wants to be befriended merely because they can check a box as an "Italian friend" or "fellow expat friend" on your list.

As with anywhere, a solid place to start is with common interests. Play tennis at home? Check to see if there are any *circoli* tennis (tennis clubs) in your area. Love to trade stories over *vino*? Seek out wine tastings and clubs. Addicted to film? Head to your local movie theatre(s) to see if they host any clubs or conferences, or browse event websites like MeetUp and InterNations to find social screenings or film discussion groups. Is a faith-based community big for you stateside? Seek one out in your new space.

Hoping to hone your Italian skills and broaden your circle? Sign up for a class and supplement your study by looking for language exchange (*scambio linguistico*) opportunities in your area. In Florence, for example, groups like Speakeasy Multilingual meet regularly and draw language learners and friend seekers of all ages and nationalities. If you're in a small town, simply becoming a regular at a bar in the main *piazza* is sure to make you a subject of fascination—and eventually, with concerted effort on your part, may introduce you to some real friends (or language exchange partners).

The expat experience can be isolating if you wait around for the world to approach you. Stateside, you most likely had to plug into your interests and put yourself out there to build friendships and community. Approach social life in Italy with similar effort. While you're sure to have warm interactions daily—"Everybody flirts in Italy!" Arlene says knowingly—accept that cultivating meaningful connections will take time. Resist the expectation for real community and relationships to arrive overnight, and slowly but surely, you will start building a second *famiglia* in Italy—just as Arlene, Sally and so many other successful dreamers have done.

Considerations for Parents

If, like David and Alatia Bach, you're making the move with children or teenagers, you will have at least one ready-made community to plug into through their schools, which helps with social integration for the whole family. The experience and pool of fellow parents is going to differ significantly depending on whether you opt for a private international school—which often cater to expats, globally minded Italians and intercultural families—or enroll in the state-run system.

The sequence of school in the public system is as follows: *asilo nido* (public daycare for older babies and toddlers; getting a spot can be highly competitive); *scuola materna* (preschool); *scuola elementare* (elementary, for ages six and up); *scuola media* (middle school, roughly from ages 11 to 14); and *scuola superiore* (high school). There are three types of high schools, meaning teens in the public system must think far ahead about the professional or academic route they hope to take. The three main classifications are *liceo* (lyceum), which has subtypes, but is overall the most comparable to the broad-based curricular experience most Americans know; *istituto tecnico* (technical institute); and *istituto professionale* (professional institute).

Beyond schools, attitudes in Italy about the division of labor in raising kids—and all that implies—are complex and vary from place to place. Though the times are a-changing, Italian extended families remain close-knit and within easy reach of each other, frequently dining together on Sundays or throughout the week. Italians who live far away from the area where they grew up continue to be a bit of an anomaly.

This carries some relevant social implications for all expats, but for parents in particular, who may be surprised to see just how deeply embedded the role of grandparents is in Italian culture. The cultural perception of *nonni* as central caretakers is something to be aware of as an expat mom or dad, since the default expectation is that most parents have free help in this form. This can impact everything from school pickup times to your playground conversations with the parents of your child's classmates.

Expat parents may be a little shell-shocked to see all the (usually positive) attention their small children—babies in particular—receive from strangers in public. The flipside of this is that comments on your parenting from well-meaning strangers is par for the course. As you prepare to make the adjustment and dive into Italian life with kids or teens in tow, know that many of the traditional expat cities have social groups and forums geared specifically at international parents who've made a major family move, as well as at intercultural couples with children. Some suggestions are listed in the Resources chapter at the end of this book.

MARY GRAY

Living the Single, Professional Life in Florence

Mary Gray was born and raised in Mississippi and originally came to Florence as a study-abroad student during college. After graduation, she decided to attempt to move to Italy full-time, though her initial plan was to stay only one year. Following a series of misadventures in Rome, she landed back in Florence in 2013, where she has been living and working ever since. A writer, journalist and writing instructor, Mary shares the perspective of a young, single professional woman in Italy. She's the author of the book *Rental Diaries: Thoughts From My Four Walls in Florence.*

Kathy McCabe: Everyone has a story of how they came to *dream of Italy*. What's yours?

Mary Gray: I don't have a drop of Italian blood or influence. The closest approximation to anything Italian in the corner of Mississippi where I was raised were red-sauce restaurants like Tellini's, where I went with my ninth-grade cross-country teammates for "carb loading." Classy!

I did grow up, though, with an eagerness to travel, and an eye toward living on this side of the pond. But I mostly fantasized about places like Paris and London. The Italian interest emerged when I took an art history course in high school. My teacher was a Renaissance fiend, and her passion was contagious. I had an inkling I wanted to study abroad in Florence before I had any idea of where I would go to college.

When I eventually came for a semester, I found language learning to be an addictive adventure, which surprised me! Being thrown into Florence and living with a host mom whose English was nonexistent made me see the real-life rewards of language learning. I felt powerful.

After that semester, I went back to the U.S. to finish my degree, applying for fellowships in Italy in the lead-up to graduation. When none of my "aim-high" approaches worked out, I enrolled in an Italian language school in Rome and found an au pairing opportunity. The au pair setup fell through quickly once I was on the ground. But since I was 22 and had nothing concrete to go back to, my parents agreed to pay my first month's rent if I could cobble things together on my own after that. I threw all my energy into surviving on the 20 hours a week I could legally work—teaching English, studying Italian, babysitting, taking on odd jobs, building up a modest writing portfolio. My friends and I took turns paying for each other's coffees, based on whoever was flushest any given week.

After a year of that, I went back to the U.S. (ironically) for the initial phase of a master's in Italian studies. A vacation after walking the Roman tightrope. My studies then brought me back to Florence, where I slowly started doing part-time work with a local magazine, *The Florentine*. Eventually I was hired full-time as an associate editor. I stayed on for about five years before going freelance in 2019. That job set the blueprint for my career as it is currently.

KM: What makes Florence a good place to be an expat?

MG: Beyond the obvious cultural and culinary perks, it is easy to be spontaneous here. Admittedly, Florence can feel small, especially after so many years in the city now. But even when I was 22 and fancy-free in Rome, I remember having to do a ton of coordination to see friends or arrange meetings. That's not necessary here. The trade-off is that you're never anonymous and you're always bound to run into someone at an inopportune moment. It's not unlike Mississippi in that way, ha!

In my experience, this city tends to draw really soulful, smart people who are hungry for life. For all the waxing poetic about living simply in Italy, I think Florence is full of people who aren't easily satisfied and who will own up to that. I don't mean that in a material sense; I mean people who want a lot of stimulation, connection and "richness" if not wealth. Many want to live in multiple places or travel a lot or create something of value. They recognize that the spaces and the streets where we spend our days add up to something. I value that in the people that surround me.

KM: No matter where you live, everyone in their 20s is making their way and making choices. What do you feel the trade-offs have been professionally and personally?

MG: I'm flattered to get this question since I'm a few months shy of 32! (May I take a "mercy year" off for the time we collectively lost to Covid-19?) Unlike many people who have made the leap, I didn't have to sell things or sever ties; instead, I was just working out the basics of building a life. Truthfully, I think my naïveté—along with my lack of a plan B—worked to my advantage!

Careerwise, I really developed as a writer and journalist here. Being fluent in Italian, while also being a good writer in English, does make you privy to stories and opportunities that parachute journalists can't necessarily get. I was able to carve out some niches and get my work read faster than I might have if I'd been a needle (a recent grad) in a haystack (say, New York media). The downside is that nine years on, I'm just beginning to move beyond living month-to-month. Money will never be my main motivator, and in Italy it can't be, but I've eaten enough canned beans in dimly lit apartments to know that pursuing it and putting it away has its advantages.

I harbor some familial guilt about living here, even though my parents have always encouraged it. I am increasingly cognizant that I'm more of an "Auntie Mame" character than a consistent presence in my nephews' lives. Being far away does make you intentional about staying in touch and making the most of your time together, though. I particularly love having family visit me.

I've gained an extraordinary community, both with people who've made Florence or Italy their long-term home and people who've passed through. Living in such a popular destination has also meant reconnecting with people whose paths probably wouldn't have crossed with mine again if I'd moved to Anywhere, USA. Doing my master's also introduced me to loads of Italy lovers stateside, since my program involved a couple of summers spent on U.S. campuses. These transgenerational, transnational friendships have benefitted both my personal well-being and my career. Living cross-culturally and forever toeing the line of insider-outsider has also taught me so much about the value of, to quote Brené Brown, seeking "belonging" over "fitting in."

KM: What is it like to be a young, single American woman in Italy?

MG: Both marvelous and maddening. For much of my life I felt fairly invisible to the opposite sex, and in Italy that changed. That shift was empowering in some ways, less so in others.

I'll spare you a dissertation on gender dynamics, but I think people can underestimate the challenges of navigating them in another culture. Particularly if you're a strong-willed woman dating men in Italy, or just dealing with them in everyday matters. I don't want to act like there's no fun to be had—there is. And I'll fully own up to the times I've embraced loony lipstick feminist Helen Gurley Brown's 1962 tip to "be brazen when helpless!" Sometimes a foreign gal does need a hand. But generally, I'm not helpless, yet I'm often assumed to be. Many Italian men can be more paternalistic than an educated American woman might like, and not just romantically. While at *The Florentine*, I would often go out with my male colleague to meet clients, and it was common for male clients to ignore me and defer to him on everything.

In Florence, you do meet a lot of women who moved primarily for a partner or spouse, or who met someone early on. Some, not all, have had smoother paths because of it. Beyond the normal "sting" that even the most confident single woman can feel when surrounded by couples, on off days, you can catch yourself resenting those who have that built-in cultural (and usually financial) help. Integration and bureaucratic odysseys are often easier when you've got the intel and unwavering support of someone who grew up here.

KM: You're a great observer of Italian life but especially of Italians themselves. What do you love about Italians?

MG: Florentines are famous for their gruffness, which can be charming or infuriating, depending on the day. Yet I think there's real substance behind the warmth and friendliness of all Italians when it's offered. I don't have much patience for the chirpy, customer-service-y "kindness" that is so common in the U.S. In Italy, there's less of that forced friendliness, so when a gesture is made, or when someone offers exceptional service, it feels like it stems from a place of joy and generosity, rather than an agenda or a sense of obligation.

KM: What's your best piece of advice for those who want to make the move?

MG: If you can't shake the desire to try it, you should probably try it. But don't look to Italy to define you. Don't let your move become the most interesting thing about you and your life. Once you move here, you're going to be surrounded by people who also live here, so it's not like it's a distinguishing characteristic. It's cool, but it's one component of your story. From time to time, I can get disheartened when loved ones stateside express pride in me for "making it work in Italy."

For more information, visit **www.verymarygray.com**

20 *Important Things* to Know About Daily Life in Italy

As I mentioned, I've found Mary Gray to be a great observer of Italian life. I asked her to share some of the nuances she's learned in more than eight years of living the expat life in Florence. This should help anyone moving to Italy get a head start on doing as the Italians do.

1. When making small talk, default to food, not the weather.

2. Always assume that you can't touch the produce. Consider it a trade-off for having easy access to fresh, local goods! Wait your turn at the veggie stand, glove up at the supermarket and count the colors and low costs among your blessings.

3. Your local bar is your neighborhood living room. Becoming a regular there is the fastest way to feel like part of the community and practice the time-honored arts of gossip and *calcio* (soccer) talk.

4. It's crude, but when you're on the go, always carry around tissue paper for emergencies. You really never know what you're going to get in an Italian public restroom. The immaculate state in which

most Italians keep their homes doesn't really translate to the corner *trattoria* or the regional train.

5. Expats and Italians alike love to bemoan bureaucracy, but Italy is a country of miracles. Just when you're ready to ditch your dream, someone swoops in with game-changing news. Chip away piece by piece, accept that "no" and setbacks are part of the adventure, and *piano, piano* (little by little), things will sort out.

6. Know that just as fortune favors the bold, miracles tend to materialize for those who learn the Italian language.

7. Julia Child said a party without cake is just a meeting. In Italy, a dinner table without wine is just a fueling station.

8. Standing in line is not really in the national DNA. But Darwinian changes might be in the cards: Covid-19 restrictions required unprecedented personal space bubbles.

9. Babies and dogs make the best icebreakers. If you have either, expect neighbors and strangers to address them before they address you!

10. Smoking is terrible for you, but in Italy, smokers always know all of the good gossip first.

11. Prepare to meet the *marca da bollo*—the Italian revenue stamp that you must attach nearly every time you sign a document or issue an invoice. You will wonder where all the nickel-and-diming stops. At some point when you are deep in the trenches of bureaucracy, you will inevitably picture treasure chests of cash from all the stamps somewhere in a politician's basement. Try not to go there: Stockpile the stamps, breathe deeply and have a Spritz in the sunshine. It all evens out!

12. Cultural Catholicism plays into everything, but carnality reigns supreme at the beach. You're likely to feel more conspicuous if you're covered up, no matter your age.

13. *Cappuccino* is a breakfast drink; *amaro* is a better after-dinner bet.

14. Cash is king in Italy (and not for the reasons you might think). Always have a few bills and coins on hand; anticipate that people will ask for smaller bills and exact change; and though this can vary, never expect to be able to use a card for any purchase less than 10€.

15. If you thought Google and Facebook had too much data on you, wait till you meet your Italian neighbors. Operate under the assumption that there are no secrets and everyone knows more than you think they do—especially the quiet ones!

16. Hanging laundry out to dry isn't just a staple of Italian postcard photography. It's a daily reality! Good news: You save energy and electricity. Bad news: You may make up the difference in fabric softener and new clothes after sun discoloration.

17. If you have a pressing inquiry, especially in matters of business, make a phone call or in-person visit. Don't send an email.

18. When you're served a plate of *spaghetti alle vongole* (or any dish with seafood), don't ask for cheese if you ever want to be invited back.

19. When you first arrive, you will wonder why everyone's so bundled up in May when the sun is out! Within a year, you will routinely gasp at the American tourists in shorts and marvel at how they aren't freezing.

20. Exaggeration is a national pastime. A light summer shower will be a *bomba d'acqua* ("water bomb") in the press. That day at the post office wasn't busy; no, there was a "giant heap of people" (*montagna di gente*) in line. That project you're proposing isn't mildly complex, it's *impossibile*. Roll with it. Enjoy the drama and find your own part to play in the Italian theater.

Renting a Home in Italy

Even if you have the means to buy property, renting is usually the way to go at the beginning, particularly if you're unsure about how long you will ultimately stay in Italy.

The Basics

A major thing to keep in mind when renting in Italy is that tenants (*inquilini*) hold many valuable rights in the tenant-landlord relationship. While this reflects well on Italy's tendency toward social protections for the most vulnerable, it comes with some drawbacks. Namely, it can mean reluctance on the part of landlords (*padroni di casa* or *proprietari*) to grant long-term contracts or to allow you to establish residency in a given property. You might equate it to the same hesitation that employers have about hiring long-term employees: Evicting a tenant, like firing someone, can be prohibitively expensive and time consuming.

Perhaps it is one reason why many property owners in popular tourist destinations like Florence and Venice opt for the short-term rental market, listing their places on Airbnb and similar portals. Generally speaking, although managing tourist rentals can be labor intensive, it's more lucrative and there's less risk for the landlord. It's little wonder, then, that so many historic centers of Italian cities are seeing long-term residents de-prioritized or even ousted from their units so that owners can convert their properties into vacation rentals.

While this is a sad state of affairs, it's a reality in many Italian (and European) cities today, even after the Covid-19 crisis and the startling phenomenon of deserted centers brought the issue back to the limelight. Damien O'Farrell estimates that in Florence, for example, some 20% of the population owns 80% of the properties—and certainly not all those coveted spaces are going to long-term, tax-paying residents.

Where to Look

Market complications aside, searching for an apartment to rent long term while still abroad is usually necessary for the purposes of visa eligibility, because you will be required to show proof of suitable accommodation when presenting your application and supporting documents. (Some schools and study programs that provide housing services may be able to help ease this process for you, if you elect to come on a student visa.) However, the Internet-based search from afar is not always easy to pull off, and you will want to be wary. If something seems too good to be true, it usually is.

Get your feet wet exploring the Italian rental market on commonly used websites like **Idealista.it, immobiliare.it, bakeca.it, casa.it** and **subito.it** The latter two are more general classifieds websites, while *Idealista* and *Immobiliare* focus exclusively on real estate. If you don't yet have solid Italian skills, using a browser like Google Chrome will allow you to auto-translate the pages enough to get the gist. Note that on those websites, some apartments are posted by private parties (indicated as *privato*; you may also see *no agenzia* or "no agency" written out). Those listed by agencies are usually denoted by a logo or indicated by name.

If you do not have Italy-based friends, contacts or hired help who can visit a rental property on your behalf while you're still stateside, it may be wise to steer clear of private negotiations and instead pursue options that are listed by real estate agencies, requesting a virtual visit if possible. For added peace of mind if you aren't fluent in Italian, you may want to reach out to an English-friendly rental agency that caters to foreigners in your situation.

Many of the major expat destination cities have these businesses in droves—but note that the rental apartments they list will typically be priced a little above standard market rate. That's not because you're an easy-target expat, but simply because these companies often provide specialized services that are out of the wheelhouse of a standard real estate agency.

For those who do not require a visa to enter Italy, the best option might be making a temporary arrangement through a vacation rental-by-owner service like Airbnb or similar, and then searching for a more permanent solution once on the ground. Once you're in Italy, you may find your temp setup is enough to your taste to become a more permanent home. It's not unheard of, in these cases, to negotiate with the owner on establishing a longer-term agreement.

But trying to take that same route when one *does* require a visa is a bit trickier. Know that a vague and short VRBO or Airbnb booking could potentially lead to problems with your application. The specific interpretation of the "suitable accommodation" requirement can vary case by case, but generally, a solid Italian rental contract drawn up that is valid for the length of your stay is the safest bet, and temp setups risk rejection at the consulate.

Types of Leases

So how do the non-temp-setup contracts actually work? Rental leases in Italy adhere to a few main types. Described as follows, there are some clear advantages and disadvantages to each.

Affitto a canone libero (free-market rental agreement): Referred to as a "4+4" contract, this is the standard Italian rental contract and yet can be surprisingly hard to come across in cities with heavy tourist and short-term rental markets. Upon expiring, it is renewed for another four years, and so on for the next four-year cycle, unless a formal letter of cancellation (*disdetta*) is sent at least six months before. Upon the first expiration, the renewal is mandatory on the landlord's end (although the tenant is free to withdraw). Landlords can object to the first auto-renewal only for highly specific and exceptional reasons. "In actual fact, it is only the landlord who is bound to the same tenant for a minimum of four years and a maximum of eight years. The tenant has much more flexibility," says attorney *Michele Capecchi.* (Although this type of agreement should be used in the majority of cases, in practice, once you see how the system works in tenants' favor, it's no surprise that you meet landlords who are hesitant about who they take on board, and often end up opting for short-term leases or renting to tourists.)

Affitto a Canone Concordato (rent-controlled agreement): The base duration in this type of "3+2" agreement is three years, and here, too, the lease is automatically renewed, and so on for each successive expiration, unless a formal letter of cancellation (*disdetta*) is sent via registered mail (*raccomandata*) at least six months before the contract's end. The key difference between this type of agreement and the *affitto a canone libero* is that the first binds the landlord for a longer period of time, but allows him or her to set the rent without specific restrictions, while a contract of *affitto a canone concordato* is less of a time commitment but sets a cap on the price of rent.

Affitto a Uso Transitorio (contract for transitory/temporary purposes): You're likely to spot lots of contracts like this in cities that are major destinations for workers and student populations—think Florence, Rome, Milan. These contracts have a minimum duration of one month and a maximum of 18 months. Be aware that the document must explicitly state why the tenant (you) only needs the property temporarily.

Contratto Per Uso Turistico (contract for tourism purposes): Be very wary of anyone who proposes a "contract for tourism purposes" when you plan to stay in an apartment longer than a few days, weeks or months. These types of contracts are designed to permit use of an apartment for

a limited time frame—a holiday or language study period, for example—
after which the owner regains his/her property. The contract will denote
the "holiday" purpose of the arrangement and will usually state that the
tenant's primary residence is elsewhere. *Capecchi* explains that while
Italian law does not clearly state a maximum duration for this type of
lease, making one beyond three months is "inadvisable."

Utilities and Fees

No matter what type of contract you obtain, it's important to be extremely
explicit—get it in writing—about whether or not utilities are included in
the monthly rent, and which ones are if so. Clarify, too, whether or not
electricity, gas and water will be in your name or in the landlord's name.
(When these utilities are left in the landlord's name—usually in shorter-term agreements—often the owner may simply come to you with a
lump sum of what you owe every few months.)

If you're moving in as a tenant in a longer-term arrangement, you
will often have to deal directly with activating your utility agreements
and moving them over to your name (the landlord or real estate agent,
if you're involving one, might help with some steps of this process to
ensure your place is primed for move-in day). If electricity and gas
meters are present but inactive in your new place, you will need to call
the suppliers and request the *subentro*, or reactivation. If instead they're
already active with a valid contract, you should request the *voltura*,
which simply transfers the contract to your name and should not take
much processing time.

Giving hard-and-fast averages on utilities and pricing is next to
impossible, since consumption, property size and other factors vary so
widely. But in general, particularly if your utilities aren't included in your
monthly rent, you should be aware of a few key elements of your potential
place before moving in. Ask the landlord about *riscaldamento autonomo*
(autonomous heating) versus *riscaldamento condominiale/centralizzato*

(central heating). In the former case, you have full control and pay only for what you consume, while in the latter, apartments in the building split the heating costs, with timing and temperature settings chosen based on building admin agreements and local laws.

Get clear on how the hot water supply works, too: The majority of apartments have their own *caldaia,* or small gas boiler, which must be checked annually, often at the tenant's expense. These boilers do not limit your hot water consumption, but if you're in a building with central heating, you may have an electric hot water heater, where the supply will run out when too many tenants are showering consecutively!

Apartments in Italy are overwhelmingly individually owned, so building business and budgeting is often overseen by either an appointed resident or an external manager (*amministratore*). Expect to pay a *condominio* (condominium) fee, a monthly extra tacked on to your rent in nearly all shared buildings. Condo fees typically include cleaning of common areas, stairwell lights and the like, but may also include extras, sometimes utilities like water. Generally, if a *condominio* fee is more than about 50€ monthly, you should be seeing something included beyond just the cursory sweeps and scrubs; amenities like elevators, for example, may significantly contribute.

When responding to rental ads, always get clarity about whether the listed price includes the condo fee. *Condominio* fees are typically found in big-city apartment buildings rather than in the countryside.

Pricing and Paperwork

Monthly rental averages are all over the map around Italy and are calculated based on factors that transcend size. Still, consider euro per square meter when comparing possibilities. Location, of course, is paramount in pricing, so if your place is close to public transport, supermarkets and shops, and in the center of town or within easy reach of it, you're likely to see that reflected in the rent.

The process of seeking an apartment or space to rent and finalizing the contract, like most bureaucratic processes in Italy, requires substantial paperwork. Particularly when signing longer-term leases, your landlord will want to see tax returns, a work contract if applicable and in some cases, character recommendations from past landlords, bosses or colleagues. In ads, you might see this requirement expressed as *solo referenziati* ("only people with references"). Freelancers should make sure their books are in order and their ducks in a row if they want to be viewed in a favorable light. For younger renters, or those whose income is not above the landlord's preferred (and likely unstated) threshold, a *garante* (guarantor) may be required.

Most renters should expect to pay a security deposit (one to two months' rent, but more in some cases), the first month's rent and, where applicable, an agency fee, usually all upon the signing of the contract.

Quirks of Renting

Florence resident Sally Carrocino, currently a renter, notes that when many people ask her for her intel on moving from the States, they're reluctant to part with their things, or overwhelmed by the thought of it. But she always tells people, "Don't put stuff in storage, because you're never going to want to go back and get it out of storage. Cut the cord, just cut the cord and do it. Bring some important things, some things that you're really in love with. But, it's just stuff, you know. You don't have to bring your mother's tea collection."

It's advice to be heeded: Shipping things internationally is rarely worth the trouble. Better to plan to rent a furnished (*arredato*) or partially furnished (*parzialmente arredato* or *semi arredato*) place. The latter, although loosely defined, can often be ideal: In her book *Rental Diaries: Thoughts From My Four Walls in Florence,* Mary Gray calls a partially furnished option "the sweet spot for foreign-born people with 4+4 contracts. It means you can forgo things like Byzantine Jesus prints in the boudoir, but don't have to buy your own refrigerator."

That may be an exaggeration of the traditional *nonna* aesthetic you can find in overly furnished places, but the extreme opposite is something to note when scrolling through ads: Often places listed as "unfurnished" (*non arredato*) won't even include built-in kitchens. Partially furnished is usually a solid compromise.

Temper your expectations about both air conditioning and dryers, as they're exceptions, not the norm, in Italy. And, if fast-functioning WiFi is a priority for you, seek out a neighborhood or area covered by *fibra ottica* (fiber-optic Internet). You will have to deal with setting up the Internet contract yourself in many cases.

THE BARTNERS

Living the Farm Life

Ashley and Jason Bartner's love affair with Italy is intertwined with their own love story: As newlyweds, these New Yorkers visited Italy in 2005 and decided to take a leap of faith in starting an *agriturismo* in a 500-year-old farmhouse in *Le Marche*. They live in the region full-time, running *La Tavola Marche*, which is composed of a B&B, a farm and a cooking school using ingredients grown on site. The Bartners pushed themselves out of their comfort zone not only by moving to Italy, but also by trading in the big city for country living, where they have learned to farm and garden.

Kathy McCabe: Did either you or your husband have a *dream of Italy*, or not really?

Ashley Bartner: Not really. It wasn't anything on our radar. We were just doing the regular grind in New York. We didn't come from families that traveled. This wasn't like, well, we always thought we would move internationally or abroad. This just happened. We thought it was the right time in our life for a change. And I think that was, more than anything, what we were looking for.

We first came to Italy in 2005 on our honeymoon, and a year and a half later, we were living in the house that we are still in today. So, we moved here in December of 2007. Italy checked things off on our list, like: learn a new language, start a garden, get our hands dirty, make our home our castle.

KM: What surprised you the most about moving to Italy?

AB: I think what surprised me the most was how welcoming the people in our area were. I mean, we knew; we both worked in hospitality for years. So, the business itself wasn't going to be a big surprise. Jason knew the kitchen; I knew the marketing and the hospitality. The garden was going to be something that we were eager to learn, and the country living.

KM: So, backing up, your *dream of Italy* started in 2005. How the heck did it end up in *Le Marche* of all places?

AB: Everyone kept saying go to *Umbria*, it's the next Tuscany. But that wasn't what we were looking for. We wanted something a bit more off the beaten path, and something where we were learning from the locals.

So then, we started to hear about and hone in on *Le Marche*. The prices were a little bit lower because *Le Marche* has long been very much a region for farming. The strategic part was not only the financial, but also, I always try to think of myself as the traveler. If we are starting to look in *Le Marche*, how far are we from train stations and airports and the breadbasket of Italy and *Emilia-Romagna*, and these different kind of food trips. We thought, "Well, this could be an undiscovered part that we could guide travelers through."

KM: I totally think of you guys as farmers now, so you were not farmers or gardeners before?

AB: We never had a garden. We didn't grow up with parents with gardens or anything. So, we just asked a lot of questions. And that was welcome. Also, we came at a time where the people our age in Italy were going away from the country life, and they weren't so interested in knowing these old recipes or spending time on a Tuesday at 10 in the morning to go forage for wild greens.

So, we ate it up and the locals didn't seem to care who they were sharing this information with. They were just happy to share it. I think, for Jason, that's been one of the most fulfilling parts of doing this, is learning to become self-sustainable, just growing your own food and being proud of that and starting it from seed and then finishing it at the table. And that feels really good.

KM: Can you summarize what *La Tavola Marche* is?

AB: *La Tavola Marche* literally means "the *Marche* table," because we feel the hub of Italian life is at the table. So, that's what our goal is, to bring people around the table, and to get to know the culture through the food and through the people, and for a real slice of life of the Italian countryside. Not just pasta and sauces class, but making sausages from scratch or a whole hog butchery. It's a bit more of a full experience.

KM: Does it matter that you're American or not? In a way, does it bring people who wouldn't be so adventurous to *Le Marche* because you're there?

AB: I think so. I think there's a comfort when you know that you're so far from home. Again, I use the stupid phrase "off the beaten path." When you're so far off the guidebooks that you want to have someone there who you can ask all your questions to, there feels a little bit of something of home about it, whether it's that we have actual queen-size beds instead of twins pushed together or whatever it may be, but there's a connection that's tangible because we have the common language.

KM: I have a feeling that you and your husband have inspired a lot of Italian dreams from guests who have come to see you. Are there some guests you remember whose lives changed not just by coming to Italy, but also by coming to your little corner of the world?

AB: Yes. Guests have come out here, seen what we've done, and were just inspired by taking a change and a risk in their life. One guest went back home and opened a haberdashery shop, because he thought, "If Ashley and Jason can move to Italy and learn a language, and do something over there, why can't I open this shop in a town that I live in already doing something that I enjoy?"

KM: I know you've also inspired at least one guest to move to Italy. You also run workshops on moving to Italy. What's the common challenge for people wanting to move to Italy?

AB: I think sometimes it is unrealistic time frames. People are in one of two categories: moving in 18 months or in five years. And most of the people who want to move in five years, we say, "Great, you guys are smart. You're planning ahead. Who knows what could be going on by then? But at least, you got the ball rolling for figuring a lot of this out." The 18 months, it's like, "Well, I hope you have money and are ready to rock and roll."

We always say have a time frame and work backwards. If you give yourself the time and work backwards and you say, "Okay, I could start collecting some of these documents right now that aren't time-sensitive." And then, as it gets closer to my visa meeting, I know I need to get these things that are going to expire.

KM: How did you get started on your business?

AB: Because we have the history in hospitality, we sat down and we wrote a serious business plan, like hundreds of pages. We always tell people to do this, because even if you don't go back to it or it doesn't even go to plan, at least you go through and ask yourself the questions, like: Do the numbers work? Does this make sense? You figure out how you're going to execute this plan, and the competition.

Where we are today is exactly what we had planned for. I think it took us a few years to get the ball rolling. It took time to make these relationships with the locals, which gives us great street cred. Otherwise, with the language barrier and the little-known information on our area, it would be hard to have that same experience. When we first moved, my sister told us, "This isn't as great as you said it was going to be." She had come to help us scrub walls and paint. I just said, "It will be." It felt like, if you build it, they will come. We knew it would take a while, but it was also why we were confident enough to pick a little-known area down a long dirt road where you have to want to come. You don't stumble upon us by any means.

KM: The self-employed visa applies to businesses like vineyards and *agriturismi* like yours. Can you explain how to get this visa?

AB: The self-employed visa requires us to have a location and the business set up. That's the *nulla osta*. Both the Chamber of Commerce and the police station need to submit a form saying that there's no contest for you to operate your business.

Sometimes what will happen is one will say, "Well, we'll sign it once the other person signs it." And then the other person says, "Well, we'll sign it when the other guy signs it." So, that's when you need a good *commercialista* (accountant and sometimes business advisor) who's a local to where you're going to be, who can maybe know someone in the office, who can call and try to smooth things out. Someone who you can trust completely and who knows how to navigate the bureaucratic waters.

KM: Are there incentives to move and buy a farm? Are they worthwhile? Are there EU grants?

AB: Well, there are these things. Is it going to be worth it? If you open your doors to the state for funding, sometimes you have to open your books in different ways as well.

The hard part with a lot of the Italian stuff is that you get it back in your taxes over the next 12 years. So, we've most often just done it ourselves and not waited for the handout. I know a lot of people who get stuck in that. We even consulted with some Italians who were starting a business in Sicily, and they just kept waiting for these Italian and EU bonuses, and they never got their projects started.

KM: Do you think now is a good time to move to Italy?

AB: I would say, use this time to really do your homework, to really learn the language, to research, research, research and keep looking at these properties. Go ahead and contact them. I don't know when the doors will be open that people can come that way to move.

For more information, visit **www.latavolamarche.com**

Buying and Renovating Property in Italy

If you've traveled to Italy enough to know that a more permanent move or connection to the peninsula is what you're after, you're probably looking at the hurdles (and joys) of owning your own property. As inspiring as Frances Mayes and the *Under the Tuscan Sun* phenomenon can be, hold your horses before you call up *House Hunters International* and tell them you're purchasing a ramshackle *Bramasole* of your own. Some aspects of setting up life in Italy can be waded through alone by the pluckiest and most patient of adventurers, but with buying property, you don't want to mess around.

Of course, the first thing that comes to mind when purchasing a property is cost. Rome-based interior designer Arlene Antoinette Gibbs advises, "There is a house for every budget. I think sometimes people think, 'This is not a dream that's attainable for me.' You don't have to be a multimillionaire. You have to be realistic. If you have a limited budget,

---

Note: The information contained in this section gives a general overview of these processes and visas, but is not intended to be comprehensive and does not constitute legal advice.

you can't say, 'I want to buy a house in *Capri* or *Portofino.*' You have to think of another region."

The Basics

If you don't have income in Italy, though, you may not get a mortgage. Because of the 2008 financial crisis and bad behavior by American banks, Italian banks are wary of lending to Americans. You will likely need to come prepared with your own money, such as leveraging a home equity loan on existing properties.

One thing to be aware of before you begin house hunting is that Italy's family-centric culture holds important implications for the real estate market, as it does for so many sectors. Properties are generally passed down within families, and one 2018 ISTAT survey revealed that 70% of Italians own their homes. Because of this, notes American-born, licensed realtor Sean Carlos (**www.seancarlos.org**)—a well-known expert in expat real estate circles for his perspective on navigating Italian home buying and renovation—the buying process usually goes smoothly.

Since so many Italians own their homes, sellers are most often motivated to sell a property because they've inherited it and do not need it. The second most common reason for selling is that the seller wants to move from the city to the countryside or vice versa.

"In Italy, inheritance law is such that a portion of your estate when you die must go to direct relatives. Exactly who gets how much depends on the relationship and the like. The result of that is that a property may have six or seven or eight owners, each with small portions of ownership," Sean says. "Mobility is a very different issue in Italy. It is much less of a factor than in the U.S. We don't have the 'cut our losses' culture here that you have in the U.S. because nobody wants to move."

Cool your jets before you make any drastic moves based on any of these realities, though. The first thing you should do is seek legal counsel on your situation and eligibility. Michael Cioffi, founder of boutique hotel *Monteverdi Tuscany*, never went about buying and renovating blindly, even in the initial stages. "The very first thing I did before I bought anything is I hired a good lawyer who is still my lawyer today, and he has closed every transaction," Michael says. "It really is important."

Also important to know straight away is that owning property in Italy does not automatically confer a right to a *permesso di soggiorno*, permanent residency, citizenship or stays beyond three months at a time. There is no unicorn permit for wealthy property owners—no "golden visa," as attorney *Michele Capecchi* describes it—nor is there a means of buying your way into the country for longer than the 90 days' stay within every 180 days allowed for American citizens. However, if you're looking to come to Italy through other avenues, such as through an elective residence visa, owning a property can help streamline the application process, since it demonstrates that you have somewhere concrete to reside upon arrival. On its own, though, it means virtually nothing for immigration.

Worth keeping in mind, too, is how the Covid-19 crisis and its short- to medium-term effects are still underway as we compile this guide. The long-term ramifications on Italy's property market remain to be seen. A December 2020 report jointly compiled by real estate agencies *Gabetti*, *Professionecasa* and *Grimaldi* found that property prices in Italy's cities dropped, on average, by -1.1% during the first nine months of 2020, relative to 2019. But the same report showed that property costs went up in non-regional capital towns and cities.

As remote work has now become a reality for so many, it and other social shifts brought on by the pandemic are likely to impact the market. Additionally, for the short to medium term, Italy's economic relaunch plan has introduced the Superbonus, a 110% tax credit on home energy efficiency improvement efforts, aiming to help revive the sector. (Non-resident property owners are also eligible to claim it.)

ʙuying Uersus Uacationing

Pandemic or no pandemic, though, a key facet of buying property in Italy has always been balancing dreams with practicalities. Home designer, television host and producer Debbie Travis is good at this. She runs regular getaways to Tuscany for groups and has been knee-deep in more than a few property purchases and adventurous renovations. Buying-versus-vacationing discrepancies are something she encourages prospective purchasers to keep in mind. "When you rent on a shorter-term trip, especially in Tuscany, you can rent these magnificent places that are 25 minutes down a dirt road, and it's amazing," Debbie says. "But not when you're living there and it's like, oh! You forgot the milk. Back to the village you go."

If you want to avoid various iterations of those "I forgot the milk" scenarios playing out over the years, it's important to get clarity up front about the place(s) you're eyeing, whether you're city-bound or have your sights set on small town life. Like Michael, *Capecchi* emphasizes that even the savviest real estate investor should not buy in Italy without legal support and asking for detailed reports on the property's physical condition.

However, given that the majority of the houses in Italy (Tuscany in particular) are super old, it's standard to sell a house as is. While the seller has to disclose structural issues or any known legal problems affecting the property to the potential buyer, the former cannot guarantee the quality of the house's systems nor that of the roof or basement.

So, if the buyer wants to be reassured regarding the (structural and legal) conditions of the property, he or she should hire a surveyor and a lawyer. In fact, attorney *Capecchi* clarifies that many foreign buyers contact him for help during this preliminary phase of due diligence, to be sure that the house they are interested in isn't concealing flaws or legal burdens.

Check for Open Claims

Once again, Italy's family-first culture comes into play. Since properties often get passed down within families, it's common for multiple names to appear on titles, and all of those listed family members need to consent to putting a property on the market. But this doesn't always happen, which means if you're not careful, you could risk putting down money for a property that isn't legitimately for sale. Before reaching this stage, get a lawyer on board who will help you to disclose potential issues and to ensure that the property does not have any open claims—*ipoteche* in Italian—from creditors. If open claims are found, the lawyer will help you to determine whether those claims or urban discrepancies can be resolved, at what cost and on what timeline.

Reviewing this will require consulting with the *catasto*, or cadaster, the Italian system of land registration, which is managed at the relevant local level. This registry also holds records of past transfers of ownership. The number of preliminary documents that need to be reviewed and collected before filing an offer justifies why you shouldn't simply rely on information provided by the seller or by the real estate agent, but should have a legal proxy.

Some properties for sale may be advertised as *da ristrutturare*, requiring renovation/restoration. The specific shades of what this means can vary, but generally they're largely uninhabitable, needing far more than a paint job and a little TLC or what's considered ordinary maintenance (*manutenzione*). In a place advertised as "requiring renovation," you may even need to get basic plumbing and electricity set up, a process that can take many months. In the meantime, you may need to purchase a generator as you and your crew go about your work. When there are no electricity or gas meters on a property, you will need to request them from the local distributor; the process and associated cost of hooking up your initial utilities is called *allacciamento*.

Double Your Budget

Multiple property owners with whom we spoke while compiling this guide have suggested that you should double whatever budget you have in mind, particularly if you plan to renovate. Debbie, who renovated her full-time home in Tuscany, urges prospective buyers to think about what it is they'll actually be doing in their dream digs. "What are you going to do there? Are you going to use it as a holiday house? Are you going to live there full-time? Are you going to have a project? Are you going to write? Are you going to do something else specific?"

Perhaps you want to rent the property out to tourists when you're not using it; if so, practical issues of access should be top of mind. Are you near an airport? Maybe you want to advertise the place as far off the beaten track, but you want the renters to be able to find you, both when seeking a vacation spot and once on the ground.

Debbie points out that it's easy to be overly romantic about purchasing property in Italy, and that you need to think not only about your own vision for the space, but also about family members, friends and the slew of potential visitors who are likely to emerge from the woodwork once they learn what you're up to. "When you buy in Tuscany," Debbie says knowingly, "suddenly everyone is your friend again and wants to come and stay."

In the same vein as our advice to take a three-month trial run, try out the type of property you'd like to live in. Combine the two! "Really try it out and try it out with friends. It's not that expensive to rent; you can rent incredible places. Go with four couples or a bunch of screaming kids and then you go, 'Well, when we get our house, I'm going to make sure they're outside. I need a barn because I need to put other people's screaming kids in the barn,'" Debbie laughs.

Searching online from abroad may give you a surface-level idea of the market, but both Debbie and Damien O'Farrell caution prospective buyers not to rely too heavily on the Internet. As with so many things in Italy, word of mouth and becoming a familiar face in the community will get you far; putting out feelers and connecting with sellers during your trial run can be a solid strategy.

"You get an idea on the Internet, but it's really very false," Debbie says. "And agents work incredibly differently in Italy than they do anywhere else. They're not very hungry. You're standing there with a suitcase full of money and they're like, 'Yeah, whatever.' The best way to go about searching is to determine the area you like and then rent something there and get to know people, the locals, the bar," where you're likely to get intel on what's coming up for sale. Using the trial run period to make friends and connections before you buy will also mean you have a network to draw upon when you're back in the States and need help with in-Italy legwork.

Italy does not have multiple listing sites (MLS) comparable to Zillow or Trulia in the U.S. Two of the main websites for browsing properties are **Immobiliare.it** and **Idealista.it**, but don't expect to find everything that's on the market in those single locations.

Sean says, "Often sellers don't commit to one agency. They list with multiple agencies, which means you might have the same property listed five times by different agencies with different prices, different data. Four of the five agencies will lose money on the listing because they won't sell it. There's not a lot of rigor in what's being listed, how it's being presented, the quality of the photos. They're photos that were taken by somebody's cell phone without thinking about the lighting, the setting, the *staging,* as it were."

When looking for a property, it's important not to treat Italy as a homogenous country. Home prices and processes will be different across small towns, big cities and everything in between. Further, you may be tempted to stretch your budget by buying in a cheaper region, but keep in mind that small towns and certain regions may be cheaper for a reason.

Property in Italy adheres to the cardinal rule of real estate: location, location, location. As Sean puts it, "You get what you pay for. If a place and a property is very desirable, like a villa with a pool in Rome, you're going to pay through the nose. If the property is somewhat modest and in a location that nobody wants for whatever reason, then it might be a bargain. People have been distracted by stories of properties with very little value in places that Italians are abandoning. People are thinking that property in Italy is cheap everywhere, and they can have something in Italy they can't have at home. Some places in *Piemonte*, they're remote, hard to get to, and maybe you're lacking Internet. Maybe lacking public services like water."

Be prepared, too, for many rural properties to offer a *real* retreat from technology. Check the coverage in your desired area before buying, if reliable Internet is a long-term priority. Internet providers will be reluctant to build new lines for one customer, and you may be in for years of pestering them before you see any movement on this.

Finding a Licensed Realtor

It might be advantageous to hire a realtor to work with while you're still abroad—but only after getting a solid referral. Note that many properties in Italy will be legitimately represented by multiple real estate agents. Keep in mind, however, that many people advertise themselves as real estate agents when they aren't licensed as such; instead, they're more like consultants. Real estate is a licensed profession in Italy, as in the U.S., but only 20% of Italian applicants pass the required exam.

Sean explains that a property finder is usually "one of two things. It's somebody working illegally who's unqualified and is trying to provide a service for which they have no training, no background. It's not legal. *Or*, it's a fully licensed, fully qualified real estate agent. So in the latter case, ultimately that's a real estate agent working as a buyer's agent as opposed to the listing agent. So that is one thing people need to be wary of, if someone's presenting themselves as an 'agent of an agent.' A property finder working with agents doesn't exist legally."

If you do end up finding a property on your own and opt for a private sale, you will still need to bring on board the right professionals to ensure that everything is as it should be—a lawyer, notary, perhaps a surveyor. If you instead work with a licensed realtor from the get-go, they can take care of assembling that team for you.

Many properties in Italy are sold by owner—perhaps even more so than in the U.S., notes Sean. Other properties are sold by a listing agent, who "in theory is working impartially for both the buyer and the seller. If I'm a buyer and I contact the listing agent, there's just one agent involved," says Sean.

Sean explains another scenario in the listing process wherein, hypothetically, "I, the buyer, don't want to do the legwork, don't want to look through listings myself, or I'm looking through listings, but I want someone who speaks my language to guide me through the process regardless of who the listing agent is, so I engage a buyer's agent who then collaborates with the listing agent."

In any case, both the buyer and seller pay a commission. There's no legally set commission, but what you as the buyer will pay to the realtor hovers around 3% of the purchase price, plus VAT (22%). The seller will pay a similar amount.

In addition, when you contact the listing agent, "you are implicitly acknowledging their contribution to putting the buyer and seller together. If you proceed to purchase, and only if you proceed to purchase, you are clearly, unless negotiated otherwise, on the hook to pay them commission. And that would complicate things should you decide you wish to have a buyer's agent help you navigate the cultural, legal and linguistic differences between your market," says Sean.

Costs and property appraisal can be overwhelming, but a good start for understanding and comparing properties for sale, as with rentals, is to examine the rate of euros per square meter. Listings will usually indicate homes' sizes in *metri commerciali* (commercial meters), which can be misleading, as the walls are factored in; the *metri calpestabili* (usable meters) are what composes the actual usable/livable space.

You will also want to be aware of the distinction between *valore commerciale* (commercial value) versus the *valore catastale* (cadastral value), which, confusingly enough, is based on a figure called the *rendita catastale* (cadastral income). The cadastral income is calculated according to factors like number of rooms, materials used, the year of construction, location and more. (If you end up renovating, the cadastral income will shift.) Ultimately, it's the cadastral value that will determine what you pay in purchase taxes and property taxes, in combination with other factors.

Making the Offer

When you finally reach the exciting phase of being in a position to make an offer, there are three main steps to keep in mind: the *proposta di acquisto* (purchase proposal), the *compromesso* (or preliminary contract) and the *rogito* (deed/closing). Generally, at the purchase proposal stage, an early deposit and a signed statement of the price being offered is required. Making a game plan with a realtor can be particularly useful here, as you might be able to oust competition by offering a heftier down payment. If the offer is ultimately accepted, the specific details of the transaction will be spelled out in the *compromesso* (also sometimes called the *contratto preliminare di acquisto*, literally "preliminary contract").

At this stage, the obligation of both parties to sign the final contract is cemented. Signing the final deed of sale will take place before a notary; this process of closing is called *rogito* (deed) or the *atto pubblico di compravendita* (final act of sale). If you are not fluent in Italian, the law requires the deed to be translated by a certified professional or that you appoint an attorney who can speak Italian and English to represent you during the notary deed and sign the contract on your behalf. The translation then becomes part of the public deed.

Taxes

Tax obligations and breaks, both in the purchase stage and in the years that follow, are, like so many things in Italy, highly dependent on individual situations. In general, a land registry tax (*imposta catastale*) will be payable (by the buyer) on all property transactions. Additional purchase taxes are paid by the buyer and will be variable depending on whether you're purchasing from a private individual, a VAT-registered company or a developer. Calculations also depend on whether or not the property will become your primary residence or a second home/holiday house.

Italian legislation offers a tax break when purchasing your *prima casa* (first home), which is understood to be a non-luxury, primary residence. Recall, though, that you can't purchase a property as a way of establishing legal residency or getting a visa. So to be eligible for this break, you'd need to either (1) be a resident with your immigration status already sorted through other means or (2) have a viable way of immigrating and establishing residency in the property's municipality within 18 months of the purchase. (Don't hedge your bets. Failing to declare residency within that allotted time frame will mean paying the difference in taxes plus a penalty.)

While all owners will pay taxes for the real estate property they own in Italy to the Italian government annually, attorney *Capecchi* clarifies that simply owning a property in Italy will not, on its own, make you subject to the country's income tax system. You become tax liable (1) if you have established your legal residency with the local municipality, (2) if you spend more than 183 days in Italy and (3) if the majority of your personal or business interests are in Italy. Therefore, owning a home in Italy can be one of the factors used in assessing whether or not Italy is your primary fiscal residence. So if you plan to spend the majority of the fiscal year in Italy, you will likely be subject to the income tax system in addition to annual property taxes.

The perk of Italian homebuying is that property taxes are usually nominal compared to those in the U.S. Sean explains, "If I'm living in Italy and have residency in a home that I own, then I don't generally pay tax on that home. As long as it's not considered a luxury property, basically. If it's a second home, then I do have to pay property tax. In other words, if it's a vacation home, my residency is in the U.S., then generally

I will be on the hook for property tax. But somebody who's going to retire to Italy and get an elective residence visa, in most cases they will not be paying property tax."

So You Want to Renovate?

If you've found your dream property and have decided to renovate, *congratulazioni* (congrats)! Buying a fixer-upper—or even just adding your touch to an already-solid property—is a challenging undertaking. But it's packed with rewards. Just be sure that before you embark on a laborious renovation project, you're clear on what the end purpose of the property will be—most likely living in the house or renting it out, perhaps as a vacation property. "We don't flip houses here," says Arlene. "If you buy property here, it has to be with the mentality that you're never going to sell it."

Buying in your home country often means buying "for the schools, for the job, for the location, safe area, all this kind of stuff," Debbie says. "But when you're buying your dream, it's very easy to see that gorgeous farmhouse and go, 'Oh my God, I'm going to be Frances Mayes, I'm going to do this, this and this,'" Debbie laughs.

And you should be excited! Still, a chief concern, from day one until job done, will be staying on top of regulations and urban planning laws related to historic and archaeological preservation. There are many in Italy, overseen by a range of local, regional and national bodies and cultural commissions.

Arlene advises, "The most important thing you need is a very good team around you, and that would include the architect. Depending on where your house is, it might be in an area that gets seismic activities, so you need a structural engineer and also a *geometra*. In America, we would call them a surveyor, but it doesn't quite describe what they do. They will be the first people actually to walk through your property, and they are the ones who pull the permits and give them to the local *comune*, or municipal hall as we would call it."

Not only will these professionals be well versed in Italian real estate law and procedures, they will also speak fluent Italian. Popular resources for culling together word-of-mouth referrals are Facebook groups such as Renovating Italy, or another called Buying Property in Italy.

Once you have your construction team, you may need design help— but not necessarily from whom you might expect. Arlene explains, "In America, if someone is a licensed interior designer, if you say, 'Okay, you want to tear down a wall,' they can do that work. In Italy, that's not the case; you can't do that. The field of interior design as we know it does not really exist in Italy. The Italians who do interiors are trained architects. They can do everything except maybe what we call soft furnishings: picking out furniture, picking out fabric, picking the wall color."

Florence-based *Danella Lucioni*, the founder of Ardium Studio and the owner-renovator of several popular vacation rental apartments, advises that if you want something done well, each contractor should be hired for his or her specialty. Think twice about fly-by-night jack-of-all-trade types who claim they can do it all. Get a *falegname* to install the doors; a *vetraio* to do custom glass; a *muratore* for walls; an *imbianchino* to paint; and a *piastrellista* or *pavimentista* to set tiles for flooring. If you have a capable and trustworthy architect overseeing your project, he or she will likely assemble this team themselves, but not all architects will apply the "specialists-only" approach if there are agreements and referral fees at play, so do your homework.

Materials and labor costs will fluctuate depending on the area you're in. What you can and can't change in your house will also vary widely by region. Tuscany, for example, is known for its stringent stipulations. Know that these can slow processes down wherever you are, and accept setbacks as part of the process.

Expect Delays

It's not just costs that should be overestimated. One thing nearly everyone who's undertaken a renovation project in Italy agrees on is that it will take longer than you expect. Discount the entire month of August and at least half of December when mapping out projected workdays, and double any timeline a contractor gives you. On the bright side, "There are significant financial incentives to renovate homes, including improving energy efficiency and, in some areas, earthquake mitigation. These incentives are very real and are worth investigating," Sean notes.

While not a hard and fast rule, you can generally expect to face more renovation obstacles and restrictions when your property is located in areas of prime patrimony, such as in a historic center or a rural landscape with special protections. Though the specific bodies you must answer to or receive permissions from will depend on the nature of your proposal, when in doubt, start at your municipal hall (the *comune* building) and work your way up. Having a grade-A architect for more ambitious renovation projects can help make knowing who to turn to easier.

One term to be aware of is *vincolo delle belle arti*, roughly translated as "fine arts obligation," and applied directly to places deemed to be of cultural interest. Even boarding up a window or knocking down a wall can be a weighty issue. Though the rules can seem needlessly restrictive while you're in the thick of things, as Debbie puts it, "When you're done, you're very happy because you know the farm over the hill is not going to suddenly be painted fluorescent pink."

While we're on the subject of pink, *Danella* cautions women overseeing renovations that the testosterone-heavy crews may readily stereotype you and be reluctant to listen. You need to get comfortable putting your foot down. "Often you will be patronized and expected not to know the difference between a screw and a nail," *Danella* says.

Whatever your gender or general know-how with renovating, part of staying on top of things and not being patronized or taken for a ride is ensuring that you get solid quotes (*preventivi*) on everything. It's an effective way to comparison shop and will help you in the planning stages. If you don't speak Italian, consider hiring an interpreter—*Danella* suggests an architecture student, who will be well versed in the lingo and lay of the land—to call and get quotes for you.

Be aware that some properties on the market may look fully habitable, yet may not technically be classified in the land registry (*catasto*) under the "A" category, which encompasses residential properties. They may be sold at seemingly bargain rates, but if you want to be able to legally live there, you're in for an expensive and lengthy conversion process.

The renovation icon herself, Frances Mayes, is not entirely convinced that Italian property bureaucracy and regulations are all that worse than their counterparts in the U.S. "It's so much easier in *Cortona* than trying to get anything done in San Francisco. Really," she says. "I mean, we don't have much bureaucracy in North Carolina where I live now, but you have to do permits for your house renovation and they take time. But it's just... a process." Trust the process, and consider that many expat renovation experiences may be colored by language barriers or lack of community to draw from for help and labor.

But the only way to get plugged into the community in the first place is to put yourself out there, and starting a renovation project is a surefire method for doing it well. "Renovating is a way into the community. You learn about all the people who are working for you and their families and it's just one of those secret benefits to moving here—the fact that with your team you really learn a lot," Frances says. "Also, it's just a magnificent sense to be restoring something to the patrimony."

The Customer Is Always Wrong

However, be sure to stay in the community's good graces as an American and a foreigner, as the philosophy of work in Italy is much different from our own. Arlene explains that "America is a very transactional culture, and if people think they're going to make money, they'll do business with you. Italy is not like that. Yes, people want to make a living and do well, but it's also about relationships. You can't just be a bulldozer. You can't have that attitude of, 'Well, the customer is always right.' That's an American thing.

In Italy, the customer is always wrong. When you get a sense of how the locals move in that world, it will make your life so much easier."

Whether you're moving into a readily habitable home and just adding on a few flourishes, embarking on a top-to-toe overhaul in a dilapidated *villino* with no running water, or something in between, it's important to be on site as much as possible. (Consider renting a property nearby if needed.) Remember that surprises are par for the course in renovations, and in historical homes, you may uncover pleasant ones like ancient latrines or old frescoes. Who'd want to miss those fun discoveries? But you're also likely to find less-welcome ones, like rotten wood ceiling beams under the *controsoffitto* (drywall ceiling).

Besides the practical importance of keeping a watchful eye on things, there are benefits for the soul when you stay close to the day-by-day action, at least in Frances' estimation. "The satisfaction is enormous because the workers here are skilled, beautiful craftsmen, and they really know what they're doing, particularly the stonemasons," she says. "They can just cut and shape that stone like it's butter and you can't believe the artistry they bring to their work."

If you manage to navigate the process, congratulations! As Sean says, "Buying a home in Italy gives one a place to hang one's hat while enjoying the Italian quality of life."

What About Those 1€ Houses?

Many media outlets have recently taken to publishing guaranteed-to-go-viral articles about countryside homes being sold for 1€ in small Italian towns in need of recovery. Cue the collective gut responses of Italy dreamers around the globe: *Yes, please! What's the catch?*

For an enjoyable but tempered look at how those 1€ house situations typically play out, Damien advises people to watch Lorraine Bracco's current series on HGTV, *My Big Italian Adventure*, which follows the actress through her triumphs and travails since buying a 1€ home in Sicily. "I think that gives people a pretty good idea of what they'd be getting into," he notes. Only, you'll be getting into the trenches without a camera crew and a captive audience at your beck and call!

As Debbie explains it, many of these towns are extremely rural. "They're in the middle of nowhere and the young people have all left, and the older population is dying off," and what you might run into is a mayor who's taken over the village, or a property or farm that's owned by a collective of 20 people. You may very well get the home in the derelict village for 1€, but typically you'll be required to show that you have "fifty grand to put down for renovations to start," Debbie says. Sean estimates that you will need even more—between 100,000€ and 200,000€ for a full renovation.

The fine print specifications of 1€ schemes can vary greatly from area to area. Some may require the renovations to be completed within three years, for example. Others may encourage or require potential buyers to propose a cultural center or business idea to bring life to the space, perhaps enhancing the appeal for prospective buyers who aren't necessarily gung-ho about making it residential, but might want the property for creative or commercial reasons.

As *Marco Dettori*, a local councilman in the Sardinian town of *Sassari*, put it in an interview with *Idealista*, "With a project like the 1€ home scheme, there are no limits. The important and fundamental thing is to make a contribution."

Attracting new blood and life to the town(s) is what the 1€ scheme is all about. Just be aware, as Damien cautions, that often "what you have is a house that's falling apart in a town that's usually nowhere near a major city." While that shouldn't necessarily be a dealbreaker— for some, it may be a dream!—it's a key consideration, particularly for issues of access (to hospitals, airports and so forth) and community resources. Most certainly, prospective 1€-home buyers who are fluent in Italian will have an easier time navigating the adventure and putting together a renovation team than someone going in with no language skills or links to the community.

And regarding links to the community, no matter where you embark on a renovation, or how much your property's list price is, Michael says, "It's really important that the people around you see you as a person who is doing it for love, or because you want to be part of that society and that culture. Not that you're an ugly American coming to change everything." If you're a prospective 1€-home buyer, consider what's calling you to it (family heritage in the area, perhaps?) and the impression that your mission will leave on the local community.

Driving in Italy

Whether with a brood in tow or solo, driving in Italy evokes images of cruising along the coast in a *Fiat 500*. Some motorway moments can be straight-up cinematic, but like every other facet of living the Italian dream, there's legwork to be done first.

For your first year of residency, you're allowed to use your American driver's license (provided it is up to date), accompanied by an International Driving Permit, which you can get at an American Automobile Association (AAA) office before departure. Governed by the 1949 Geneva Convention on Road Traffic, the permit is valid for one year from the date of issue, and at publication time costs $20 to obtain.

Once you have been a resident in Italy for a year, you will need to get your Italian driver's license. You can begin this process as early as you like. The one-year residency rule is a cap, not a minimum. But given all the other paperwork and adjustments to be made, and Italy's pedestrian-oriented lifestyle, it's not particularly common for expats to embark on this mission in year one.

Taking the Test

The U.S. has no reciprocal driving agreements with Italy, so unfortunately, American citizens have no fast-track conversion process for validating their licenses on Italian soil. You must pass a road exam and a theory test—in Italian—before getting an Italian *patente B* license. Eighteen is the legal age to drive a car (category B vehicle). Before attempting the process, you should already have your *carta d'identità* (identity card) and, if you are a non-Italian or EU citizen, your *permesso di soggiorno* (permit of stay) in order.

Do not attempt to take the test without taking a series of courses at your local *autoscuola* (driving school), which will help you with obtaining your *foglio rosa* (learner's permit) from the *motorizzazione civile* (department of motor vehicles). If that sounds like teenager territory, don't be put off: The exam is notorious for tripping up even native Italian speakers. In 40 true/false questions, it tests your knowledge of the *codice della strada* (Highway Code), and there is no English option. While going through an *autoscuola* might seem like an unnecessary expense or even an embarrassment, it's bound to save you time and money in the long run; having to retake the test means having to repay fees.

Beyond test preparation, too, schools help take care of bureaucratic hoop-jumping and paperwork that needs filing with the *motorizzazione civile.* Enrollment fees and class hours might vary widely depending on your geographical location and other factors, but expect to spend at least several hundred euro. When comparing schools, ask if the fees are comprehensive and what they include—paperwork stamps (*marche da bollo*), class instruction hours, medical exams and so forth.

If you are not familiar with driving a manual transmission car, take the opportunity to learn. While in some special circumstances you may be able to take your road exam in an automatic transmission car, you may then be restricted to driving only automatics, which could become problematic. This could also exacerbate the limitations and potential insurance complications that you will already be facing as a *neopatentato* (newly licensed driver), a status all drivers hold for the first three years of having their license.

Drivers up to age 50 will have to renew their licenses only once every 10 years; between 50 and 70, every five years; between 70 and 80, every three years; and 80 and older, every two years.

Buying a Car

Buying a new car in Italy will entail paperwork that the dealership handles, working with the area *Agenzia di Pratiche Auto* (similar to the motor vehicle bureau, and overseeing separate-but-related issues to the *motorizzazione civile,* which is most comparable to the DMV). These costs will be factored into the sticker price of the automobile. On your end, you will need to submit your *codice fiscale* (tax code), residence certificate (*certificato di residenza*), a valid form of identification for vehicle registration with the *motorizzazione civile* and an insurance document. Insurance should be arranged prior to finalizing the purchase.

Broadly, the two main car insurance options in Italy are *casco* (comprehensive), which is expensive and not popular among average Italians, and *responsabilità civile* (third party). You may want add-ons for situations like theft and fire (*furto* and *incendio*), *infortuni del conducente* (coverage for the driver when deemed responsible for an accident) and the usually modestly priced *servizio assistenza* (roadside assistance).

If buying a secondhand vehicle from a private seller or a dealership, take similar precautions as you would in the U.S., asking about mileage, recent servicing information (*tagliandi*), the expiration date of the car tax (*bollo*) and the engine power (*potenza*), which should be noted in the vehicle's logbook (*libretto*). You and the seller can turn to an *Agenzie di Pratiche Auto* (**agenziapraticheauto.it**) in your area for assistance with paperwork; the Automobile Club d'Italia's PRA (*Pubblico Registro Automobilistico*) office is also equipped to help with this, including finalizing the transfer of ownership (*passaggio di proprietà*). When an individual buys a new or used vehicle in the concessionaria (car shop), the seller will handle all the bureaucracy on behalf of the client. When the car is purchased from a private individual, all the paperwork (namely the *pubblico registro* and the *assicurazione*) falls on the buyer.

All cars that are more than four years old must have a *revisione* (roadworthiness test) carried out every two years. This can be done at authorized garages and is different from a standard servicing or tire rotation as they will be checking highly specific safety criteria. Your car's *libretto* (logbook) will be stamped upon completion and you should always keep it in your glove compartment for any potential roadside checks.

Leasing a Car While Visiting

If you will be in Italy longer than 21 days, but you're not an EU citizen or EU resident, you may want to explore leasing a car rather than renting. To lease a car, you must be a non-EU citizen/resident, at least 18 (there are no maximum age requirements) and lease the car for at least 21 days. If you qualify, you will get a brand-new car that you can pick up and drop off anywhere in Europe. Leasing has several benefits: There is no cost for extra drivers; it's often more affordable than long-term renting or buying; unlimited mileage; the ability to reserve and pre-pay in the U.S.; and excellent insurance coverage with no deductible, including for damage and breakdowns.

This may seem too good to be true, but it's really a win-win situation for both you and European rental car companies. The leasing program originates from a law unique to France that adds 20% value-added tax (VAT) to brand-new cars for both individual buyers and rental car agencies. Consequently, rental car companies are stuck paying that 20% VAT—unless they lease a brand-new car to a tourist, then buy it back and rent it to their customers as a slightly used car.

This means that all leased cars will be French makes, including Peugeot, Citroen and Renault, most of them with a manual transmission and a steering wheel on the left-hand side. Companies such as Auto Europe and Kemwel arrange the lease, including getting the car to you. While all cars originate in France, you don't have to pick it up or drop it off in France—you can pick it up in Italy, for a slightly higher rate.

Phineas Orazio McCabe

Bringing Your Pet to Italy

Whether a dog, cat or exotic animal, pets are important members of the family. If you're moving to Italy or living there part-time, you will of course be interested in bringing your pet with you. Pets can be a great way to meet locals and make friends. Retiree Sally Carrocino, who brought her dog with her when she moved to Florence, says having Zoe around helped her integrate into her new city. "Having a dog is the best," she says. "We all speak dog."

In some parts of Italy, pets, especially cats and dogs, are viewed differently from in the U.S. Many residents of big cities like Rome, Milan and Florence give their pets the elegant royal treatment, taking them everywhere and pampering them. However, many in the south and some rural areas find that the farming traditions of Italy influence how they feel about pets. Traditionally, animals lived on the first floor of the house or outdoors, while people lived on the second floor. Many pet owners in rural areas keep their dogs and cats outdoors, either chained in the yard or in a doghouse.

As a result of these more traditional attitudes, there are a lot of stray animals in Italy, and shelters—which are all no-kill facilities—and animal rescues are always full of pets needing good homes. So if you're not bringing a pet to Italy, there are many who would be so happy to be rescued if you decided to pursue that route. (To learn more about adopting a pet from Italy, see our article on Sicilian animal rescue *Animalsicilia*, *Helping the Strays of Sicily*, in the December 2017/January 2018 issue of *Dream of Italy*.)

So, how do you get your pet from the U.S. to Italy? Service animals are, of course, allowed to board the plane with you, but guidelines for emotional support animals vary. In January 2021, the U.S. Department of Transportation stopped requiring airlines to accommodate emotional support animals on board with their owners, and many airlines have changed their policies as a result. However, as of when this book was printed, some airlines still allow emotional support animals on board, including Air France, Lufthansa and KLM. Each airline has different requirements regarding the type of emotional support animal allowed, weight and height, and other factors.

Animal transport companies will also arrange flights for your pet to ensure your furry friend arrives safely, whether they fly in the cabin or in the hold. One reputable company that was recommended to *Dream of Italy* is Air Animal Pet Movers (**www.airanimal.com**). Animal transport companies help your pet fly on commercial passenger airlines and assist you in completing paperwork. Air Animal Pet Movers, for example, advises its network of veterinarians on how to fill out the paperwork and what different countries' pet immigration requirements involve.

If pets meet the airline's size and weight requirements, they can travel as "accompanied baggage" (i.e., linked to a passenger's ticket—either you or a staff member from the pet moving company) in the cabin or in the luggage hold beneath the plane. For this option, the ballpark cost with Air Animal Pet Movers would be between $500 and $1,000, including the pet carrier, airline fees and documents.

Pets can also be shipped as air cargo if the airline or destination country does not allow them to be transported as luggage, if they exceed the airline's size and weight requirements or if they are unaccompanied by a passenger. Pet moving companies can also arrange air cargo shipments, including documents, pet carrier, export/import costs, airline and fuel fees, and any costs required by the destination country. With Air Animal Pet Movers, air cargo costs range from $2,500 to $7,500.

If your pet can't fly on board with you, and you can't bear the thought of putting them in cargo, you can arrange to charter a private plane from your hometown to Italy or a destination close by. Flying a chartered plane is, of course, expensive, but sharing the plane with other pet owners helps reduce the cost significantly. The Facebook groups Chartered Air Travel With Pets and US/UK Dog & Pet Repatriation Private Charter Jet Group help pet owners meet and coordinate flights to international destinations. The cost can be around $8,000 per person with pets, one way.

Current travel requirements for cats and dogs include a microchip, an up-to-date rabies vaccine and a European Community veterinary certificate. Travelers can bring a maximum of five pets into Italy as long as they fall within the categories of dogs, cats, birds, rodents and reptiles. Pets do not need a pet passport to travel from the U.S. to Italy or vice versa, but they will need an EU pet passport to travel within Europe. There is no required quarantine for pets traveling to Italy.

Filling out your pet's paperwork can be confusing and time consuming, and your veterinarian's office may not be familiar with the requirements or know how to complete the forms. Similarly, information found through a quick Google search can be misleading or out of date. Consequently, some travelers have been turned away because of minor errors in their pets' paperwork or missing requirements. To make sure your paperwork is complete and up to international standards, you may want to work with a company that specializes in transporting pets abroad. These companies will help you and your vet with the paperwork and other requirements before you leave the U.S.

You can also seek advice on paperwork, requirements and more from travelers and expats in Facebook groups such as Expats in Italy.

Final Note

KATHY McCABE

This rather lengthy book is filled with ideas on how to make your unique *dream of Italy* come true. If you've read through to the end, that's a great sign of your commitment!

"I didn't want to wake up someday and think, 'I wish I did. I wish I did. I wish I did that,'" Sally Carrocino says.

Our Italian dreams can take so many forms, but the most important thing to do is to *take action* to make your *dream of Italy* come true as we travel, transform and thrive.

The *Dream of Italy* formula is simple.

Travel: Travel virtually through our TV shows or on the ground in real life and discover what Italians do better than the rest of us.

Transform: Apply the principles of the Italian lifestyle to your own life and start dreaming bigger.

Thrive: Live a happier and healthier life where you are now or in your new home in Italy.

Happy dreaming . . . and doing!

Resources

Here are websites for many of the resources mentioned throughout the book as well as some additional websites and publications. This is just the tip of the iceberg but should get you started in exploring these topics further.

INTRODUCTION

Dream of Italy **Magazine** (www.dreamofitaly.com/magazine): *Dream of Italy* began as a subscription travel newsletter. It is now a glossy digital and print magazine with more than 180 issues online available to members. If you're not a member, join at **www.dreamofitaly.com/join**

Dream of Italy: Travel, Transform and Thrive **TV Special** (www.dreamof italy.com/ttt): Find out how and when to watch the TV special on PBS or via streaming.

Dream of Italy: Travel, Transform and Thrive **Book** (www.dreamofitaly. com/tttbook): Any additional resources related to the book will be listed here.

Dream of Italy: Travel, Transform and Thrive **Podcast** (www.dreamofitaly. com/podcast): More interviews on topics from travel to ancestry to living like an Italian.

Dream of Italy **Travel Service** (www.dreamofitaly.com/travel): Have one of Kathy's hand-picked travel planners create a dream itinerary and book all of your travel arrangements!

THE LAND

Sierra Club (www.sierraclub.org): An outdoor organization with chapters in all 50 U.S. states, promoting environmental conservation, hiking trails and other outdoor activities.

Agriturismo.com: Database of farmhouse stays (*agriturismi*) around Italy, organized by region.

***Native Wine Grapes of Italy* by Ian D'Agata:** A well-indexed and comprehensive book providing historical, anecdotal and scientific accounts of Italy's hugely diverse grape varietals and their connection to their territory of origin.

***Vino Italiano: The Regional Wines of Italy* by Joseph Bastianach and David Lynch:** The most comprehensive American-written guide to Italy's 300 growing zones, 361 authorized grape varieties and 200 of the top producers.

Tenuta Il Palagio (www.il-palagio.com and www.facebook.com/TenutailPalagio): Use these links to explore Sting and Trudie Styler's estate in Tuscany with more information on how to rent villas on the property, visit the wine shop and order the wine and other products to be delivered to your home.

UNESCO World Heritage Sites (https://whc.unesco.org): Explore the dozens of Italian sites that the United Nations has protected.

Blue Flag Beaches (www.blueflag.global): A map of Italy's cleanest and most eco-friendly beaches.

Official National Parks (www.mite.gov.it/pagina/elenco-dei-parchi): A list of Italy's national parks, maintained by the Ministry of Ecological Transition.

Parks, Protected Areas and Preserves (www.parks.it): A more comprehensive list of all of the national and regional parks nationwide, as well as marine protected areas and nature preserves.

Orange Flag Towns (www.bandierearancioni.it): A list of the municipalities in Italy noted by the Italian Touring Club for excellence in hospitality, tourism and sustainability.

Seeds From Italy (www.growitalian.com): Order heirloom seeds imported from Italy to grow your own Italian garden! Save 10% with *Dream of Italy* discount code: dreamgarden

FOOD

American Heart Association Guide to the Mediterranean Diet (www. heart.org/en/healthy-living/healthy-eating/eat-smart/nutrition-basics/ mediterranean-diet): Explore the benefits of the Mediterranean diet.

Blue Zones (www.bluezones.com): Information, including books and a documentary, on areas of the world that have a higher-than-average population of centenarians.

The Blue Zones Solution **by Dan Buettner**: A book detailing why people in the Blue Zones live longer and how to live like them.

Tenuta Il Palagio **(www.il-palagio.com and www.facebook.com/ TenutailPalagio)**: If you're in Tuscany, visit the *Il Palagio* Wine Shop for fresh local produce, olive oil, wine, honey and more. Eat at the new *pizzeria* and wine shop.

Cesarine.com: Enjoy an authentic regional meal in the home of a local Italian family. These home cooks are incredible!

Eating Europe (www.eatingeurope.com): Urban food tours in Rome and Florence; owned by American expat Kenny Dunn.

Taste Florence (www.tasteflorence.com): Food and wine tours with our friend American expat Toni Mazzaglia in Florence.

Vinitaly **(www.vinitaly.com)**: An international wine and spirits exhibition, held annually in April, that attracts thousands of wine professionals from around the world.

Salone del Gusto (www.terramadresalonedelgusto.com): A biannual gastronomy exhibition featuring food artisans from around Italy and held in Turin.

Slow Food (www.slowfood.com): The Slow Food movement began in Italy and has expanded globally. It focuses on local food, native food practices and cultures and sustainability.

Carpigiani Gelato University (www.gelatouniversity.com): *Gelato*-making courses ranging from basic to advanced, including online classes.

La Scienza in Cucina e l'Arte di Mangiar Bene *(Science in the Kitchen and the Art of Eating Well)*: A definitive, timeless classic of Italian cooking published in 1891 by *Pellegrino Artusi*.

The Essentials of Classic Italian Cooking by Marcella Hazan: Another more modern classic, this one by the woman who taught America that "Italian food" doesn't mean spaghetti and meatballs.

Gambero Rosso (www.gamberorosso.it): Website for multimedia editorial group publishing guidebooks, articles, periodicals, broadcasts and more focused on fine Italian wine, food and travel.

Great Italian Chefs (www.greatitalianchefs.com): Recipes and tips from great Italian chefs, but also a wealth of information in English on regional food specialties, what to try where and more.

U.S. Farmers Market Directory (www.ams.usda.gov/local-food -directories/farmersmarkets): National directory of farmers markets in the U.S. run by the USDA.

Gustiamo.com: Great source for ordering Italian specialty foods for home delivery in the U.S.

FAMILY

Also see **Ancestry and Citizenship** (page 265)

National Italian-American Foundation (www.niaf.org): Celebrating the heritage of Italian-Americans and their contributions to the U.S.

MumAbroad (www.mumabroad.com): Useful information for English-speaking parents living in western Europe, with some extensive Italy-specific sections.

Third Culture Kids, Revised Edition: The Experience of Growing Up Among Worlds by **David Pollock:** Handy book for parents navigating raising children between cultures.

ART AND CULTURE

UNESCO Intangible Cultural Heritage List (ich.unesco.org/en/lists): A list of Italy's Intangible Cultural Heritage practices recognized by the United Nations.

Italian Ministry of Culture (www.beniculturali.it): Government website in Italian for state museums, archaeological sites and more.

Vatican Museums (www.museivaticani.va): Explore the museums of Vatican City and learn how to plan your visit.

The *Uffizi* Galleries (www.uffizi.it): No cultural visit to Italy and no visit to Florence is complete without exploring one of the greatest art collections in the world. Book tickets ahead or hire a guide.

Artigianato e Design Vicenza (www.cnavenetovest.it): Held annually, this craft fair showcases artisan-made pieces including ceramics, woodworking, textiles and papercraft.

Mostra dell'Artigianato di Firenze (www.mostrartigianato.it): This annual craft fair pays homage to Florentine artisan tradition and highlights Italian craftsmanship.

Umbria Jazz (www.umbriajazz.it): Held twice a year, this jazz festival is one of the world's biggest and attracts major jazz musicians.

Ravello **Festival** (www.ravellofestival.com): Originally a tribute to composer Richard Wagner, the *Ravello* Festival has grown into a summerlong celebration of music and the arts.

Italian Historic Houses Network (www.dimorestoricheitaliane.it): A list of historic houses and castles open to the public.

Artribune (www.artribune.com): One of the most widely read Italian publications on contemporary art and culture.

Il Giornale dell'Arte (www.ilgiornaledellarte.com): A monthly periodical and website (in Italian) on art and culture, produced in Turin and a sister publication of *The Art Newspaper.*

The Agony and the Ecstasy **by Irving Stone**: The classic biographical novel of *Michelangelo.* It is considered the most compelling portrait of the world's greatest artist.

The Divine Comedy (La Divina Commedia) **by Dante Alighieri:** This long narrative poem journeying through Hell, Purgatory and Paradise is the quintessential piece of Italian literature.

Leonardo da Vinci **by Walter Issacson**: An excellent biography of the 15th-century's quintessential "Renaissance man."

Dream of Italy **Magazine Recommended Tour Guides** (www.dreamof italy.com/tourguides): Meet the local tour guides, specializing in art and culture, that we have recommended over the years.

Paola Vojnovic (www.paolavojnovic.com): A Renaissance art historian and guide, Paola specializes in Florentine art.

Smarthistory.org: Search works of art by city or artist to plan your visit in advance.

BEAUTY

I Borghi Più Belli d'Italia (www.borghipiubelliditalia.it): Website in Italian and English for an association promoting the heritage and landscapes of small Italian towns.

PACE OF LIFE

In Praise of Slowness by **Carl Honore**: A book dedicated to exploring a slower pace of life and what drives people to "the cult of speed."

Città Slow (www.cittaslow.it): A slow travel movement focused on local traditions, slower pace of life and sustainability.

Slow Europe (www.sloweurope.com): Travel forums for people who want to travel at a slower pace.

PASSION

Dario Cecchini (www.dariocecchini.com): Lover of *Dante* and perhaps the most famous butcher in all of Italy. He was featured in the Tuscany episode of *Dream of Italy* and embodies passion!

MOVEMENT

Worldwide Opportunities on Organic Farms (www.wwoof.net): Volunteer to help out on an organic farm in exchange for accommodations.

Workaway (www.workaway.info): Community for culture exchange and working vacations.

Tourissimo (www.tourissimo.travel): Walking, hiking and biking tours across Italy.

AllTrails (www.alltrails.com/italy): Search for hiking and walking trails by location, length and difficulty.

COMMUNITY

Also see **Finding Your Community** (page 271)

***Bowling Alone: The Collapse and Revival of American Community* by Robert Putnam:** A book exploring the importance of interpersonal connections in our lives.

Meetup.com: Join others in your community to explore your interests. There are meetups for everything from Italian language learning to hiking.

Nextdoor.com: If you can't meet your neighbors in person, meet them virtually, at least at first.

CELEBRATIONS

***Dream of Italy* Events Calendar** (www.dreamofitaly.com/events): A searchable database of some of our favorite events and festivals throughout Italy.

Sagre in Italia (www.sagreinitalia.it): Italian database of traditional fairs and festivals (*sagre*) around Italy.

Eventi in Toscana* by *Toscana Tascabile (www.eventiintoscana.it): Extensive event listings for the region of Tuscany.

Romeing (www.romeing.it): One of the more thorough English guides to events and lifestyle in Rome and surrounding areas.

Mass at the Vatican (www.papalaudience.org/papal-mass): Reserve tickets to attend Mass with the Pope at St. Peter's Basilica.

***Dream of Italy: Tuscan Sun* TV Special** (www.dreamofitaly.com/tuscan -sun-special): Watch Kathy and Frances Mayes celebrate the *Giostra dell'Archidado* in *Cortona*, dressed in medieval costumes.

SENSE OF HOME

Dream of Italy **Travel Magazine** (www.dreamofitaly.com/magazine): Find recommended villa and apartment rental agencies as well as specific individual properties throughout Italy.

Home Exchange (www.homeexchange.com): Swap homes with an Italian family—you stay in their home while they stay in yours.

TRAVEL

Dream of Italy **Travel Magazine** (www.dreamofitaly.com/magazine): Find recommended villa and apartment rental agencies as well as specific individual properties throughout Italy.

Dream of Italy **Travel Service** (www.dreamofitaly.com/travel): Have one of Kathy's hand-picked travel planners create a dream itinerary and book all of your travel arrangements!

Dream of Italy **Book Club** (www.facebook.com/groups/64038432312 9501): Share recommendations of books to inspire your Italian dreams and travel. Live book club meetings with authors.

Dream of Italy: Travel, Transform and Thrive **TV Special** (www.dreamof italy.com/ttt): Find out how and when to watch the TV special on PBS or via streaming.

Dream of Italy **TV Show** (www.dreamofitaly.com/tv-show): With 12 episodes, each in a different part of Italy, the TV show will let you travel virtually with Kathy and Italian locals as your guides.

ANCESTRY AND CITIZENSHIP

Castelvetere sul Calore **Episode of** *Dream of Italy* (www.dreamofitaly .com/castelvetere): Watch the episode where Kathy and her late parents revisit her ancestral hometown and learn more about genealogy and citizenship.

U.S. National Archives (www.archives.gov/research): Find naturalization records for your Italian-American ancestors.

Lo Schiavo Genealogica (www.italyancestry.com): Ancestry and citizenship services offered by Melanie Holtz.

Ancestry.com: This is the world's largest online family history resource.

FamilySearch.org: A free and comprehensive genealogy website with ancestral records and tutorials on how to interpret documents. FamilySearch works with the Italian National Archive to update and transfer records from Italian databases. The site is run by the Church of Jesus Christ of Latter-Day Saints and has millions of searchable images of records.

Antenati (www.antenati.san.beniculturali.it): Italian archive of family records.

Italian Parish Records (www.italianparishrecords.org): Digital database of Italian church records.

Gaetano Petrillo (www.thewinebus.it): Whether you're looking to experience wine or meet your long-lost family, my friend *Gaetano Petrillo* is your guy in *Campania.*

My Bella Basilicata (www.mybellabasilicata.com): Ancestry research in southern Italy provided by expat Valerie Fortney.

Italian Consulates in the U.S. (www.bit.ly/italianconsulates): List of Italian consulates in the U.S. and the embassy and their areas of jurisdiction.

Capecchi Legal (www.capecchilegal.com): Attorney *Michele Capecchi,* LL.M.'s law firm is based in Florence and specializes in family relocation and dual citizenship.

U.S. Citizenship and Immigration Services (www.uscis.com): Find naturalization records for your Italian-American ancestors.

TRANSFORMATION

Debbie Travis (www.debbietravis.com and www.tuscangetaway.com): Author, interior designer and television personality Debbie Travis hosts life-changing retreats at her home in the Tuscan countryside.

Sheri Salata (www.sherisalata.com): Sheri Salata, former executive producer of *The Oprah Winfrey Show*, is a noted author and hosts online workshops and retreats in Italy that can help you transform your life.

Glenn Main (www.themainpoint.com): Glenn Main founded his company, The Main Point, to help privately held business owners with strategic problem solving and planning.

Sarah Centrella (www.sarahcentrella.com): Master life coach and best-selling author of the book *#Futureboards*, Sarah Centrella is making her *dream of Italy* come true.

David Bach (www.davidbach.com): Best-selling financial author David Bach teaches us how to plan and save for our dreams. He moved with his family to Florence for a "radical sabbatical."

MOVING TO ITALY

Damien O'Farrell (www.damienofarrell.com): Damien has coached 10,000 people in moving to Italy. His free email newsletter is a great resource.

Capecchi Legal (www.capecchilegal.com): Attorney *Michele Capecchi*, LL.M.'s law firm is based in Florence and specializes in family relocation and dual citizenship.

AngloInfo.com: A website and database for English speakers living abroad in 30 different countries, filled with practical advice, guides, local services and products.

The Grown-Up's Guide to Running Away From Home: Making a New Life Abroad by **Rosanne Knorr:** Some basics on things to consider (mostly practicalities) before moving abroad in midlife or later.

JustLanded.com: Practical information on the ins and outs of building a life overseas.

Tales From a Small Planet (www.talesmag.com): A collection of mostly first-person essays and experiences from around the globe offering insight into "what it's really like to live there," shedding light on some of the near-universal challenges and triumphs expats experience.

VISAS AND IMMIGRATION

Capecchi Legal (www.capecchilegal.com): Attorney *Michele Capecchi,* LL.M.'s law firm is based in Florence and specializes in family relocation and dual citizenship.

Study in Italy (www.studyinitaly.esteri.it): Government-run website on studying in Italy with information about student visas.

Ministry of the Interior (www.interno.gov.it): Official website of the Ministry of the Interior and a place to watch for news of the *decreto flussi* (flow decree).

Il Portale Immigrazione **(Immigration Portal)** (www.portaleimmi grazione.it): Official website for processes related to the issuance and renewal of permits of stay (*permessi di soggiorno*). Run by the Ministry of the Interior, the Italian postal system and ANCI; currently only in Italian.

European Union Blue Card (www.apply.eu): Details on the special European visa for highly skilled workers. It is similar to the U.S. Green Card.

Ministry of the Interior—Department of Civil Liberties and Immigration (www.nullaostalavoro.dlci.interno.it): Website for submission of *nulla osta* application.

Investor Visa for Italy (www.investorvisa.mise.gov.it): Information on the new two-year investor visa.

Italian Consulates in the U.S. (www.bit.ly/italianconsulates): List of Italian consulates and the embassy in the U.S. and their areas of jurisdiction.

U.S. Consulates in Italy (it.usembassy.gov): List of U.S. consulates and the embassy in Italy and their services.

LIFE IN ITALY

Rosetta Stone (www.rosettastone.com): Language-learning software.

Conversation Exchange (www.conversationexchange.com): Website to find real-life or virtual language tandem partners.

Online Italian Club (www.onlineitalianclub.com): Free Italian language-learning resources, including worksheets and listening exercises.

Tia Taylor YouTube Channel (www.youtube.com/user/tiataylor-makeup): Young Milan-based expat's channel has a bit of humor and life-in-Italy videos, but is worth exploring for Tia's frank assessments and recounting of personal experiences and processes in Italy, from getting a mortgage to opening a *partita IVA* (VAT number).

Rental Diaries: Thoughts From My Four Walls in Florence **by Mary Gray:** Humorous and truthful take on apartment living in Florence.

Ultimate Italy (www.facebook.com/groups/ultimateitaly): Facebook group run by relocation expert Damien O'Farrell to share positive stories about Italy.

WORK LIFE

Cambridge English (www.cambridgeenglish.org/teaching-english/teaching-qualifications/celta): Information on CELTA, the Certificate in

Teaching English to Speakers of Other Languages (according to the site, three out of four English-teaching jobs require a CELTA certification).

Teaching English in Italy (www.teachingenglishinitaly.com): Weekend TEFL courses in Florence with certification that can be used elsewhere.

FAO Employment Listings (www.fao.org/employment): Food and Agriculture Organization of the United Nations (Rome-based) job listings.

Wanted in Rome (www.wantedinrome.com/classified): Mostly English-speaking jobs in Rome.

Wanted in Milan (www.wantedinmilan.com/classified): Mostly English-speaking jobs in Milan.

The Florentine **Classifieds** (www.theflorentine.net/classifieds): English-friendly jobs in Florence and Tuscany.

Bakeca.it: Website in Italian that offers classified ads including jobs.

Subito.it: Website in Italian that offers classified ads including jobs.

Business Italy Marketplace (www.facebook.com/groups/businessitaly-classifieds): Facebook group run by relocation expert Damien O'Farrell for Italian businesses to advertise services and jobs.

HEALTHCARE

Italian Ministry of Health (www.salute.gov.it): Government website of the Ministry of Health, currently only in Italian, though select pages pertaining to foreign citizens may be found in English.

U.S. Embassy and Consulates in Italy: Medical Assistance (www.it.usembassy.gov/u-s-citizen-services/doctors/): Helpful healthcare-related resources and listings of English-speaking doctors and medical providers compiled by the U.S. Embassy in Rome and the Consulates in Florence, Milan and Naples.

World Health Organization—Italy (www.euro.who.int/en/countries/ italy): Health-related news and information out of Italy.

Doctors in Italy (www.doctorsinitaly.com): Digital database of English-speaking doctors for travelers and expats in Italy.

Medicare Interactive (www.medicareinteractive.org): A general website powered by the Medicare Rights Center with an ample section on Medicare coverage while abroad.

FINDING YOUR COMMUNITY

Expats in Italy (www.facebook.com/groups/AnyexpatITALY): Popular Facebook group for expats living in Italy.

American International League of Florence (www.ailoflorence.org): Charitable organization running a number of important fundraisers and cultural events throughout the year in the Florence area.

American International Women's Club of Naples (www.facebook.com/ AmericanInternationalWomensClubOfNaples): Social and networking club for women in the Naples area.

ARCI—*Associazione Ricreativa e Culturale Italiana* (www.arci.it): The largest Italian secular nonprofit, with nearly 5,000 cultural community centers (*circoli*) spread around the country. Website (in Italian) includes a searchable database.

Caritas (www.caritas.org): An international Catholic nonprofit focused on serving the needy.

International Women's Forum, *Bologna* (www.iwfbologna.com): Women's club of *Bologna*.

Girl Gone International (www.girlgoneinternational.com): Non-Italy-specific platform for women (mostly younger to middle age) with chapters around the world.

InterNations (www.internations.org): Non-Italy-specific expat platform but with a number of chapters around Italy, and catering to a mostly 40+ demographic.

Speakeasy Multilingual, Florence (www.speakeasymultilingual.com): Language exchange and social group meeting regularly in Florence, varying in ages and nationalities.

Expats Living in Rome (www.expatslivinginrome.com): Active group founded by *Patrizia De Gregorio* and hosting regular meetups for all ages.

Volunteers and Consultants Network, Rome (signup link: **www.groups.io/g/VCNRome**): Email listserv originally designed for UN organization consultations working in Rome temporarily but now featuring classifieds, events and information relevant to the international community in and around Rome.

Toastmasters Italy (www.toastmastersitalia.it): International group with focus on improving public speaking has numerous local chapters around Italy.

RENTING, BUYING AND RENOVATING

Countrywide Websites to Look for Rentals: www.immobiliare.it; www. idealista.it; www.bakeca.it; www.subito.it; www.casa.it

Sean Carlos (www.seancarlos.org): Sean is an American-born, Italian-licensed real estate agent offering his services throughout the country.

Property Guides (www.propertyguides.com/italy): A good general resource for those taking their first steps toward buying property in Italy and seeking general information.

Agenti Immobiliari Abilitati **(www.agentiimmobiliariabilitati.it)**: Searchable database (in Italian only) with publicly available information on real estate agents, including their registration status at the *Camera di Commercio* (Chamber of Commerce)—best accompanied by a final verification directly with the relevant *Camera di Commercio*.

Buying Property in Italy (www.facebook.com/groups/BuyingProperty inItaly): Useful and English-first Facebook group founded by Sean Carlos.

Catasto Explainer (www.seancarlos.org/en/resources/catasto -explained): Helpful article on Sean Carlos' website covering the basics of the Italian *catasto* (land registry) system.

Tax Incentives, Deductions and Credits (www.agenziaentrate.gov.it/ portale/web/guest/aree-tematiche/casa/agevolazioni): These vary year-to-year but can really add up for a homeowner.

DRIVING

International Driving Permit (IDP) (www.aaa.com): If you live in the U.S., the easiest way to get this document is through the American Automobile Club.

Real-Life Stories of Getting an Italian Driver's License (www. questadolcevita.com/blog/getting-an-italian-drivers-license-is-a-rite-of-passage): One of our favorite Italy bloggers, Jasmine Mah, shares her lived-to-tell-about-it tale and shares links to the success stories of other expats.

Automobile Club of Italy (www.aci.it/i-servizi/guide-utili/guida-pra-tiche-auto/importare-un-veicolo.html): The ACI's website lists rules for importing vehicles to Italy.

Countrywide Websites for Buying Cars: www.bakeca.it; www.subito.it

Italian Car Agency (www.agenziapraticheauto.it): Look for the local office to help you with paperwork in purchasing a car.

AutoEurope (www.autoeurope.com): AutoEurope lets foreign drivers lease brand-new cars within Europe. You may be able to save 5% with the *Dream of Italy* discount code: 72002261

Kemwel (www.kemwel.com/car-leasing-in-europe): Another company that arranges long-term car leases in Europe.

PETS

Animalsicilia (www.facebook.com/Animalsicilia): An animal rescue based in Sicily that cares for stray dogs and cats. Some of these pets are available for international adoption.

Air Animal Pet Movers (www.airanimal.com): A recommended company that will help arrange flights, logistics and paperwork for your pets.

Chartered Air Travel with Pets (www.facebook.com/groups/232240235092427): A Facebook group to help pet owners join together to charter private flights abroad.

US/UK Dog & Pet Repatriation Private Charter Jet Group (www.facebook.com/groups/271983317342001): Another Facebook group for pet owners to coordinate flights, focused on the U.S. and the U.K.

Expats in Italy (www.facebook.com/groups/AnyexpatITALY): A Facebook group for expats living in Italy, with advice on all aspects of Italian life, including pets.

Italian Embassy in the U.S. (it.usembassy.gov/embassy-consulates/rome/sections-offices/foreign-agricultural-service/pet-travel-faqs-italy-u-s/): The official website of the Italian Embassy lists rules for taking your pet from the U.S. to Italy.

European Union Pet Requirements (europa.eu/youreurope/citizens/travel/carry/animal-plant/index_en.htm): An official EU website lists requirements for pets traveling to Europe.

Expats in Italy (www.facebook.com/groups/AnyexpatITALY): A Facebook group for expats living in Italy, with advice on all aspects of Italian life, including pets.

Acknowledgments

It would be impossible to truly thank *all* of the incredible people who played a part in the making of the TV special *Dream of Italy: Travel, Transform and Thrive* and this companion book. The list, if I ever had long enough, would start with the warm and generous Italians I have met throughout the country, who have been my teachers in the meaning of Italian life, and life itself! *Dream of Italy* began life in September 2002 as a subscription travel newsletter. A humble *grazie mille* must go out to the many subscribers who have believed in this dream and still do (now a glossy magazine) and supported it from the very start!

To turn a publication into a public television TV series has been a daunting task. It would not be possible without the sponsors who fund this unique travel programming. My deepest appreciation goes out to the sponsors of this special including *De Cecco, Monteverdi Tuscany,* VIETRI, *Lo Schiavo Genealogica* (ItalyAncestry.com), Seeds From Italy, Pinnacle Communication Service, Toscana Restaurant (Los Angeles), Mark & Sandy Amorello and Joseph J. Bell, Esq. TV is labor intensive and a wonderful crew of Italians and Americans came together to film this production. A grateful shout-out to Chuck Smith and Brian Sheehan, who helped me finish the final product in a bizarre pandemic-filled year.

Heartfelt thank yous must go to Sting, Trudie Styler, Francis Ford Coppola, Frances Mayes, the Bach family, Arlene Antoinette Gibbs and Sally Carrocino, who all eloquently shared their thoughts on what makes life in Italy so captivating. *Michele Capecchi* and Damien O'Farrell aptly shared practical advice for making a new life in Italy.

I am still in awe that Frances Mayes wrote such an eloquent foreword to this book. What a dream come true from a woman and writer I admire deeply.

I'd like to also thank Ed Mayes and *Rossella de Filippo* (who runs *Palazzo Margherita*) for their support. I meet the most wonderful people through this work and count actor Joe Mantegna at the top of that list. Thanks to Joe for generously agreeing to support *Dream of Italy* and public television by co-hosting the pledge breaks with me.

I've long admired journalist Mary Gray, who is based in Florence. She's a great reporter and simply a beautiful writer. Mary was essential to the more than 80 pages of this book devoted to the process of moving to and living in Italy.

Another key member of the *Dream of Italy* team and the team producing this book is Elaine Murphy. Elaine has been the associate editor of *Dream of Italy* for more than a decade. We've worked on so much content together but I think this has been our most daunting project.

Throughout the filming of the special and production of the book, some of my hardest years personally and professionally, I was blessed with a fantastic assistant, Stephanie McClendon. She truly kept every-thing humming along.

When I needed a little more help with some chapters, I wondered who could just jump in and do a great job? Two fantastic women came to mind—Jane Fullerton Lemons and *Maria Pradissitto*. They both helped make parts of the book more creative and precise.

There is so much material in these pages and I relied heavily on the sharp eye of Sharon Berman, who has also been the proofreader for the magazine, to make sure every word was perfect.

Karen Sheets de Gracia patiently designed this book and is behind the new design of the *Dream of Italy* Magazine. She's so talented and always easy to work with.

I can't end without thanking my constant companion during both the editing of the TV special and the writing of this book. My wire fox terrier Phineas Orazio McCabe aka Finney spent many hours in a dark edit suite curled up under the desk or by my side on many a coffee shop patio in Denver, Aspen and Vail, as I wrote these pages. He has been my saving grace.